ATLAS

RETURN OF THE THREE DIMENSIONAL MAN

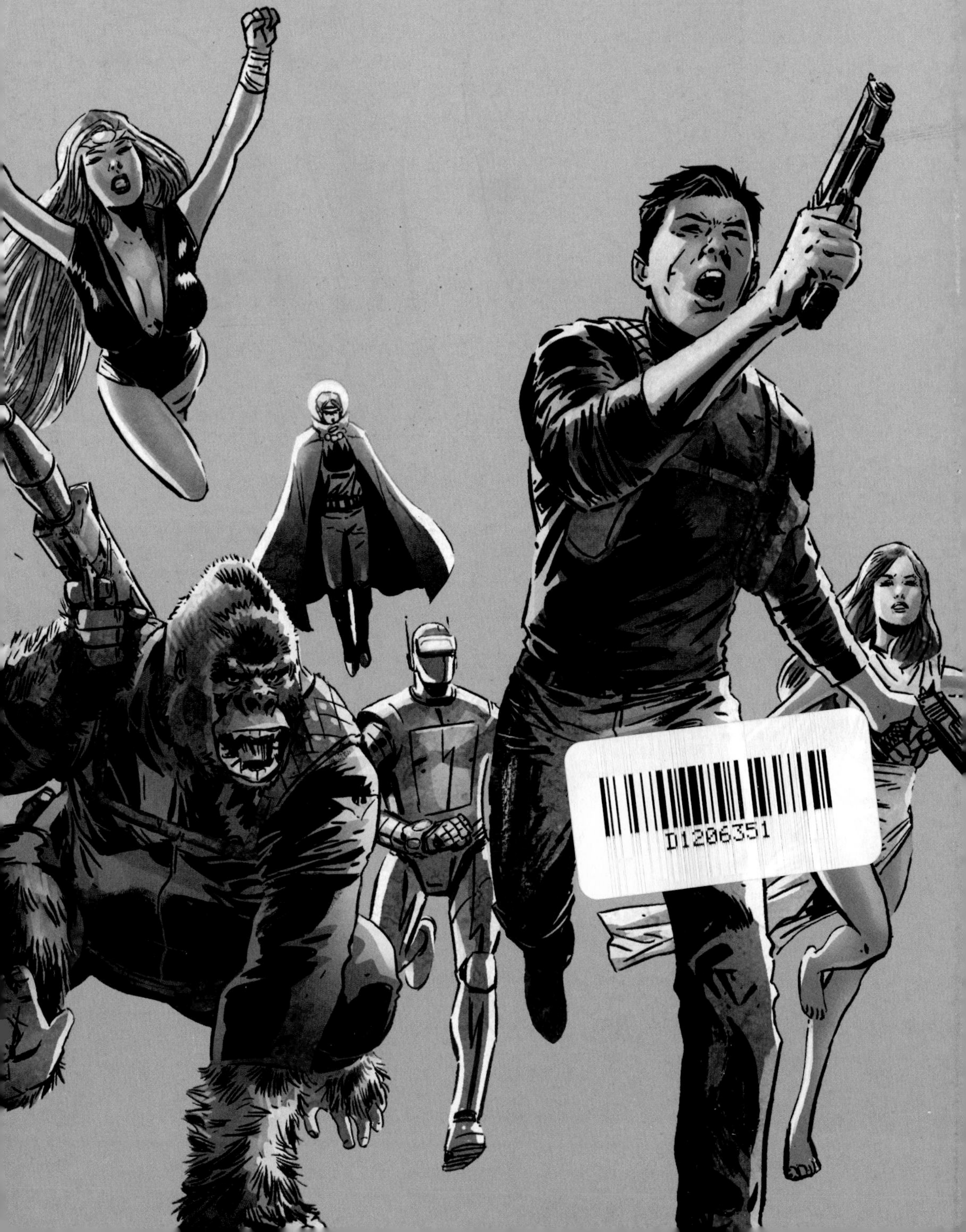

ATLAS

RETURN OF THE THREE DIMENSIONAL MAN

"GODMARKED"
WRITER: JEFF PARKER
ARTIST: GABRIEL HARDMAN
COLORISTS: ELIZABETH BREITWEISER, WIL QUINTANA,
& SOTOCOLOR'S J. ROBERTS
LETTERER: TOM ORZECHOWSKI
COVER ARTISTS: ADI GRANOV, MICHAEL BIEREK
& ALEX GARNER

"HEROES FOR THE AGES"
WRITER: JEFF PARKER
ARTISTS: GABRIEL HARDMAN
& GIANCARLO CARACUZZO
COLORIST: ELIZABETH BREITWEISER
LETTERER: ED DUKESHIRE
COVER ARTISTS: BRYAN HITCH, KARL KESEL
& PAUL MOUNTS

"The Return of the Three Dimensional Man"
Writer: Jeff Parker
Artists: Gabriel Hardman, Ramon Rosanas & Jeff Parker
Colorists: Elizabeth Breitweiser, Ramon Rosanas, Jim Charalampidis & Jeff Parker
Letterer: Ed Dukeshire
Cover Artists: Terry Dodson & Rachel Dodson; Carlos Pacheco & Christina Strain; Carlo Pagulayan, Jason Paz & Wil Quintana; Jae Lee & June Chung; and Carlo Pagulayan, Jason Paz & Dave McCaig

Assistant Editors: Jordan D. White & Michael Horwitz
Associate Editor: Nathan Cosby
Editor: Mark Paniccia

Collection Editor & Design: Cory Levine
Editorial Assistants: James Emmett & Joe Hochstein
Assistant Editors: Matt Masdeu, Alex Starbuck & Nelson Ribeiro
Editors, Special Projects: Jennifer Grünwald & Mark D. Beazley
Senior Editor, Special Projects: Jeff Youngquist
Senior Vice President of Sales: David Gabriel

Editor in Chief: Joe Quesada
Publisher: Dan Buckley
Executive Producer: Alan Fine

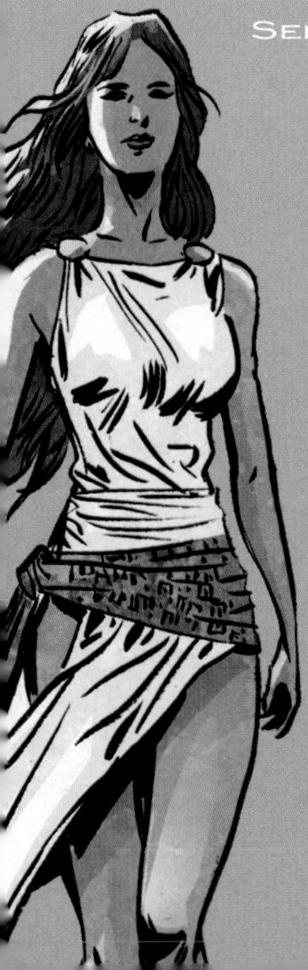

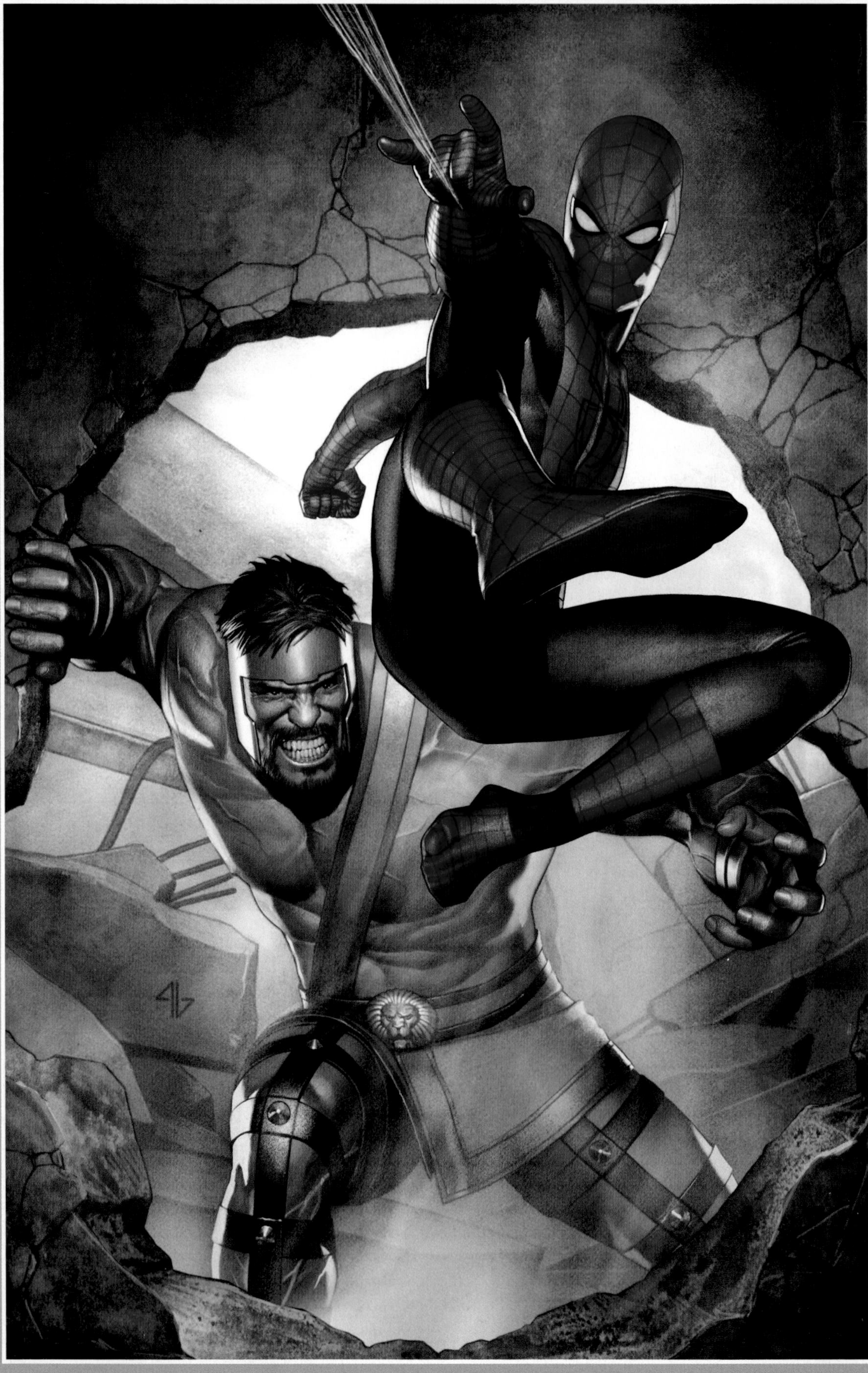

Assault on New Olympus Prologue

JIMMY WOO	THE URANIAN	VENUS	NAMORA	M-11	GORILLA MA...
LEADER OF THE SECRET EMPIRE KNOWN AS ATLAS	BOB GRAYSON, TELEPATH AND TECH	AN HONEST-TO-GOSH SIREN	ATLANTEAN PRINCESS, COUSIN OF NAMOR	KILLER ROBOT, "REFORMED"	KEN HALE, GUY THAT'S A GORILLA

THEY ARE A TEAM OF 1950s ADVENTURERS RE-FORMED TO BATTLE EARTH'S GREATEST THREATS, WHILE UNDER THE GUISE OF AN EVIL ORGANIZATION BASED UNDERNEATH SAN FRANCISCO. THEY ARE THE

AGENTS OF ATLAS

RECENTLY...

THE AGENTS USED A MODIFIED CEREBRA (THE X-MEN'S MUTANT-DETECTING MACHINE) TO FIND THEIR MISSING TEAMMATE, VENUS. * UNFORTUNATELY, THEY FOUND HER...

*SEE X-MEN VS. AGENTS OF ATLAS #1-#2

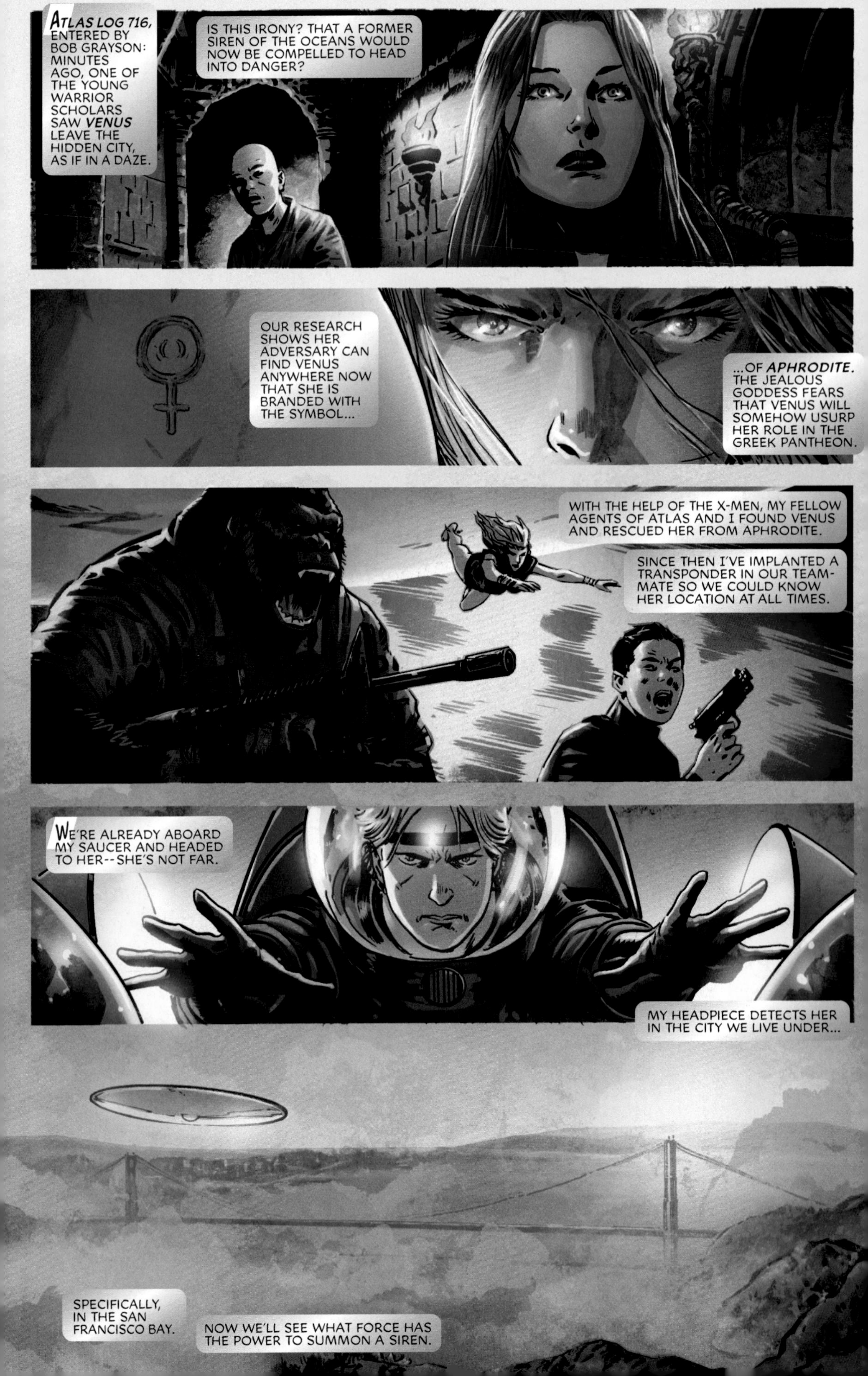
ATLAS LOG 716, ENTERED BY BOB GRAYSON: MINUTES AGO, ONE OF THE YOUNG WARRIOR SCHOLARS SAW VENUS LEAVE THE HIDDEN CITY, AS IF IN A DAZE.
IS THIS IRONY? THAT A FORMER SIREN OF THE OCEANS WOULD NOW BE COMPELLED TO HEAD INTO DANGER?
OUR RESEARCH SHOWS HER ADVERSARY CAN FIND VENUS ANYWHERE NOW THAT SHE IS BRANDED WITH THE SYMBOL...
...OF APHRODITE. THE JEALOUS GODDESS FEARS THAT VENUS WILL SOMEHOW USURP HER ROLE IN THE GREEK PANTHEON.
WITH THE HELP OF THE X-MEN, MY FELLOW AGENTS OF ATLAS AND I FOUND VENUS AND RESCUED HER FROM APHRODITE.
SINCE THEN I'VE IMPLANTED A TRANSPONDER IN OUR TEAM-MATE SO WE COULD KNOW HER LOCATION AT ALL TIMES.
WE'RE ALREADY ABOARD MY SAUCER AND HEADED TO HER--SHE'S NOT FAR.
MY HEADPIECE DETECTS HER IN THE CITY WE LIVE UNDER...
SPECIFICALLY, IN THE SAN FRANCISCO BAY.
NOW WE'LL SEE WHAT FORCE HAS THE POWER TO SUMMON A SIREN.

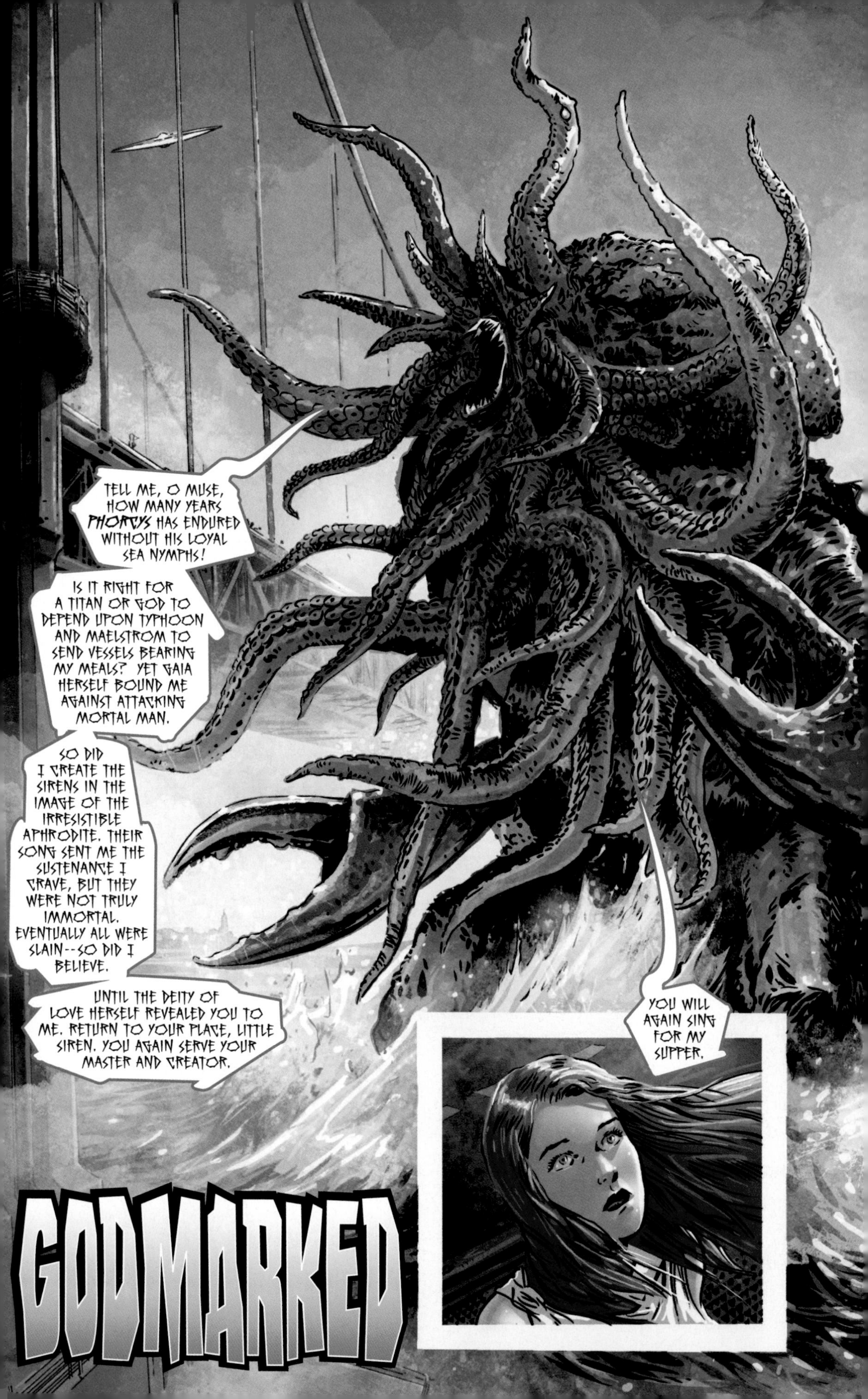
TELL ME, O MUSE, HOW MANY YEARS PHORCYS HAS ENDURED WITHOUT HIS LOYAL SEA NYMPHS!
IS IT RIGHT FOR A TITAN OR GOD TO DEPEND UPON TYPHOON AND MAELSTROM TO SEND VESSELS BEARING MY MEALS? YET GAIA HERSELF BOUND ME AGAINST ATTACKING MORTAL MAN.
SO DID I CREATE THE SIRENS IN THE IMAGE OF THE IRRESISTIBLE APHRODITE. THEIR SONG SENT ME THE SUSTENANCE I CRAVE, BUT THEY WERE NOT TRULY IMMORTAL. EVENTUALLY ALL WERE SLAIN--SO DID I BELIEVE.
UNTIL THE DEITY OF LOVE HERSELF REVEALED YOU TO ME. RETURN TO YOUR PLACE, LITTLE SIREN. YOU AGAIN SERVE YOUR MASTER AND CREATOR.
YOU WILL AGAIN SING FOR MY SUPPER.
GODMARKED

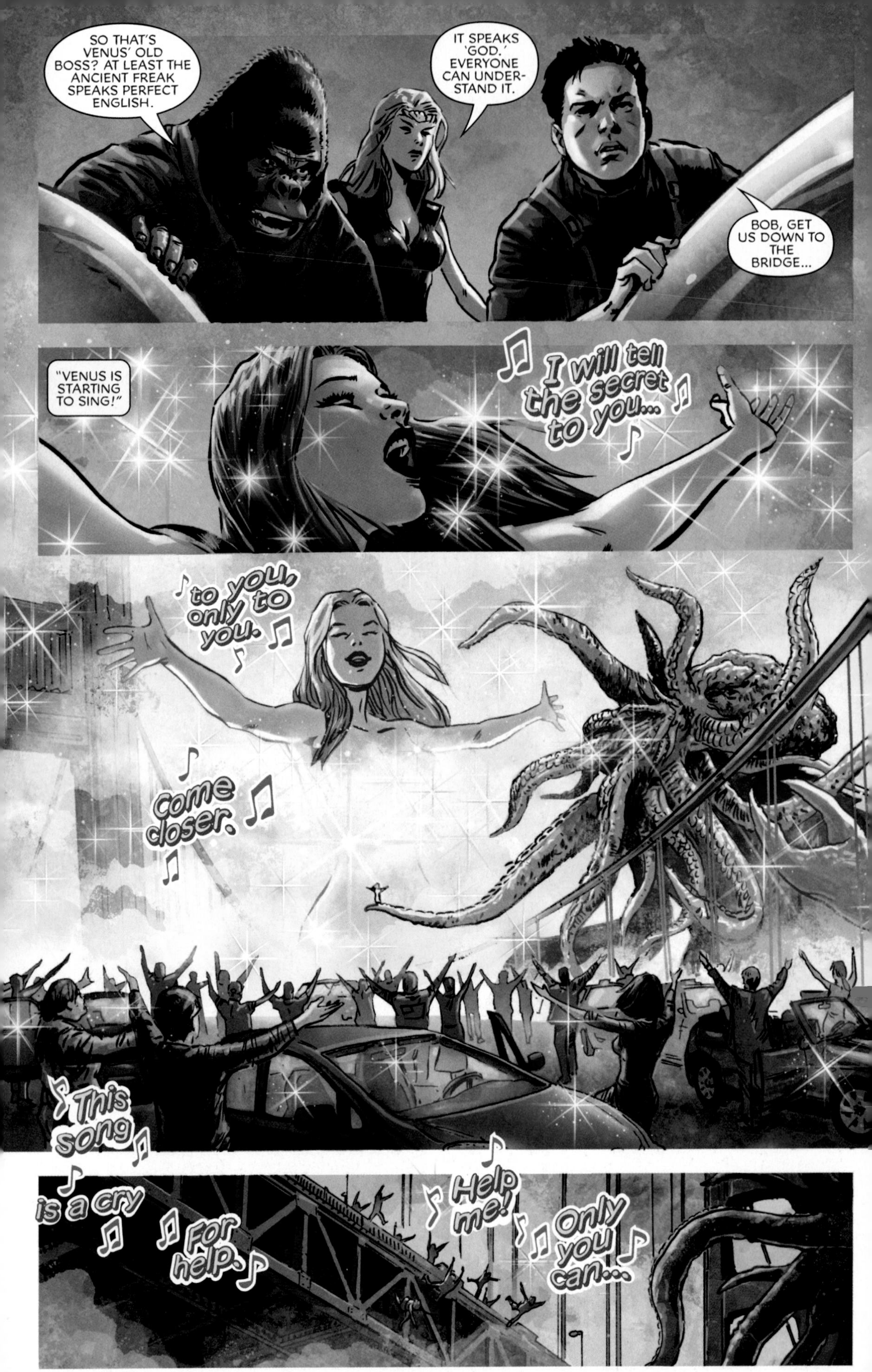
SO THAT'S VENUS' OLD BOSS? AT LEAST THE ANCIENT FREAK SPEAKS PERFECT ENGLISH.
IT SPEAKS 'GOD.' EVERYONE CAN UNDER-STAND IT.
BOB, GET US DOWN TO THE BRIDGE...
"VENUS IS STARTING TO SING!"
I will tell the secret to you...
to you, only to you.
Come closer.
This song is a cry
For help.
Help me!
Only you can...

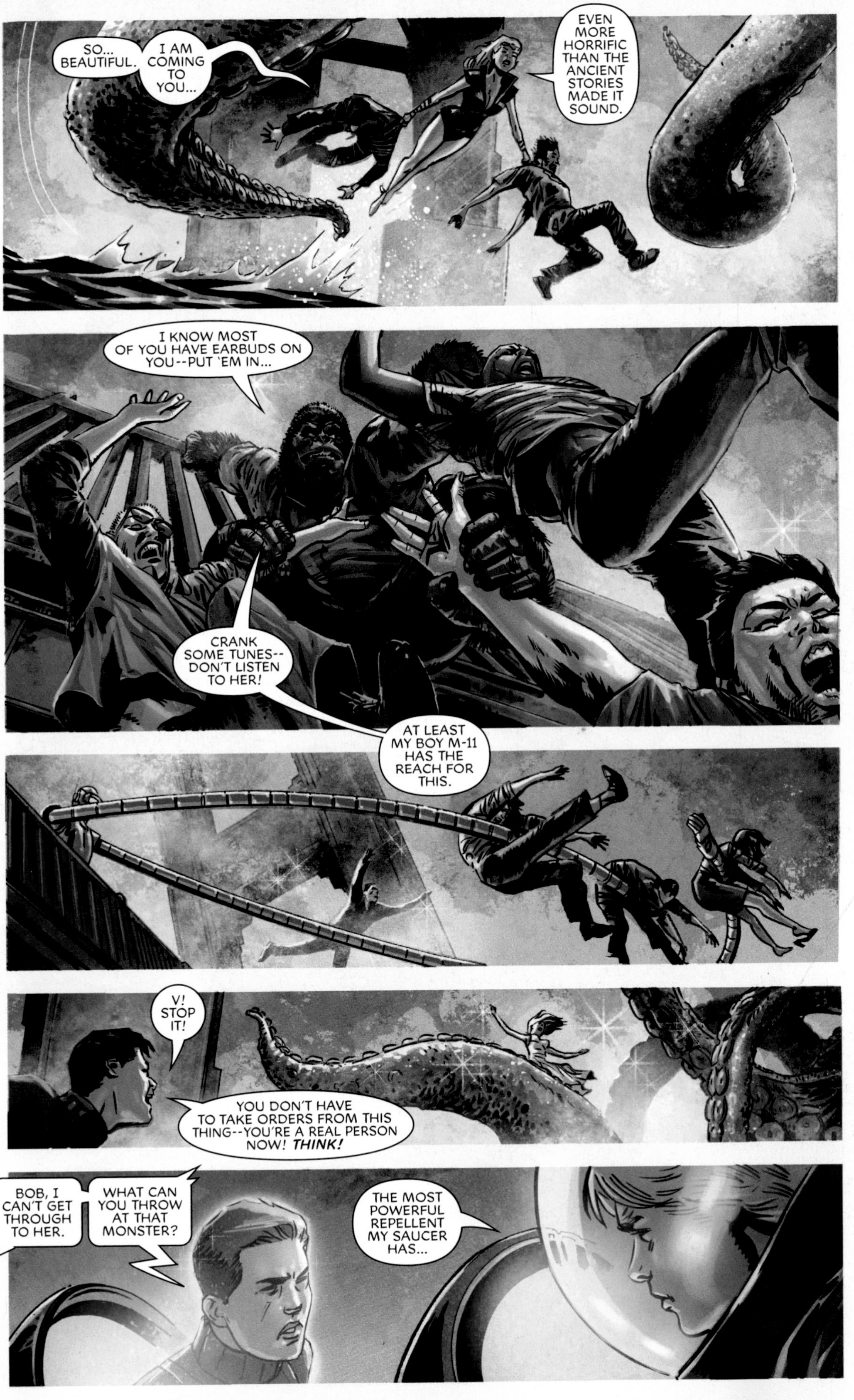
SO... BEAUTIFUL.
I AM COMING TO YOU...
EVEN MORE HORRIFIC THAN THE ANCIENT STORIES MADE IT SOUND.
I KNOW MOST OF YOU HAVE EARBUDS ON YOU--PUT 'EM IN...
CRANK SOME TUNES--DON'T LISTEN TO HER!
AT LEAST MY BOY M-11 HAS THE REACH FOR THIS.
V! STOP IT!
YOU DON'T HAVE TO TAKE ORDERS FROM THIS THING--YOU'RE A REAL PERSON NOW! THINK!
BOB, I CAN'T GET THROUGH TO HER.
WHAT CAN YOU THROW AT THAT MONSTER?
THE MOST POWERFUL REPELLENT MY SAUCER HAS...

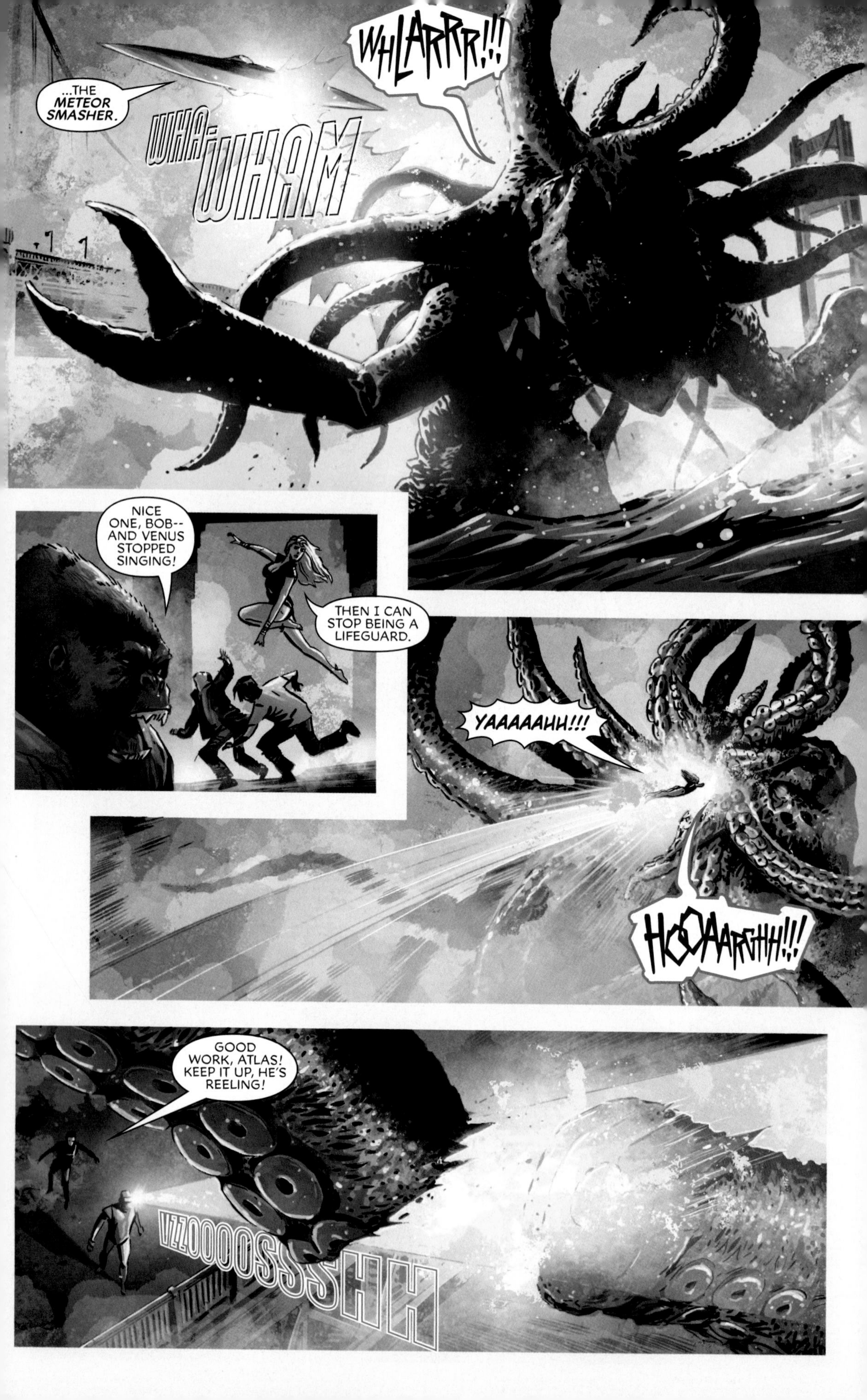

...THE METEOR SMASHER.
WHA-WHAM
WHLARRR!!!
NICE ONE, BOB-- AND VENUS STOPPED SINGING!
THEN I CAN STOP BEING A LIFEGUARD.
YAAAAAHH!!!
HOOAARGHH!!!
GOOD WORK, ATLAS! KEEP IT UP, HE'S REELING!
VZZOOOOSSSHH

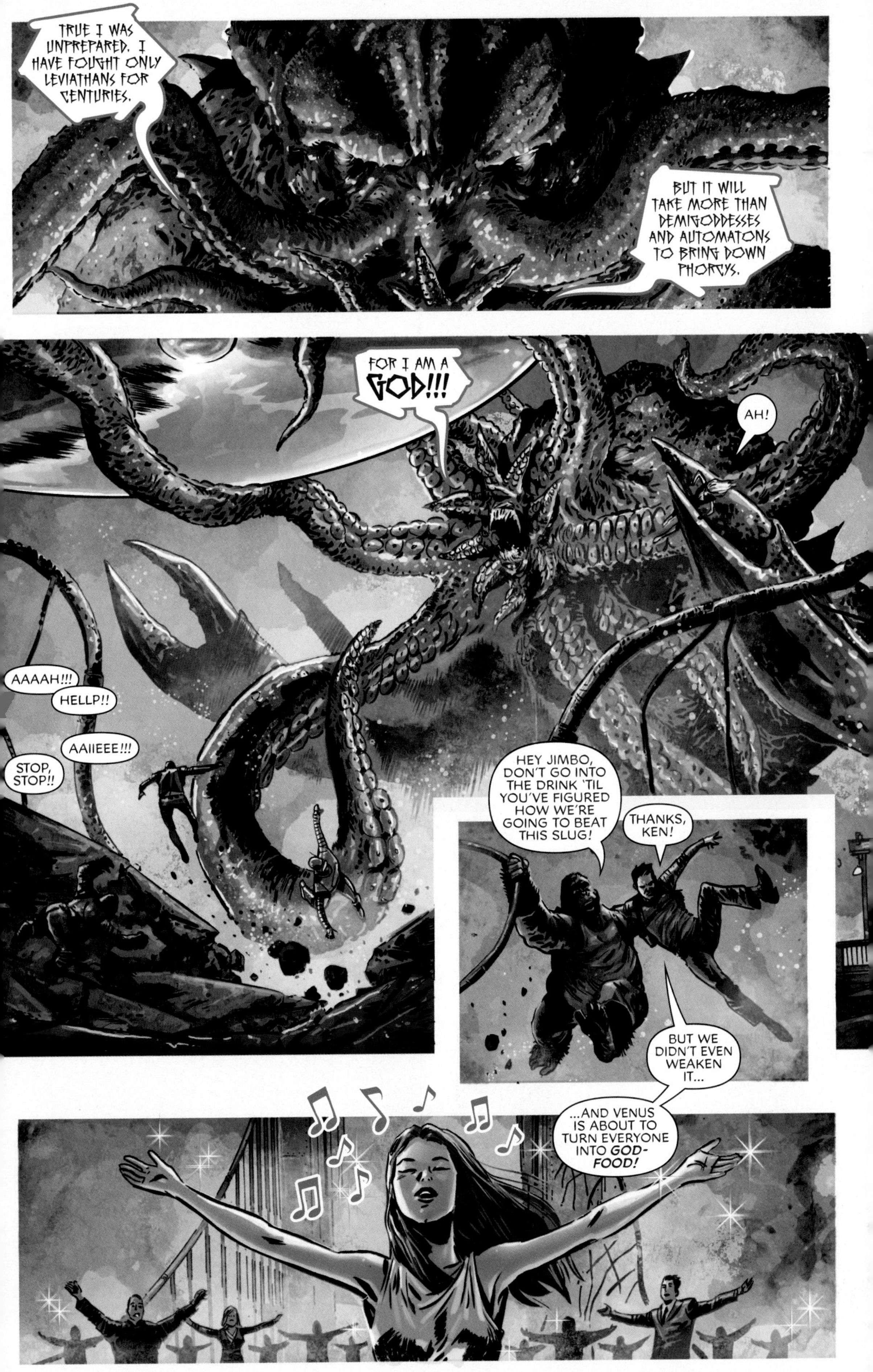

TRUE I WAS UNPREPARED. I HAVE FOUGHT ONLY LEVIATHANS FOR CENTURIES.
BUT IT WILL TAKE MORE THAN DEMIGODDESSES AND AUTOMATONS TO BRING DOWN PHORCYS.
FOR I AM A GOD!!!
AH!
AAAAH!!!
HELLP!!
AAIIEEE!!!
STOP, STOP!!
HEY JIMBO, DON'T GO INTO THE DRINK 'TIL YOU'VE FIGURED HOW WE'RE GOING TO BEAT THIS SLUG!
THANKS, KEN!
BUT WE DIDN'T EVEN WEAKEN IT...
...AND VENUS IS ABOUT TO TURN EVERYONE INTO *GOD-FOOD!*

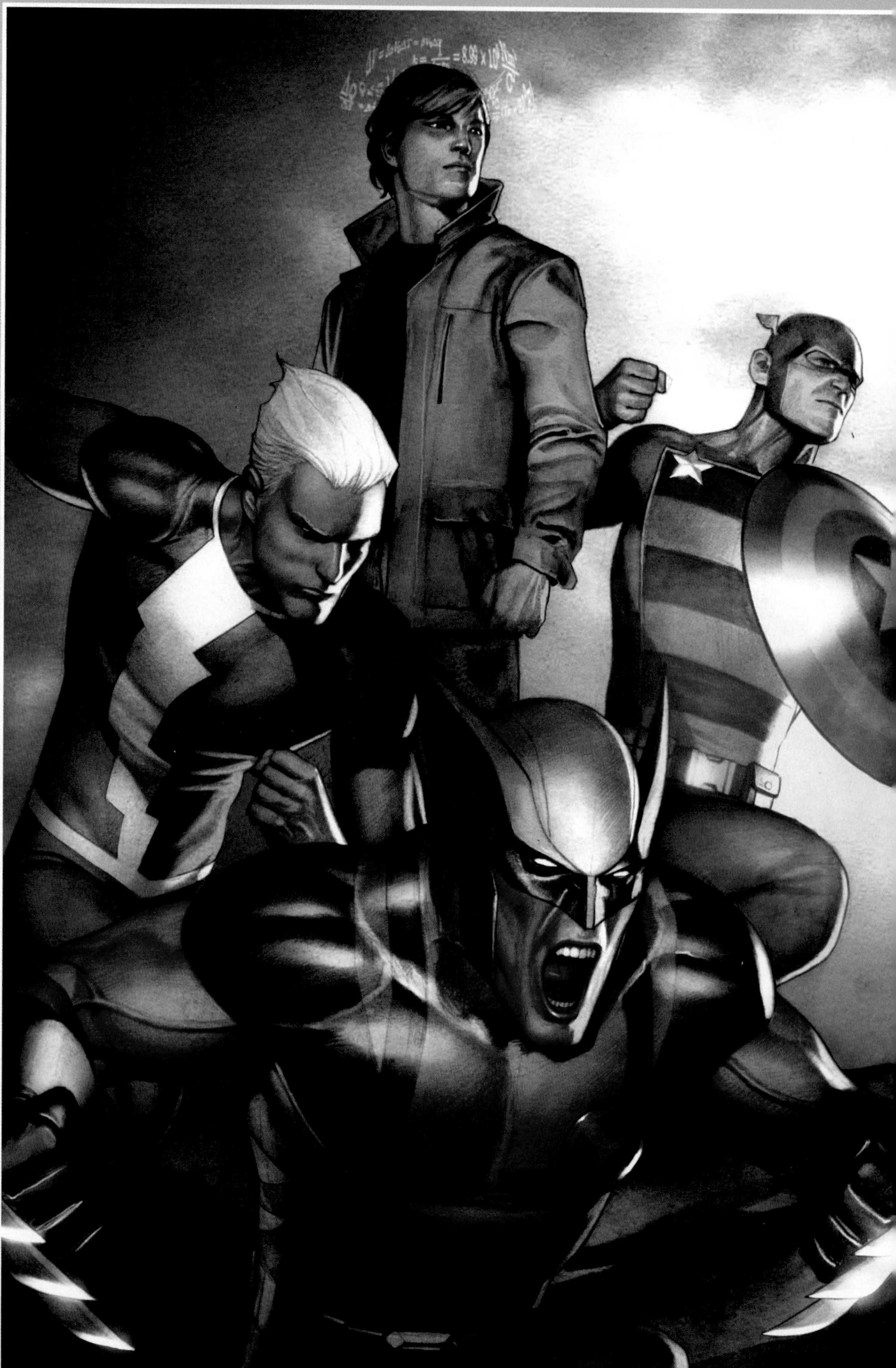

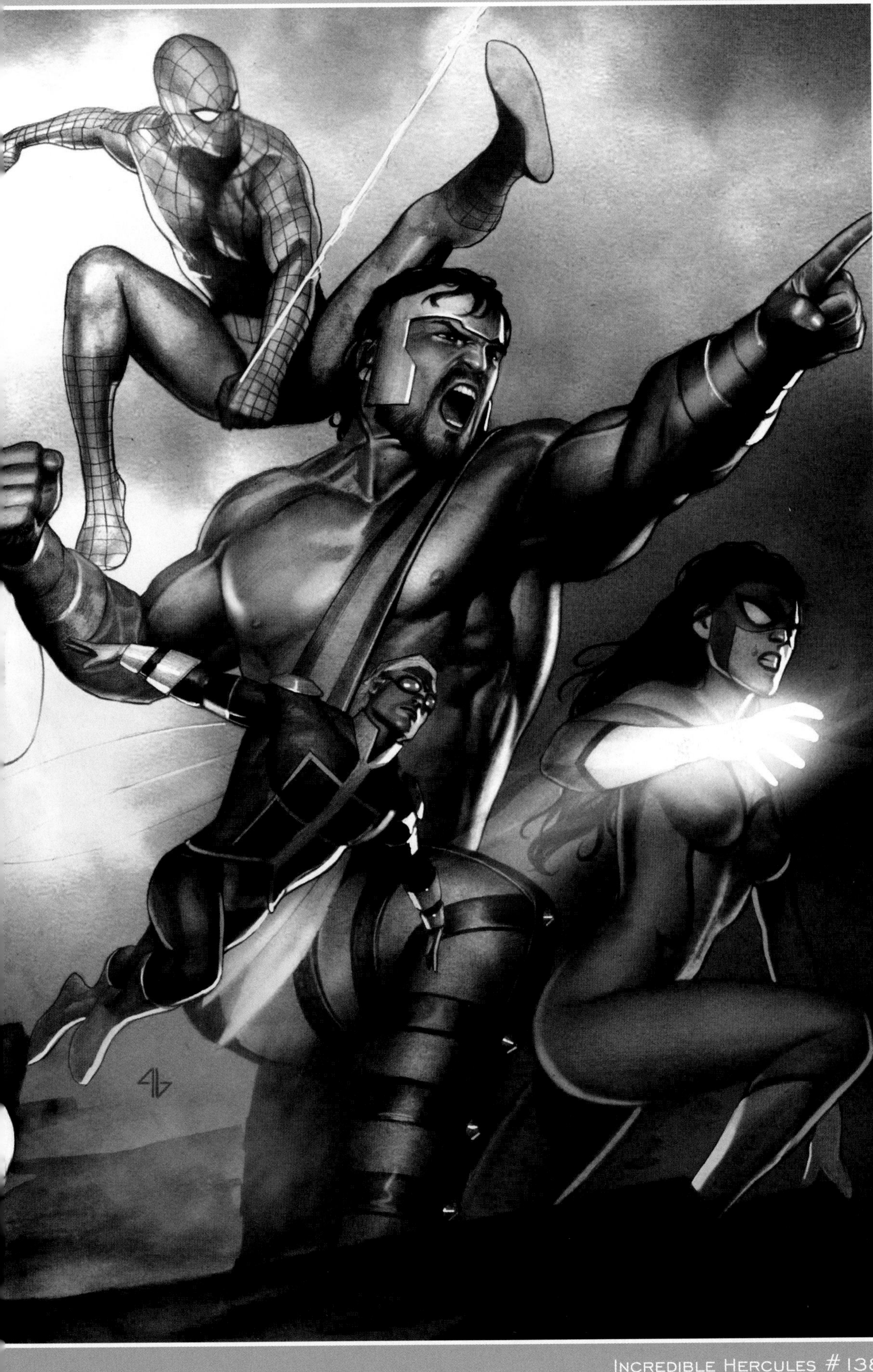
AB

Incredible Hercules # 138

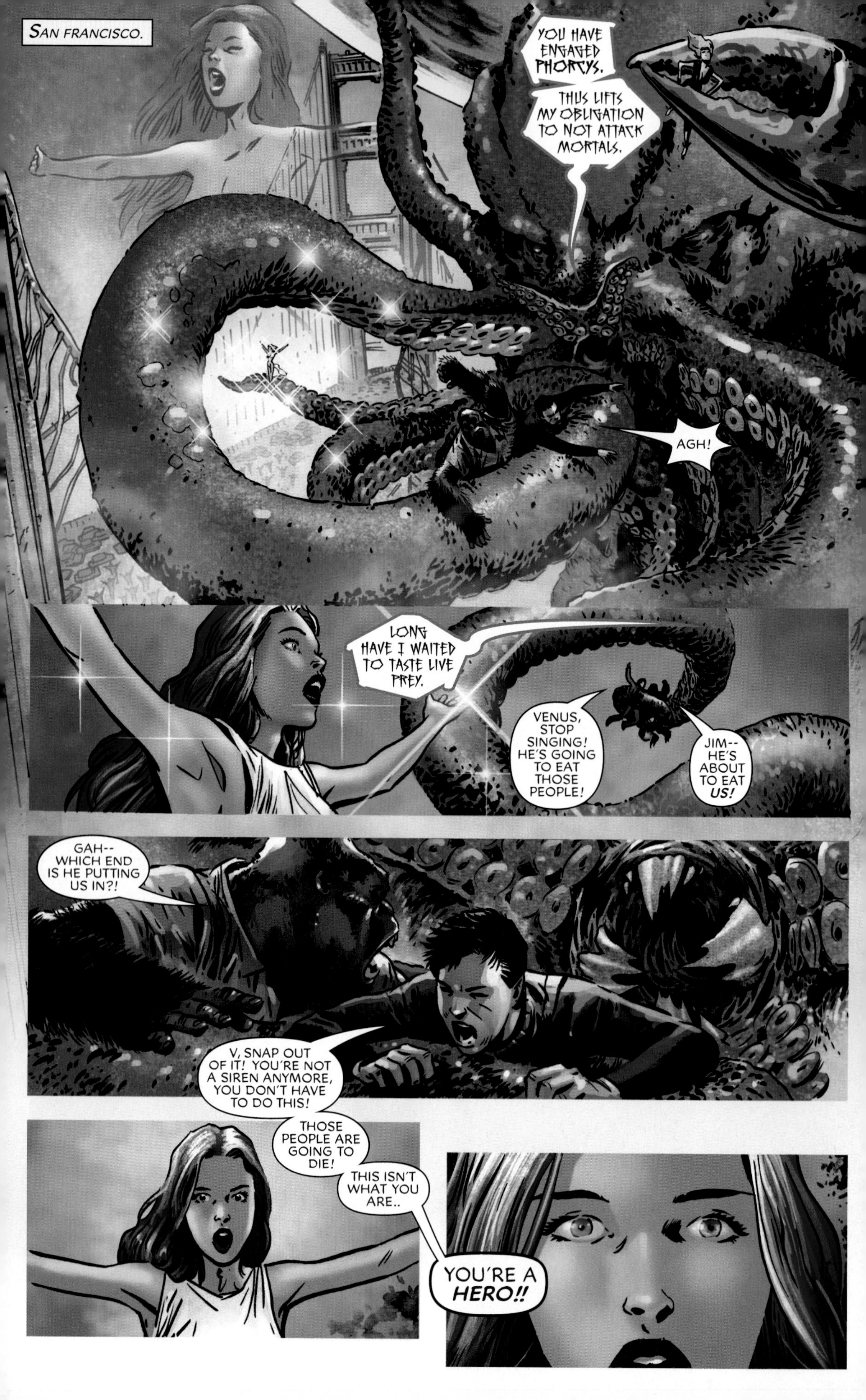

SAN FRANCISCO.
YOU HAVE ENGAGED PHORCYS.
THUS LIFTS MY OBLIGATION TO NOT ATTACK MORTALS.
AGH!
LONG HAVE I WAITED TO TASTE LIVE PREY.
VENUS, STOP SINGING! HE'S GOING TO EAT THOSE PEOPLE!
JIM-- HE'S ABOUT TO EAT US!
GAH-- WHICH END IS HE PUTTING US IN?!
V, SNAP OUT OF IT! YOU'RE NOT A SIREN ANYMORE, YOU DON'T HAVE TO DO THIS!
THOSE PEOPLE ARE GOING TO DIE!
THIS ISN'T WHAT YOU ARE..
YOU'RE A HERO!!

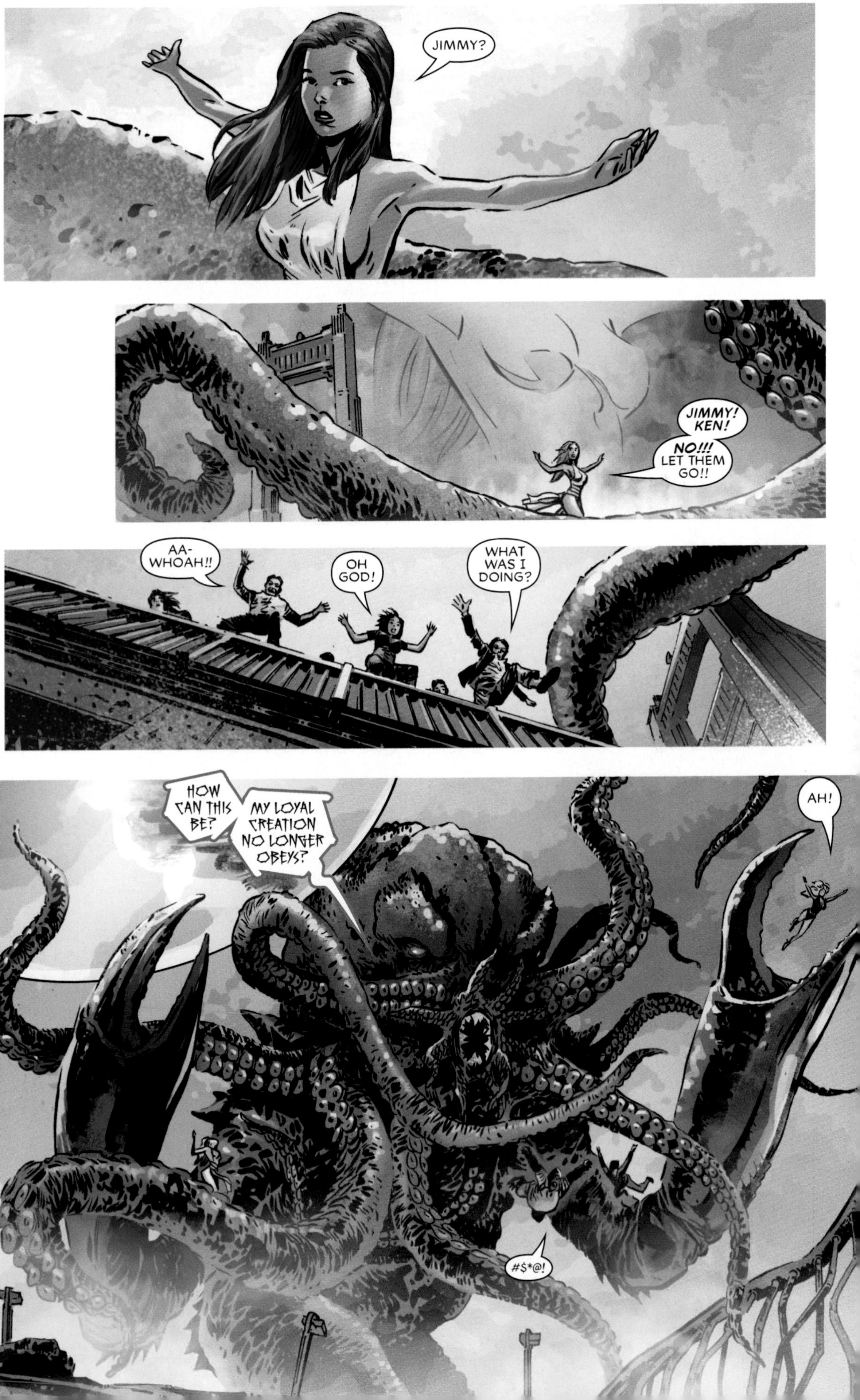
JIMMY?
JIMMY! KEN!
NO!!! LET THEM GO!!
AA-WHOAH!!
OH GOD!
WHAT WAS I DOING?
HOW CAN THIS BE?
MY LOYAL CREATION NO LONGER OBEYS?
AH!
#$*@!

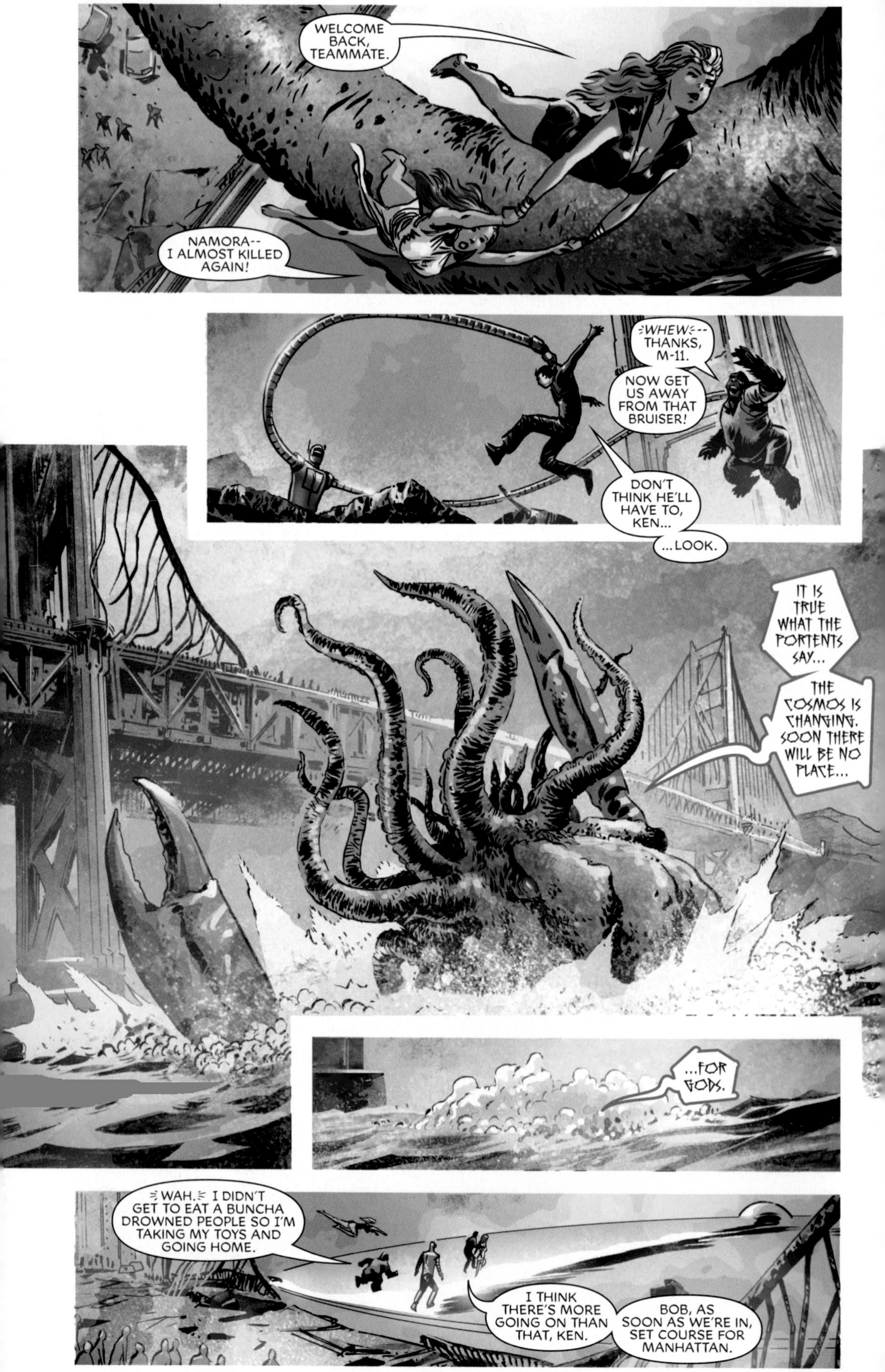

WELCOME BACK, TEAMMATE.
NAMORA-- I ALMOST KILLED AGAIN!
WHEW-- THANKS, M-11.
NOW GET US AWAY FROM THAT BRUISER!
DON'T THINK HE'LL HAVE TO, KEN...
...LOOK.
IT IS TRUE WHAT THE PORTENTS SAY...
THE COSMOS IS CHANGING. SOON THERE WILL BE NO PLACE...
...FOR GODS.
WAH. I DIDN'T GET TO EAT A BUNCHA DROWNED PEOPLE SO I'M TAKING MY TOYS AND GOING HOME.
I THINK THERE'S MORE GOING ON THAN THAT, KEN.
BOB, AS SOON AS WE'RE IN, SET COURSE FOR MANHATTAN.

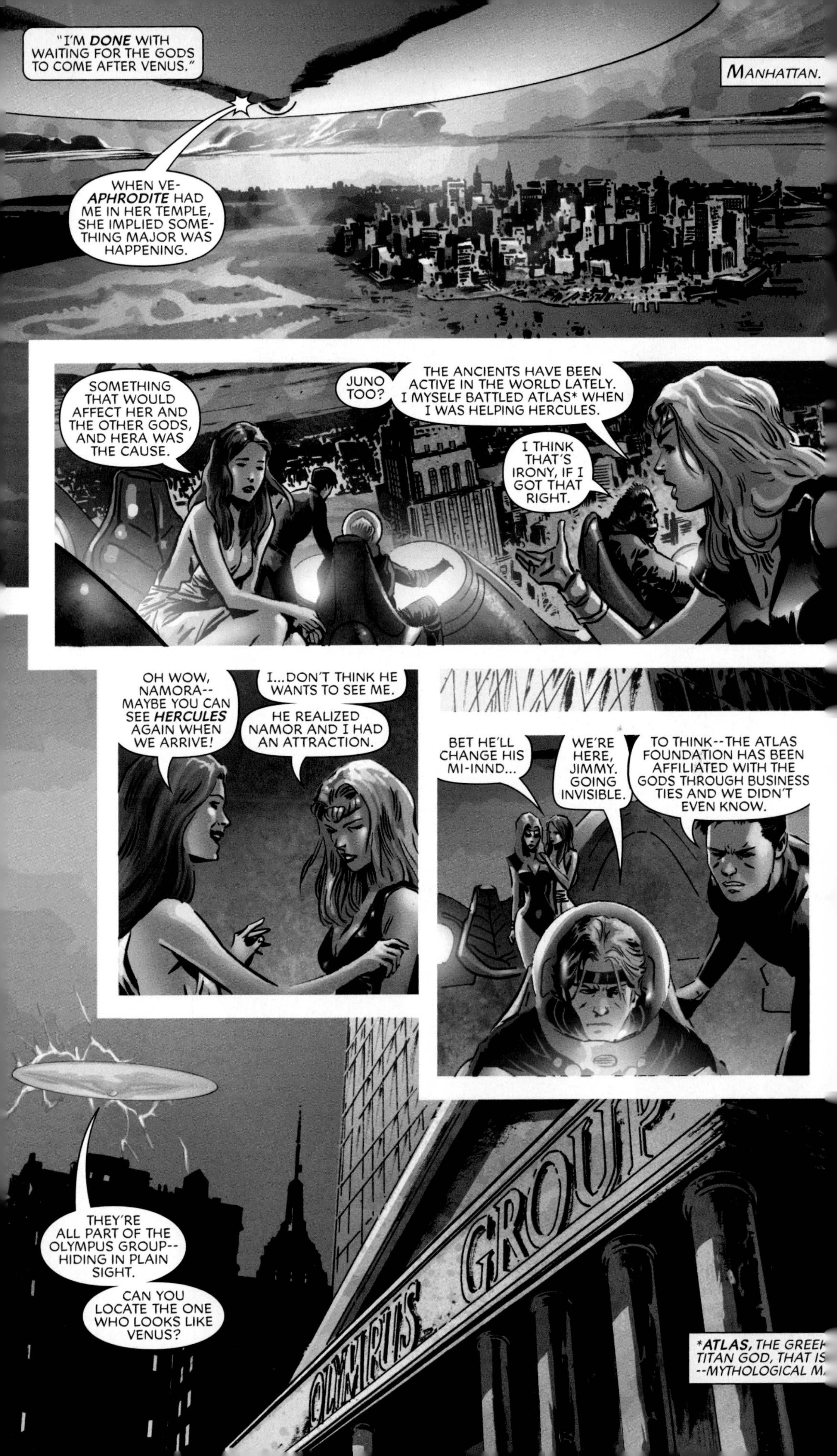
"I'M DONE WITH WAITING FOR THE GODS TO COME AFTER VENUS."
MANHATTAN.
WHEN VE- APHRODITE HAD ME IN HER TEMPLE, SHE IMPLIED SOMETHING MAJOR WAS HAPPENING.
SOMETHING THAT WOULD AFFECT HER AND THE OTHER GODS, AND HERA WAS THE CAUSE.
JUNO TOO?
THE ANCIENTS HAVE BEEN ACTIVE IN THE WORLD LATELY. I MYSELF BATTLED ATLAS* WHEN I WAS HELPING HERCULES.
I THINK THAT'S IRONY, IF I GOT THAT RIGHT.
OH WOW, NAMORA-- MAYBE YOU CAN SEE HERCULES AGAIN WHEN WE ARRIVE!
I...DON'T THINK HE WANTS TO SEE ME.
HE REALIZED NAMOR AND I HAD AN ATTRACTION.
BET HE'LL CHANGE HIS MI-INND...
WE'RE HERE, JIMMY. GOING INVISIBLE.
TO THINK--THE ATLAS FOUNDATION HAS BEEN AFFILIATED WITH THE GODS THROUGH BUSINESS TIES AND WE DIDN'T EVEN KNOW.
THEY'RE ALL PART OF THE OLYMPUS GROUP-- HIDING IN PLAIN SIGHT.
CAN YOU LOCATE THE ONE WHO LOOKS LIKE VENUS?
OLYMPUS GROUP
*ATLAS, THE GREEK TITAN GOD, THAT IS --MYTHOLOGICAL

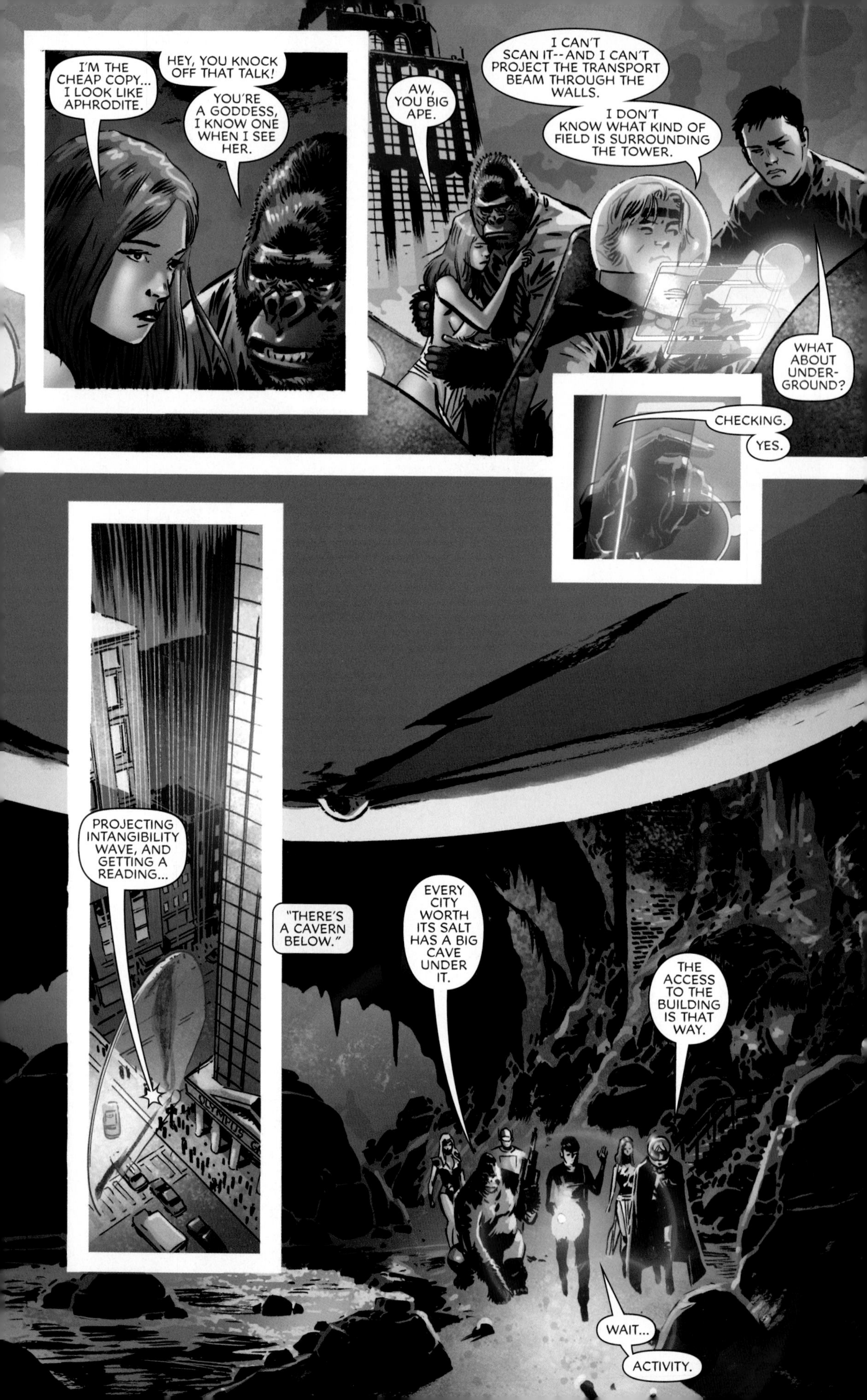

I'M THE CHEAP COPY... I LOOK LIKE APHRODITE.
HEY, YOU KNOCK OFF THAT TALK!
YOU'RE A GODDESS, I KNOW ONE WHEN I SEE HER.
AW, YOU BIG APE.
I CAN'T SCAN IT--AND I CAN'T PROJECT THE TRANSPORT BEAM THROUGH THE WALLS.
I DON'T KNOW WHAT KIND OF FIELD IS SURROUNDING THE TOWER.
WHAT ABOUT UNDER-GROUND?
CHECKING.
YES.
PROJECTING INTANGIBILITY WAVE, AND GETTING A READING...
"THERE'S A CAVERN BELOW."
EVERY CITY WORTH ITS SALT HAS A BIG CAVE UNDER IT.
THE ACCESS TO THE BUILDING IS THAT WAY.
WAIT...
ACTIVITY.

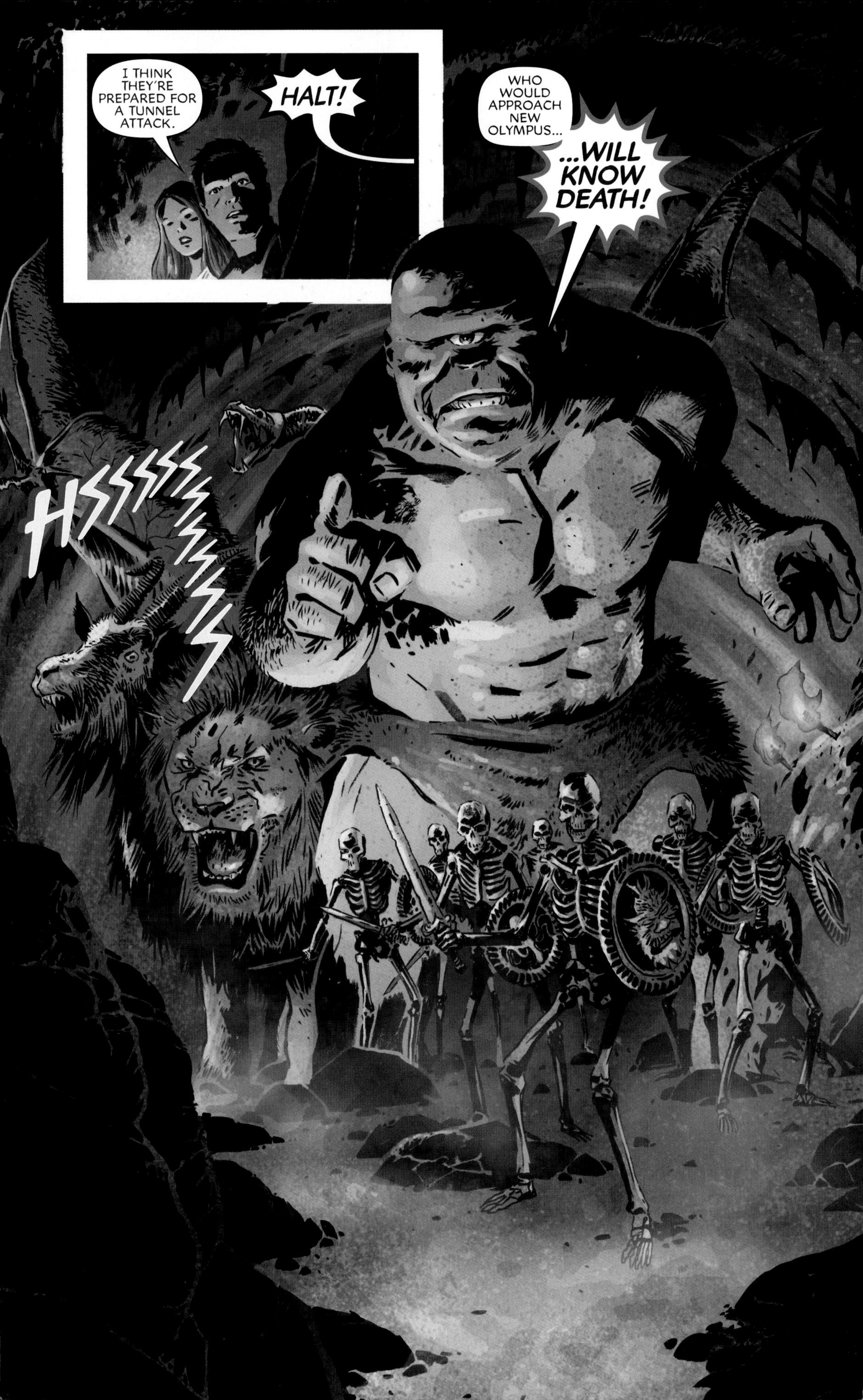
I THINK THEY'RE PREPARED FOR A TUNNEL ATTACK.
HALT!
WHO WOULD APPROACH NEW OLYMPUS...
...WILL KNOW DEATH!
HSSSSSSSSSSSS

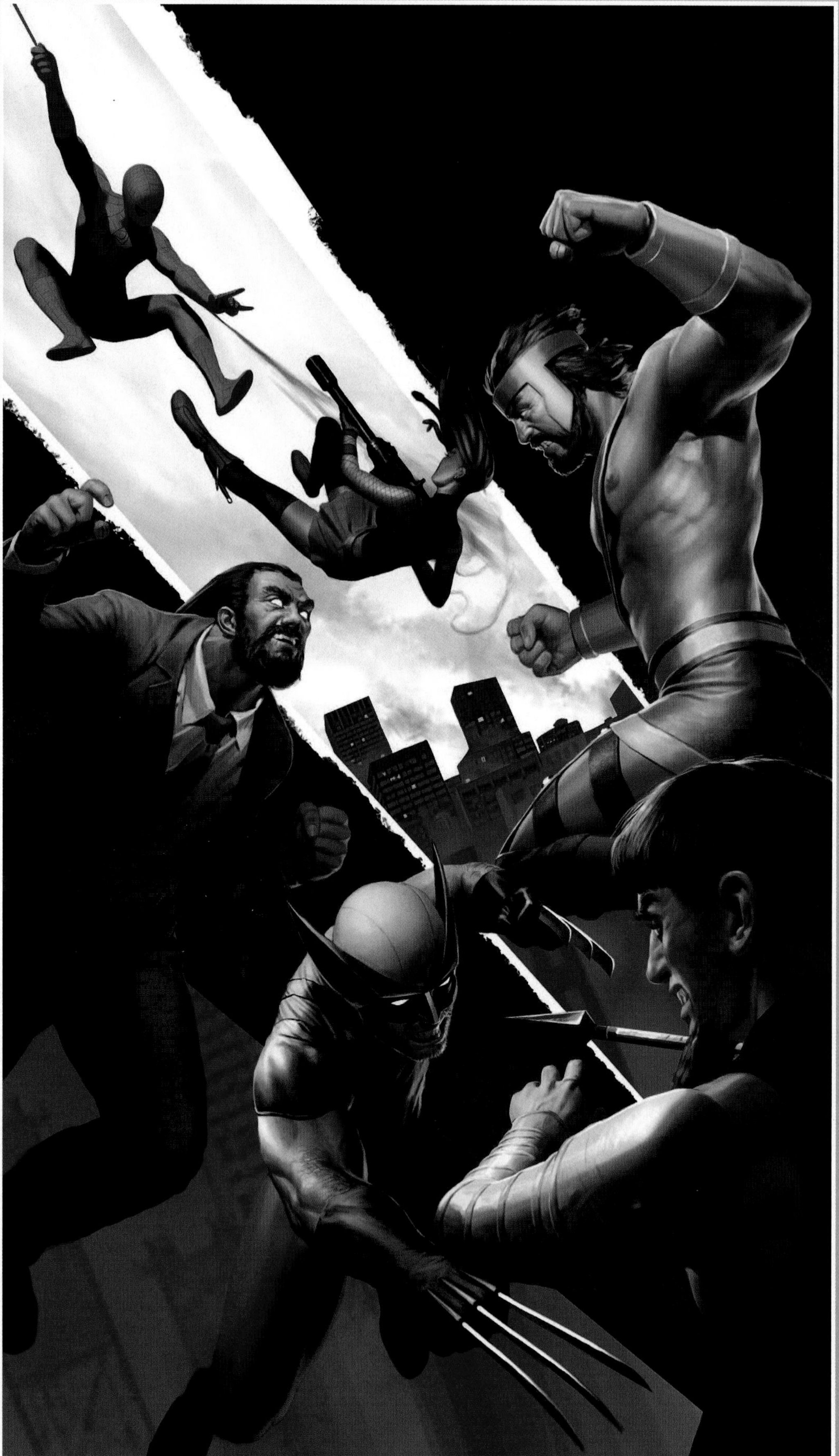

Incredible Hercules #139

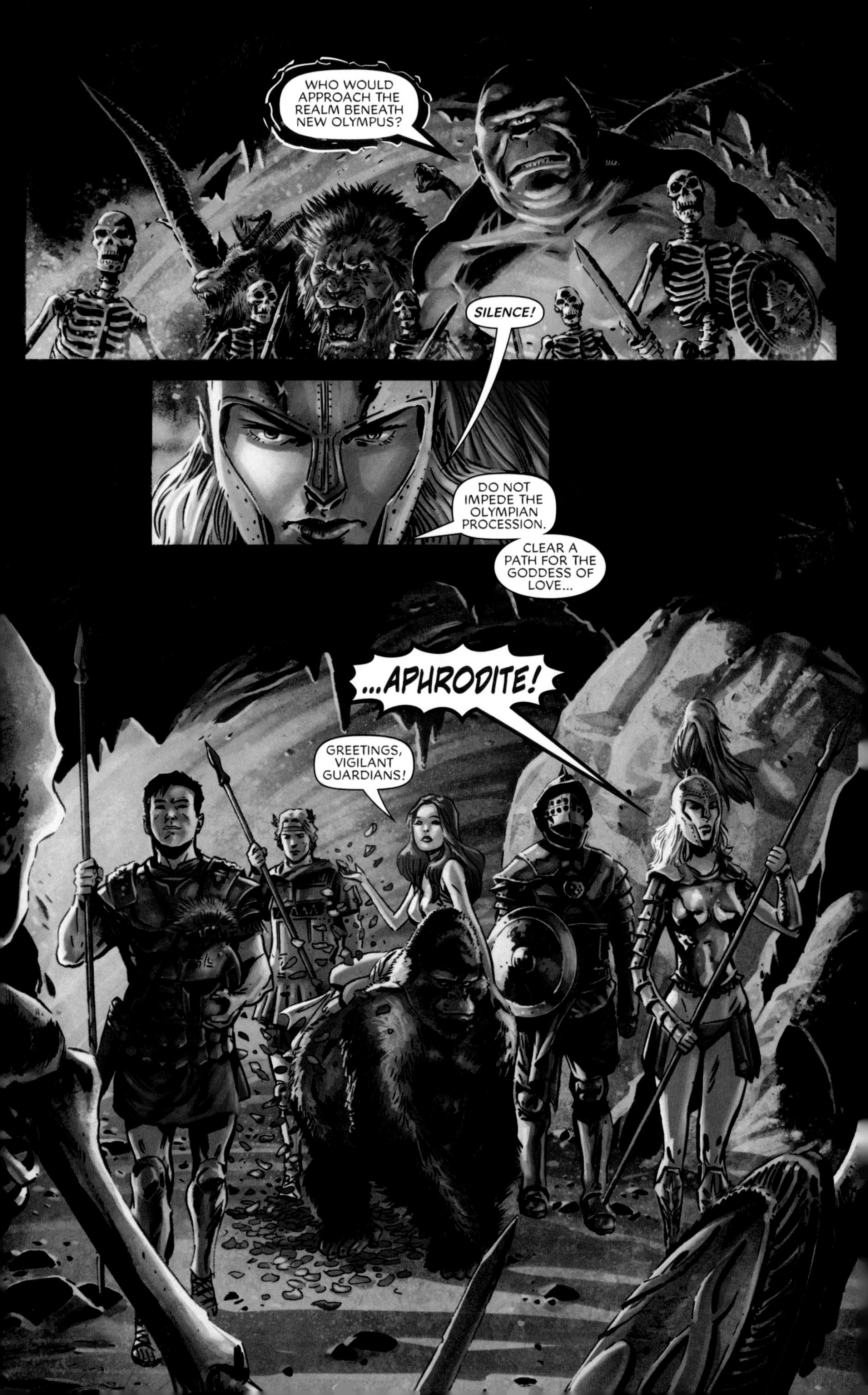
WHO WOULD APPROACH THE REALM BENEATH NEW OLYMPUS?
SILENCE!
DO NOT IMPEDE THE OLYMPIAN PROCESSION.
CLEAR A PATH FOR THE GODDESS OF LOVE...
...APHRODITE!
GREETINGS, VIGILANT GUARDIANS!

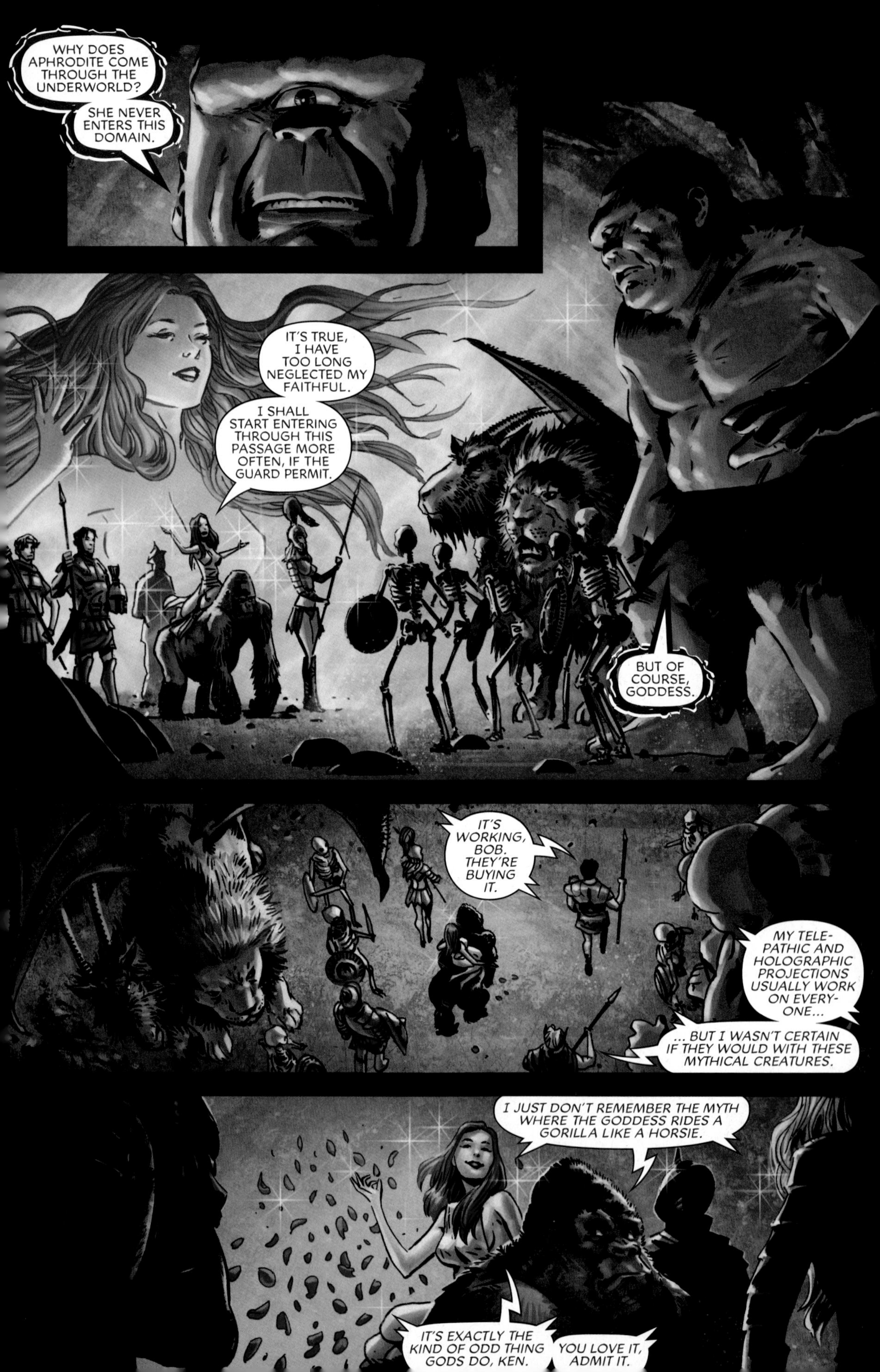
WHY DOES APHRODITE COME THROUGH THE UNDERWORLD?
SHE NEVER ENTERS THIS DOMAIN.
IT'S TRUE, I HAVE TOO LONG NEGLECTED MY FAITHFUL.
I SHALL START ENTERING THROUGH THIS PASSAGE MORE OFTEN, IF THE GUARD PERMIT.
BUT OF COURSE, GODDESS.
IT'S WORKING, BOB. THEY'RE BUYING IT.
MY TELE-PATHIC AND HOLOGRAPHIC PROJECTIONS USUALLY WORK ON EVERY-ONE...
... BUT I WASN'T CERTAIN IF THEY WOULD WITH THESE MYTHICAL CREATURES.
I JUST DON'T REMEMBER THE MYTH WHERE THE GODDESS RIDES A GORILLA LIKE A HORSIE.
IT'S EXACTLY THE KIND OF ODD THING GODS DO, KEN.
YOU LOVE IT, ADMIT IT.

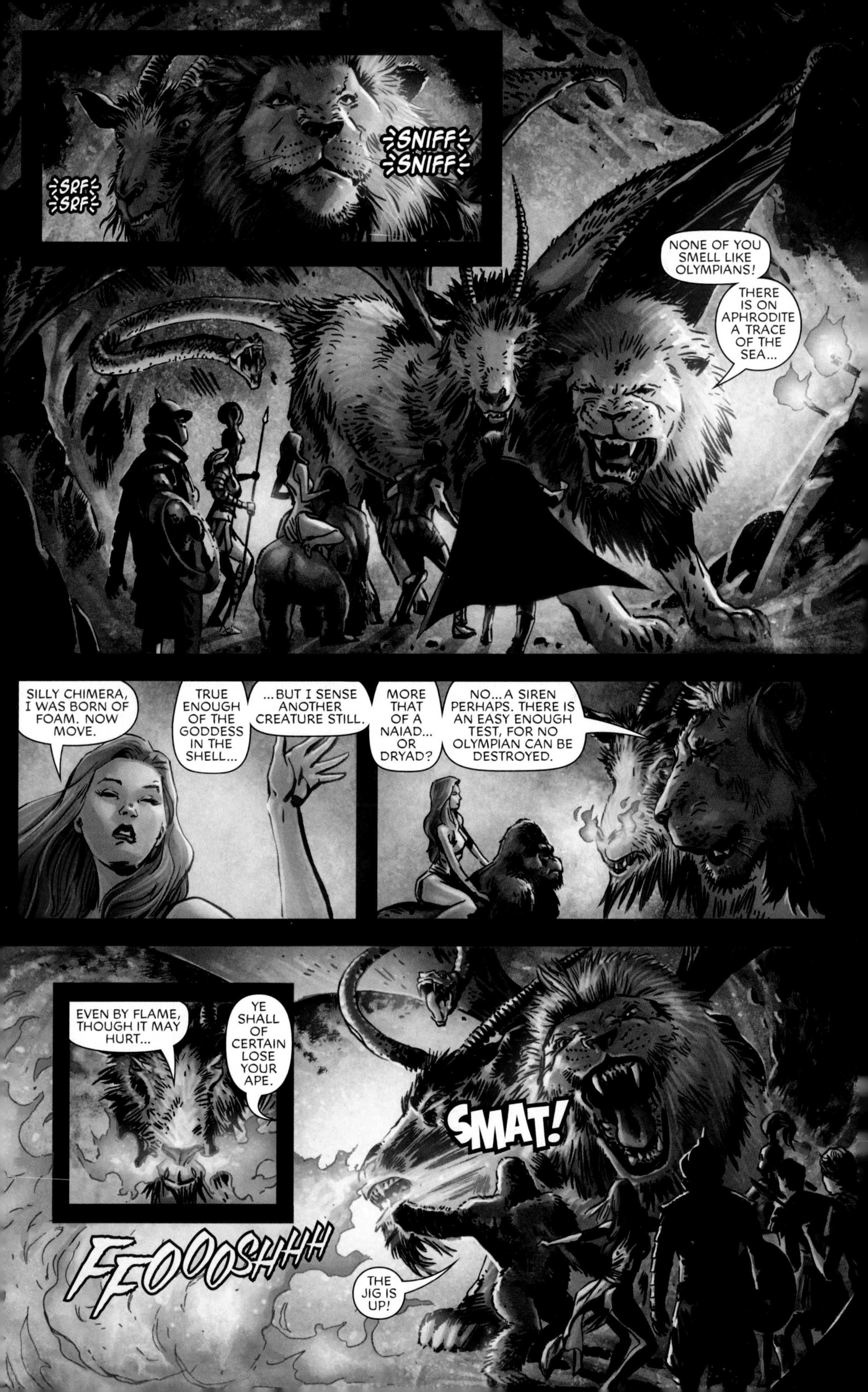
SRF SRF
SNIFF SNIFF
NONE OF YOU SMELL LIKE OLYMPIANS!
THERE IS ON APHRODITE A TRACE OF THE SEA...
SILLY CHIMERA, I WAS BORN OF FOAM. NOW MOVE.
TRUE ENOUGH OF THE GODDESS IN THE SHELL...
...BUT I SENSE ANOTHER CREATURE STILL.
MORE THAT OF A NAIAD... OR DRYAD?
NO...A SIREN PERHAPS. THERE IS AN EASY ENOUGH TEST, FOR NO OLYMPIAN CAN BE DESTROYED.
EVEN BY FLAME, THOUGH IT MAY HURT...
YE SHALL OF CERTAIN LOSE YOUR APE.
SMAT!
FFOOOSHHH
THE JIG IS UP!

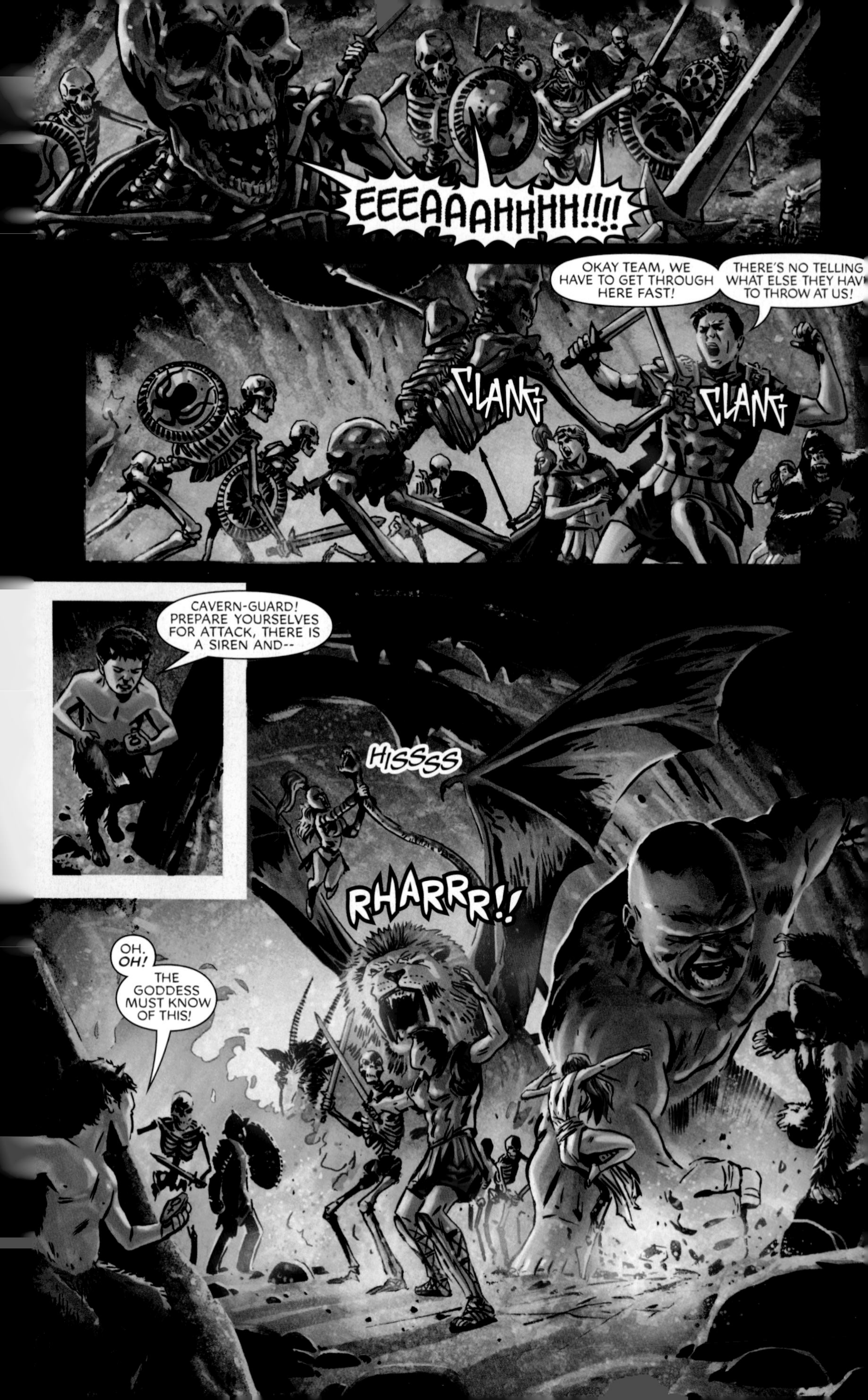
EEEAAAHHHH!!!!
OKAY TEAM, WE HAVE TO GET THROUGH HERE FAST!
THERE'S NO TELLING WHAT ELSE THEY HAV TO THROW AT US!
CLANG
CLANG
CAVERN-GUARD! PREPARE YOURSELVES FOR ATTACK, THERE IS A SIREN AND--
HISSSS
RHARRR!!
OH. OH! THE GODDESS MUST KNOW OF THIS!

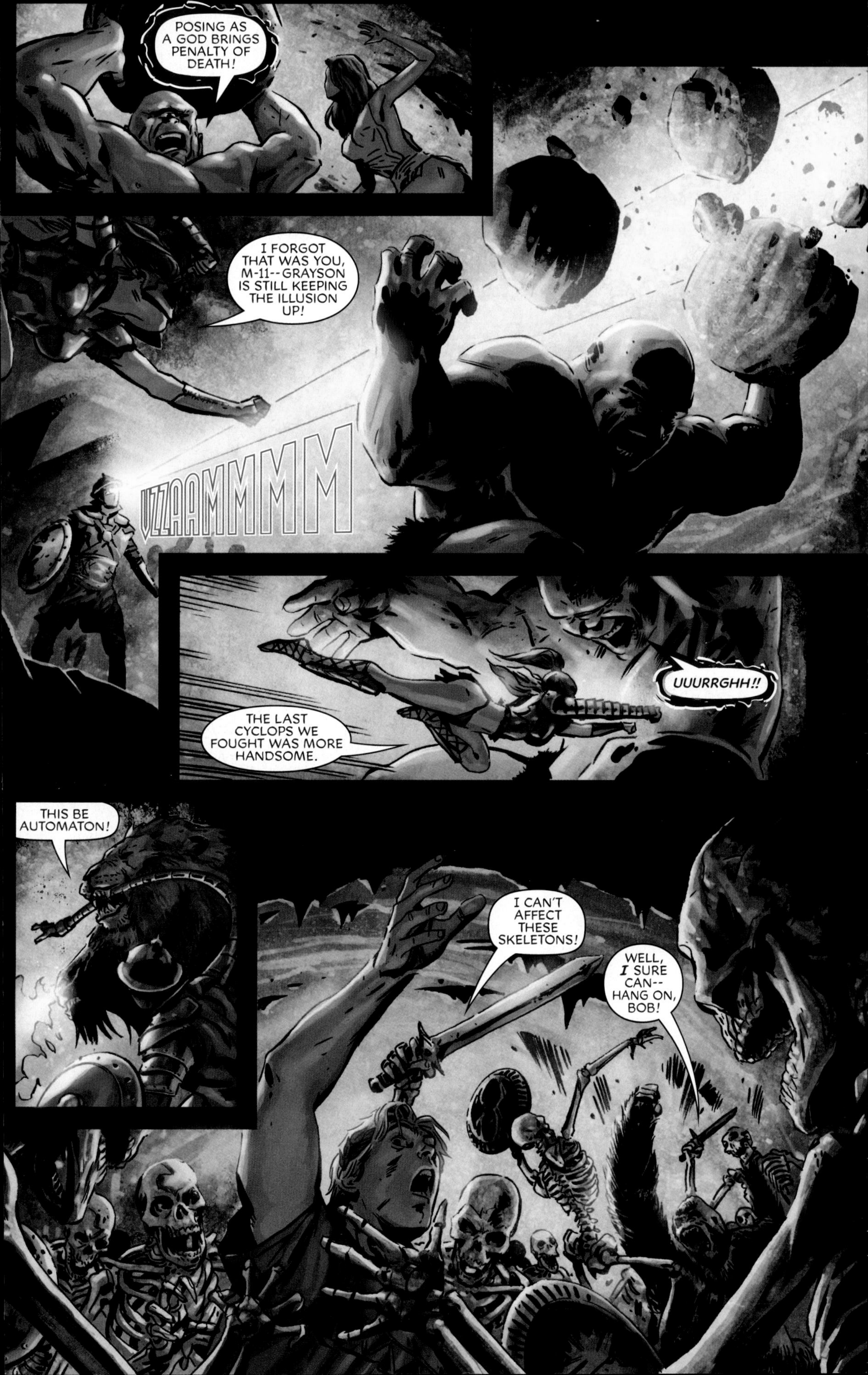
POSING AS A GOD BRINGS PENALTY OF DEATH!
I FORGOT THAT WAS YOU, M-11--GRAYSON IS STILL KEEPING THE ILLUSION UP!
VZZAAMMMMM
UUURRGHH!!
THE LAST CYCLOPS WE FOUGHT WAS MORE HANDSOME.
THIS BE AUTOMATON!
I CAN'T AFFECT THESE SKELETONS!
WELL, *I* SURE CAN--HANG ON, BOB!

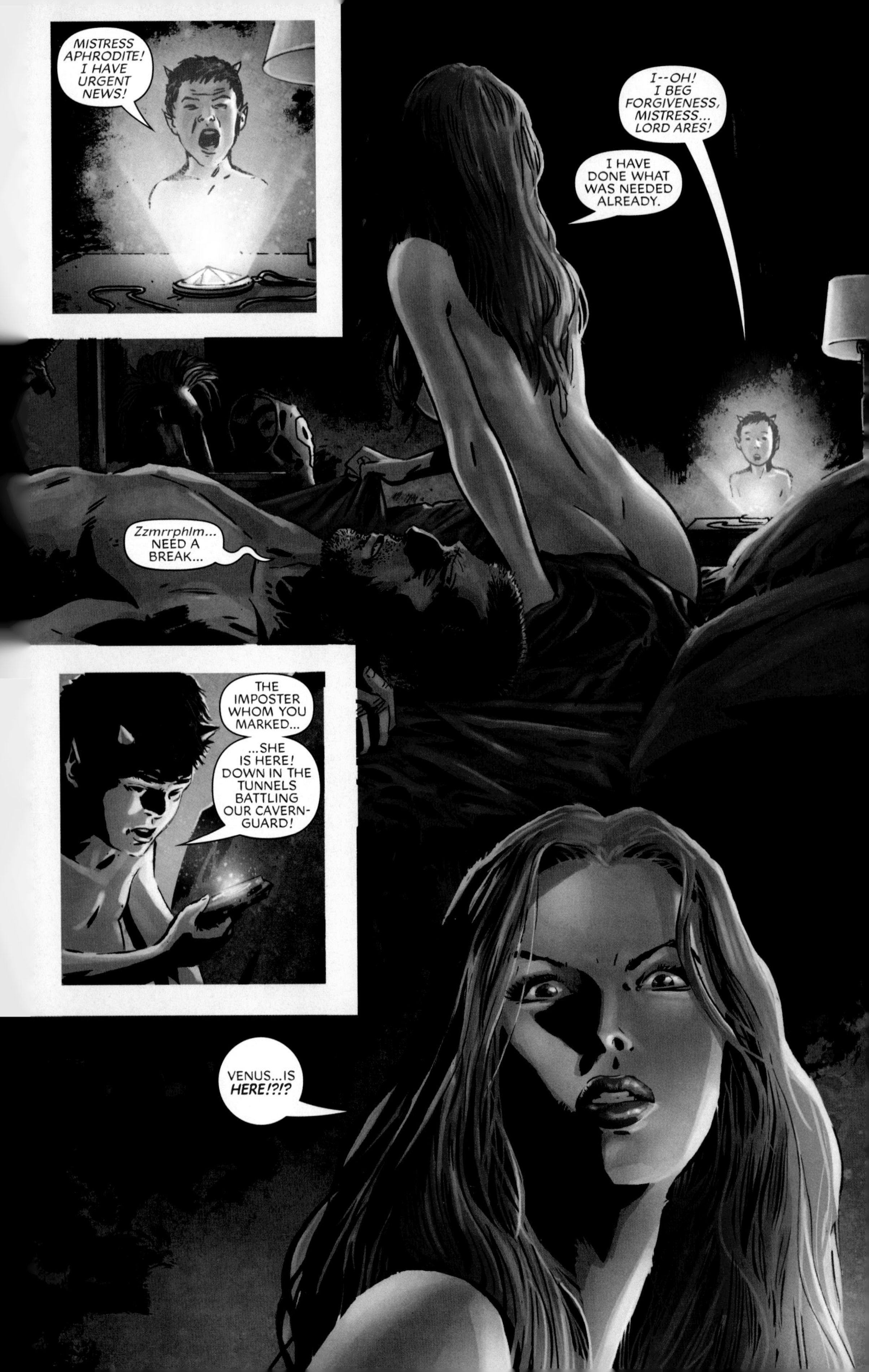
MISTRESS APHRODITE! I HAVE URGENT NEWS!
I--OH! I BEG FORGIVENESS, MISTRESS... LORD ARES!
I HAVE DONE WHAT WAS NEEDED ALREADY.
Zzmrrphlm... NEED A BREAK...
THE IMPOSTER WHOM YOU MARKED...
...SHE IS HERE! DOWN IN THE TUNNELS BATTLING OUR CAVERN-GUARD!
VENUS...IS HERE!?!?

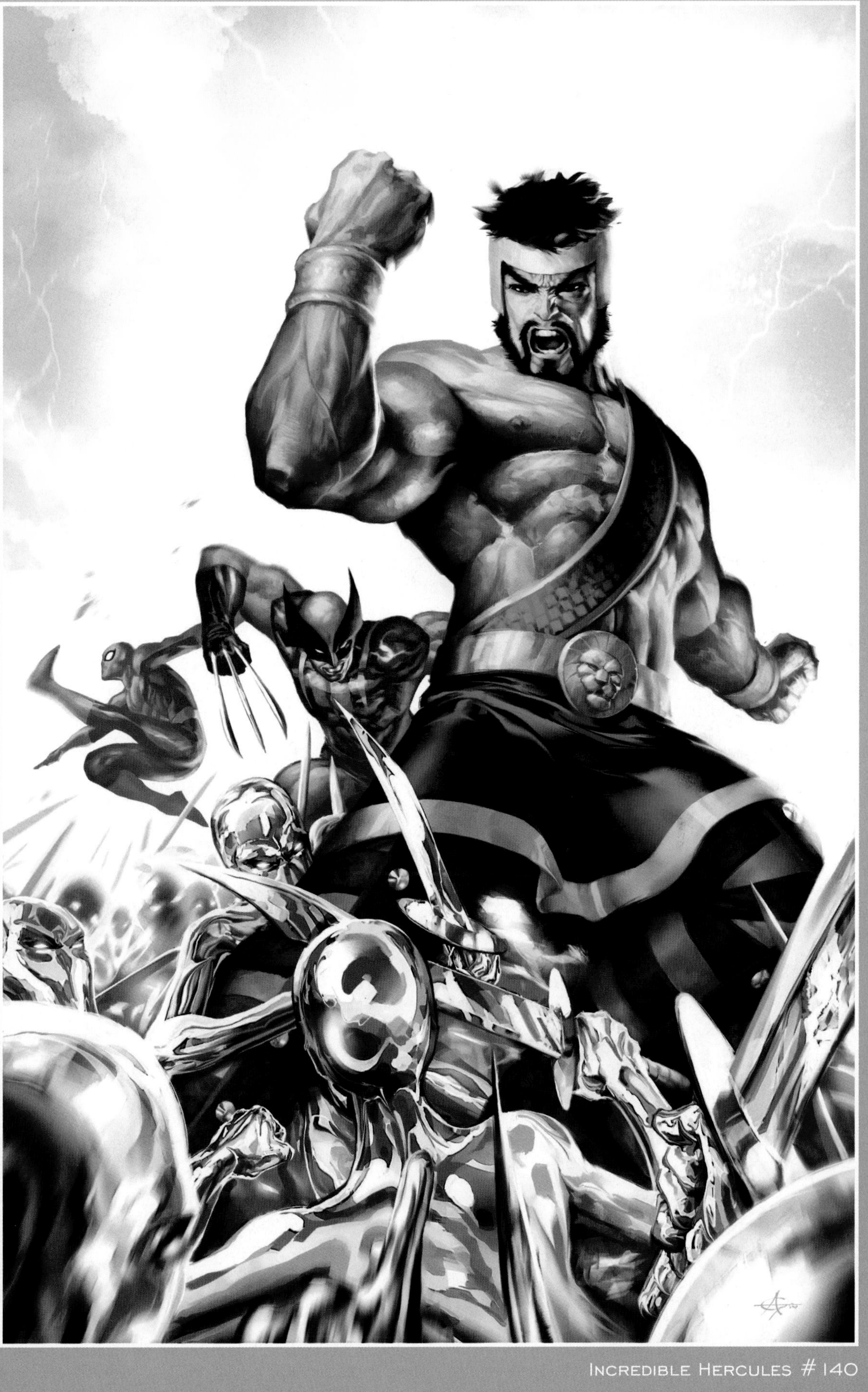

Incredible Hercules # 140

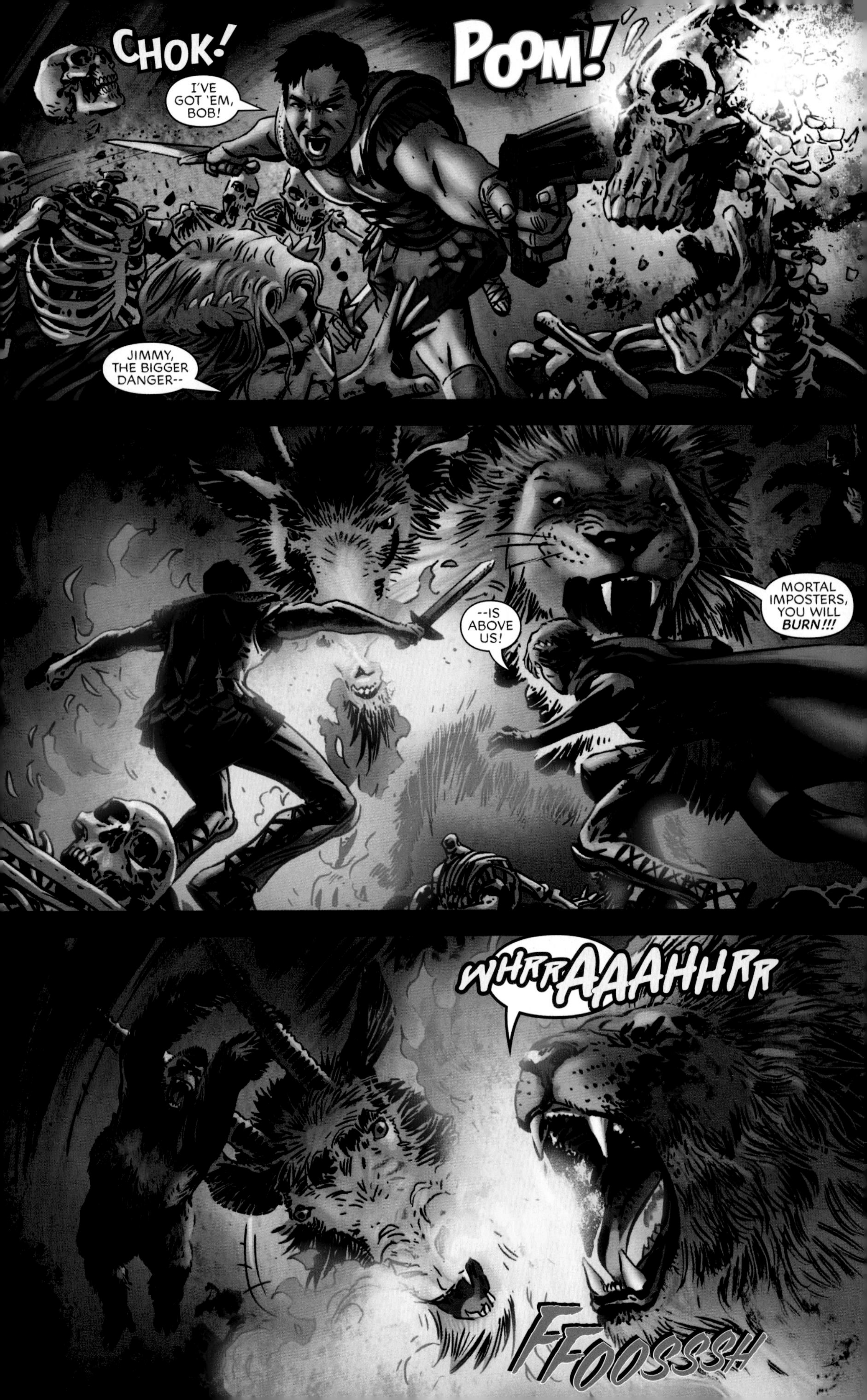
CHOK!
I'VE GOT 'EM, BOB!
POOM!
JIMMY, THE BIGGER DANGER--
--IS ABOVE US!
MORTAL IMPOSTERS, YOU WILL BURN!!!
WHRRRAAAHHRR
FFOOSSSH

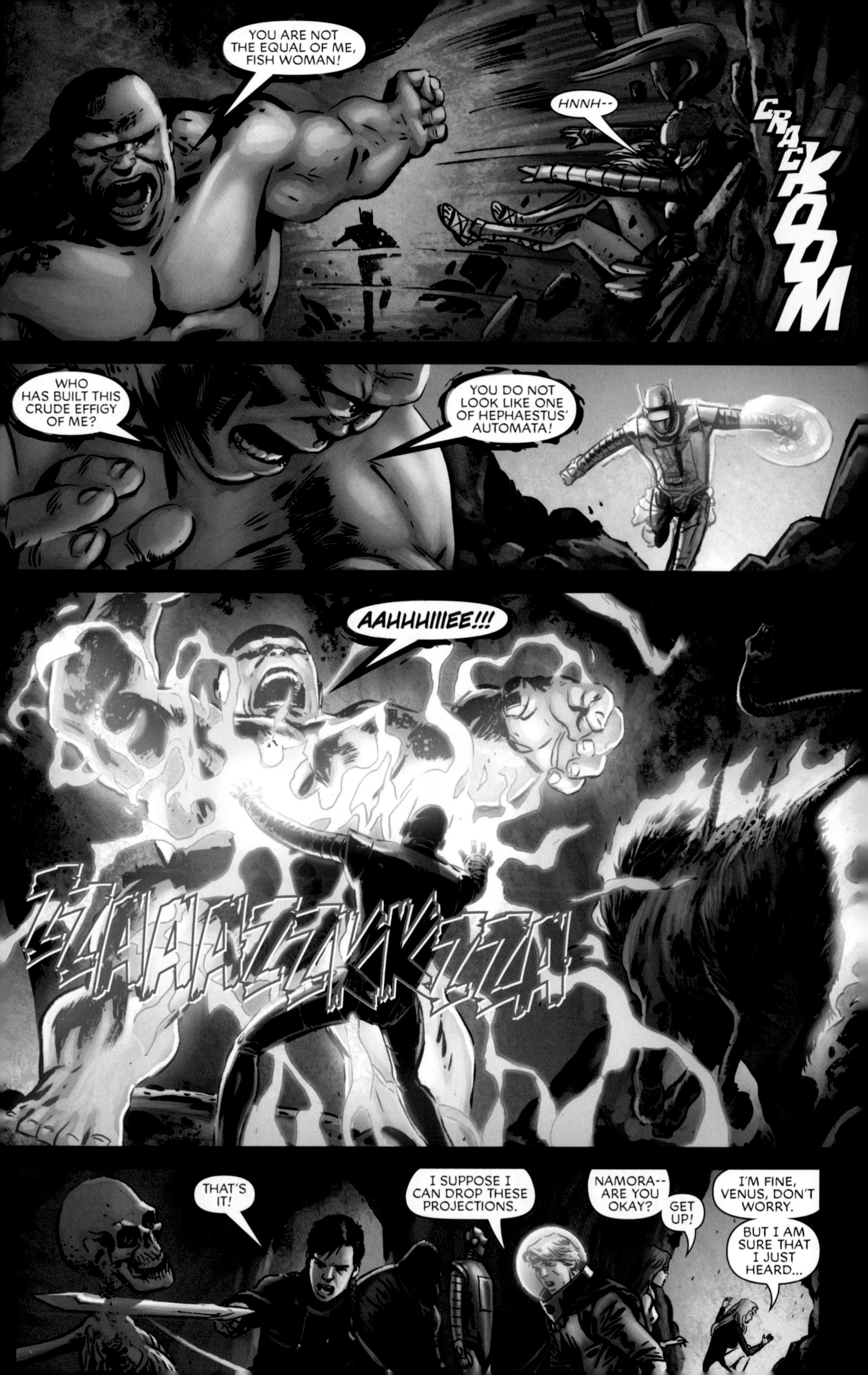
YOU ARE NOT THE EQUAL OF ME, FISH WOMAN!
HNNH--
CRACKOOM
WHO HAS BUILT THIS CRUDE EFFIGY OF ME?
YOU DO NOT LOOK LIKE ONE OF HEPHAESTUS' AUTOMATA!
AAHHHIIIEE!!!
ZZAAAZZAKKZZZA
THAT'S IT!
I SUPPOSE I CAN DROP THESE PROJECTIONS.
NAMORA-- ARE YOU OKAY?
GET UP!
I'M FINE, VENUS, DON'T WORRY.
BUT I AM SURE THAT I JUST HEARD...

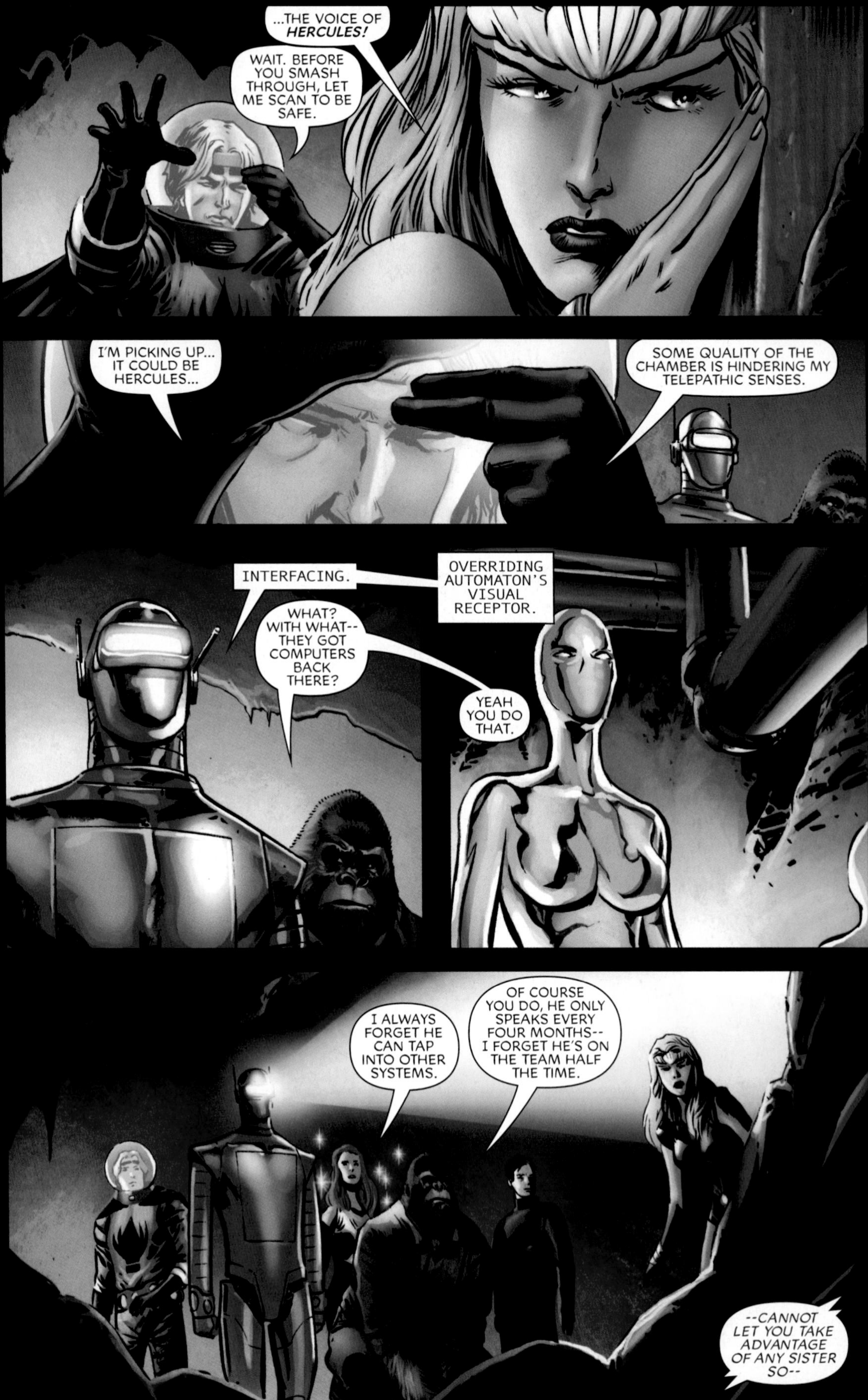
...THE VOICE OF *HERCULES!*
WAIT. BEFORE YOU SMASH THROUGH, LET ME SCAN TO BE SAFE.
I'M PICKING UP... IT COULD BE HERCULES...
SOME QUALITY OF THE CHAMBER IS HINDERING MY TELEPATHIC SENSES.
INTERFACING.
OVERRIDING AUTOMATON'S VISUAL RECEPTOR.
WHAT? WITH WHAT-- THEY GOT COMPUTERS BACK THERE?
YEAH YOU DO THAT.
I ALWAYS FORGET HE CAN TAP INTO OTHER SYSTEMS.
OF COURSE YOU DO, HE ONLY SPEAKS EVERY FOUR MONTHS-- I FORGET HE'S ON THE TEAM HALF THE TIME.
--CANNOT LET YOU TAKE ADVANTAGE OF ANY SISTER SO--

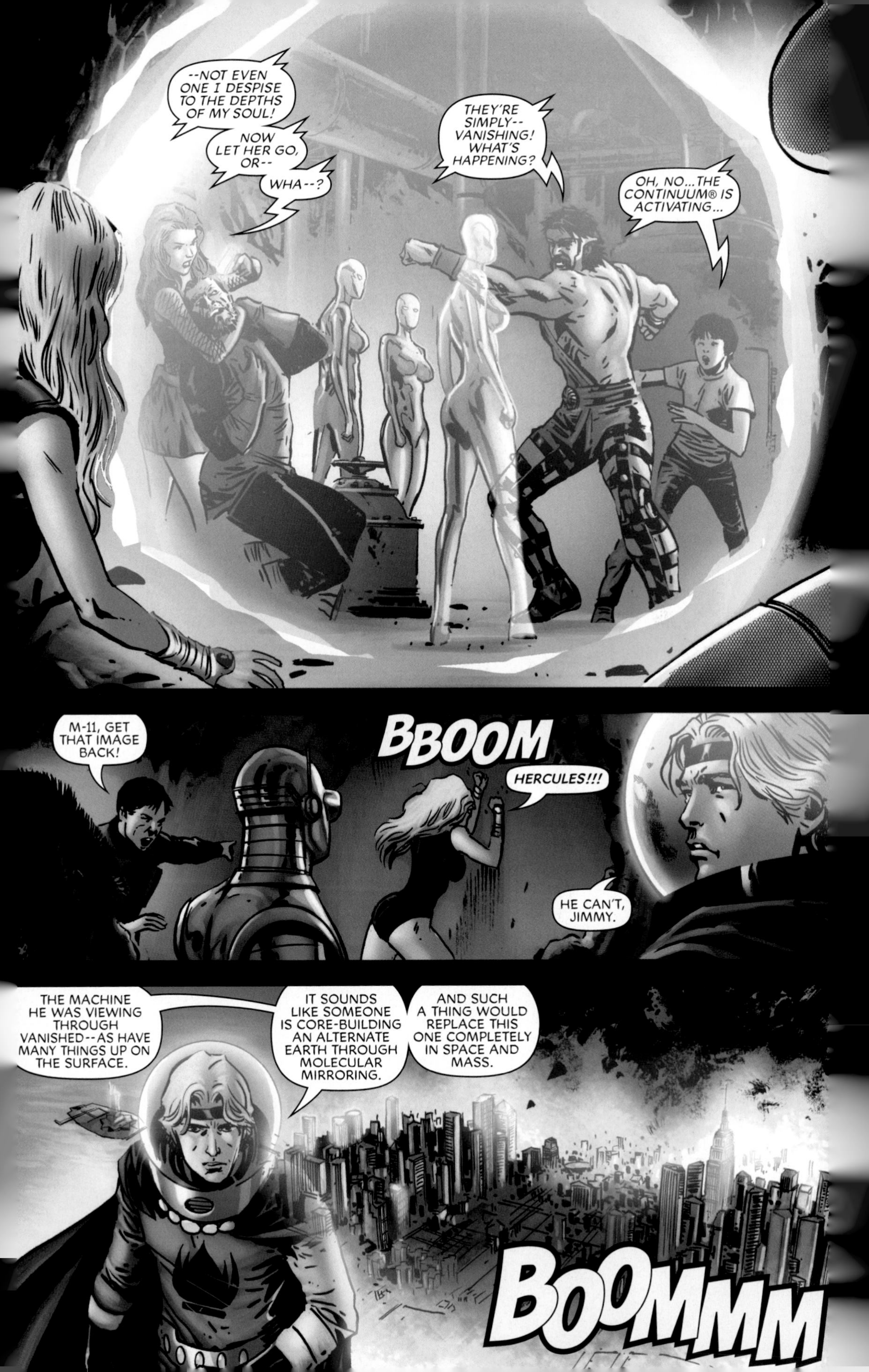
--NOT EVEN ONE I DESPISE TO THE DEPTHS OF MY SOUL!
NOW LET HER GO, OR--
WHA--?
THEY'RE SIMPLY-- VANISHING! WHAT'S HAPPENING?
OH, NO...THE CONTINUUM® IS ACTIVATING...
M-11, GET THAT IMAGE BACK!
BBOOM
HERCULES!!!
HE CAN'T, JIMMY.
THE MACHINE HE WAS VIEWING THROUGH VANISHED--AS HAVE MANY THINGS UP ON THE SURFACE.
IT SOUNDS LIKE SOMEONE IS CORE-BUILDING AN ALTERNATE EARTH THROUGH MOLECULAR MIRRORING.
AND SUCH A THING WOULD REPLACE THIS ONE COMPLETELY IN SPACE AND MASS.
BOOMMM

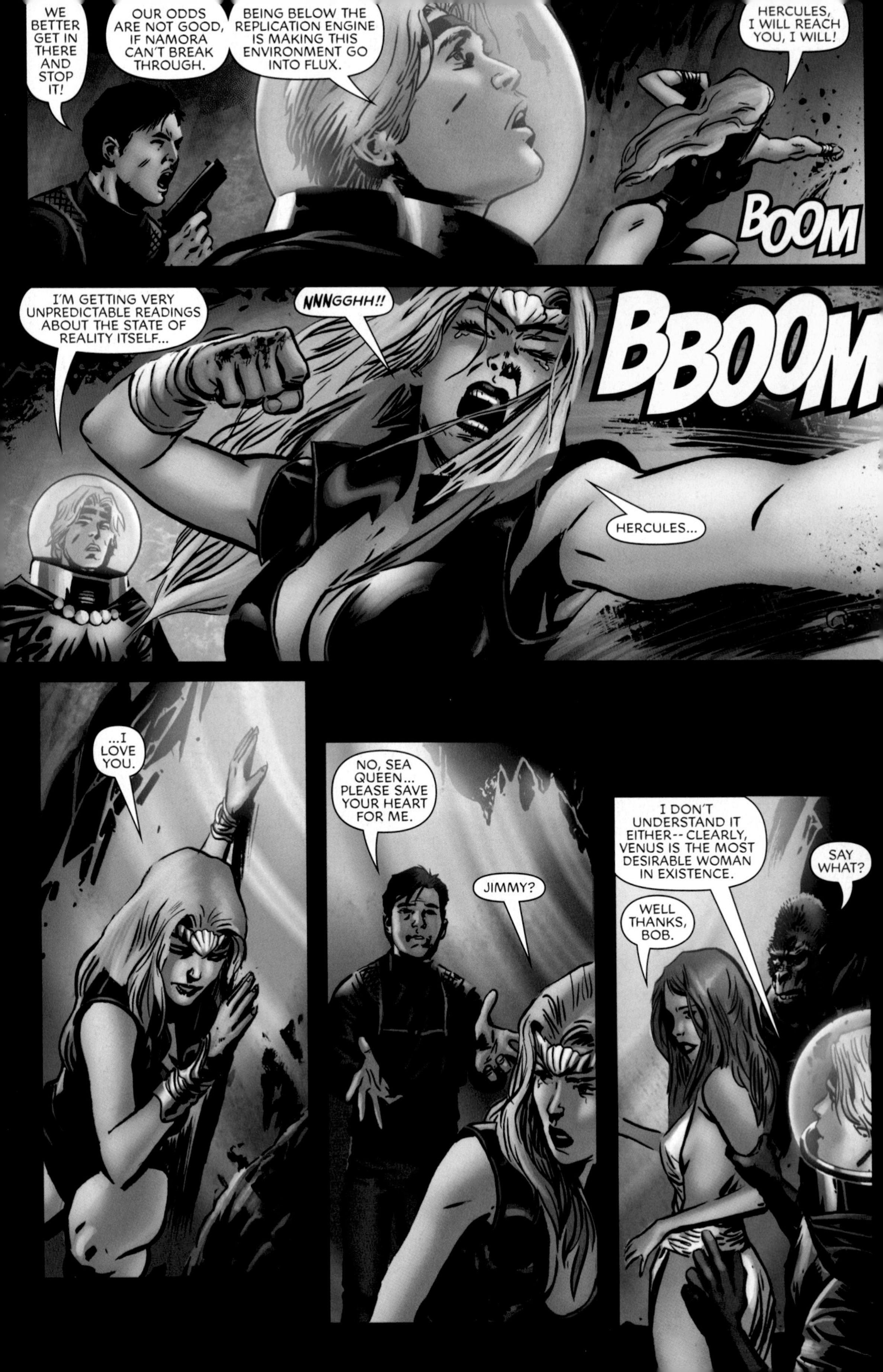
WE BETTER GET IN THERE AND STOP IT!
OUR ODDS ARE NOT GOOD, IF NAMORA CAN'T BREAK THROUGH.
BEING BELOW THE REPLICATION ENGINE IS MAKING THIS ENVIRONMENT GO INTO FLUX.
HERCULES, I WILL REACH YOU, I WILL!
BOOM
I'M GETTING VERY UNPREDICTABLE READINGS ABOUT THE STATE OF REALITY ITSELF...
NNNGGHH!!
BBOOM
HERCULES...
...I LOVE YOU.
NO, SEA QUEEN... PLEASE SAVE YOUR HEART FOR ME.
JIMMY?
I DON'T UNDERSTAND IT EITHER-- CLEARLY, VENUS IS THE MOST DESIRABLE WOMAN IN EXISTENCE.
SAY WHAT?
WELL THANKS, BOB.

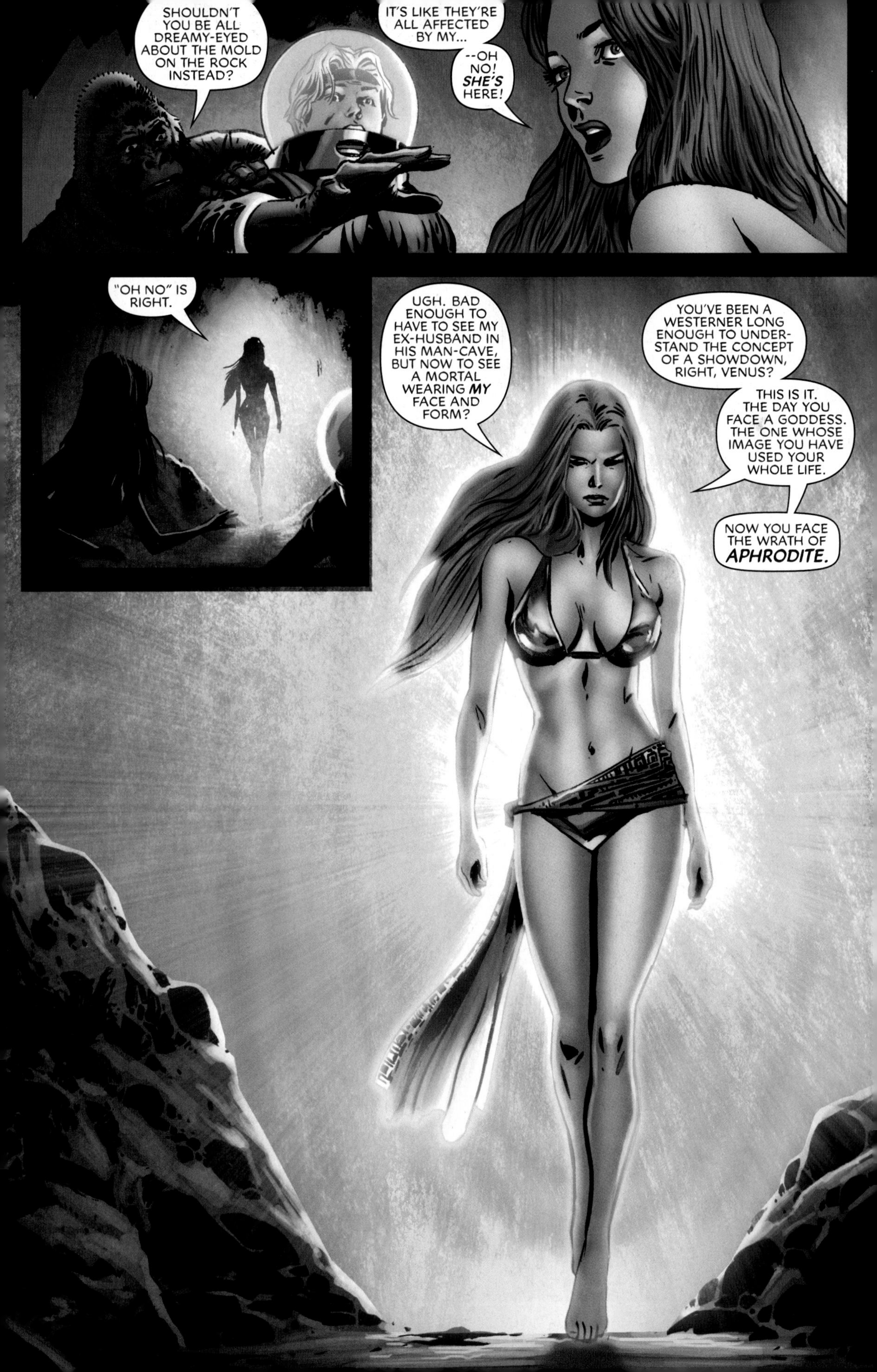
SHOULDN'T YOU BE ALL DREAMY-EYED ABOUT THE MOLD ON THE ROCK INSTEAD?
IT'S LIKE THEY'RE ALL AFFECTED BY MY...
--OH NO! *SHE'S* HERE!
"OH NO" IS RIGHT.
UGH. BAD ENOUGH TO HAVE TO SEE MY EX-HUSBAND IN HIS MAN-CAVE, BUT NOW TO SEE A MORTAL WEARING *MY* FACE AND FORM?
YOU'VE BEEN A WESTERNER LONG ENOUGH TO UNDER-STAND THE CONCEPT OF A SHOWDOWN, RIGHT, VENUS?
THIS IS IT. THE DAY YOU FACE A GODDESS. THE ONE WHOSE IMAGE YOU HAVE USED YOUR WHOLE LIFE.
NOW YOU FACE THE WRATH OF ***APHRODITE.***

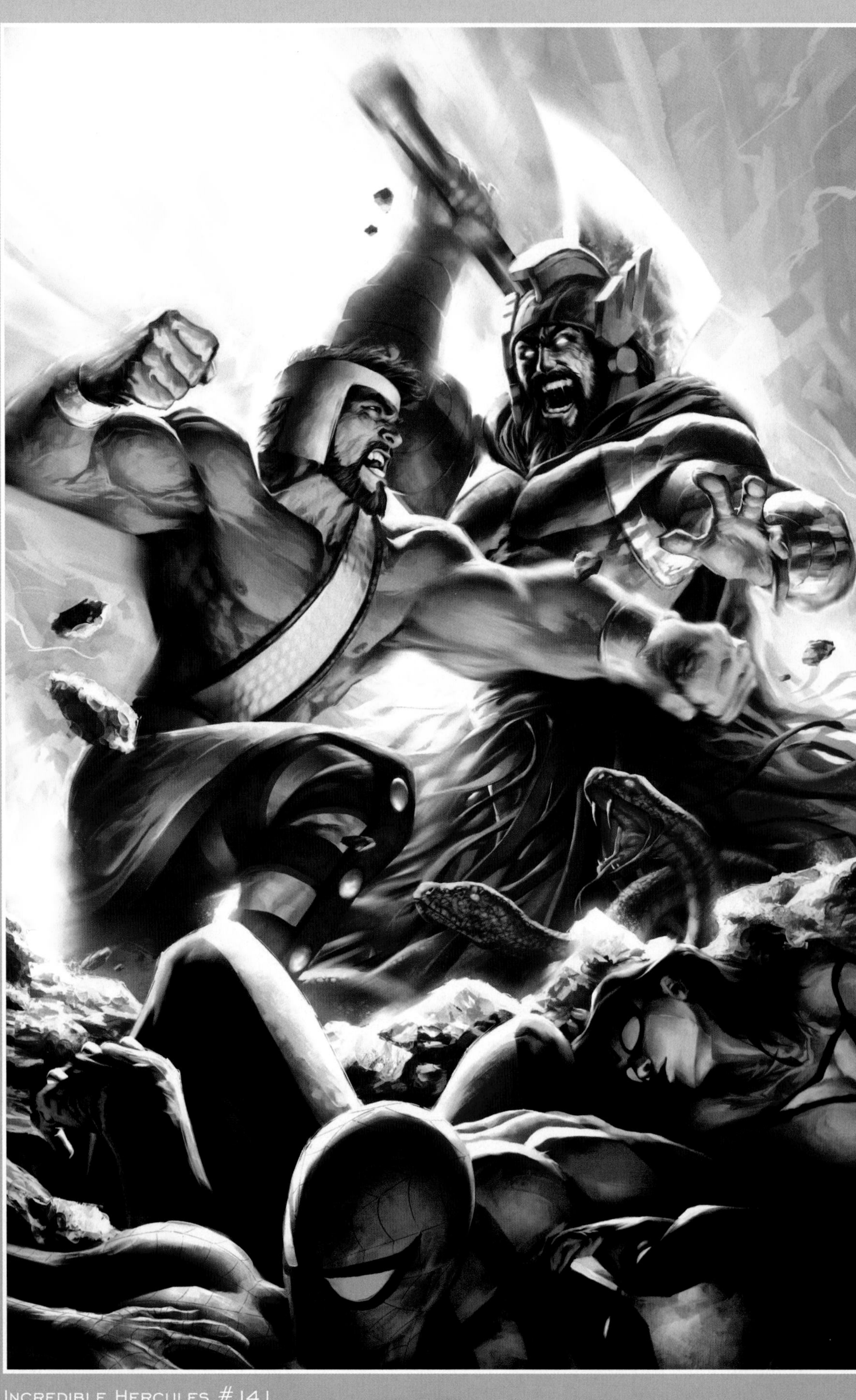

Incredible Hercules #141

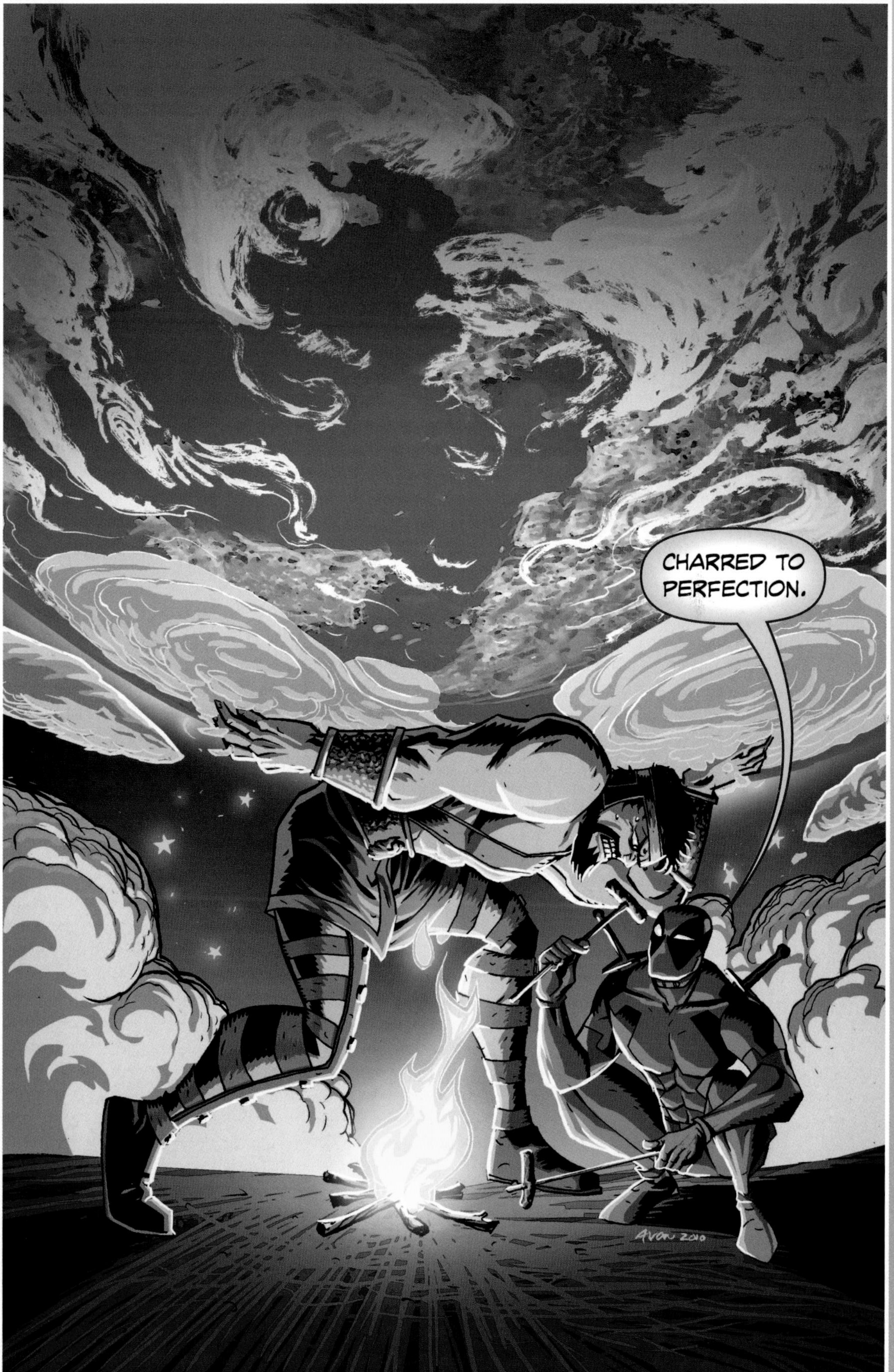
CHARRED TO PERFECTION.
AVON 2010

Incredible Hercules #141 Deadpool Variant by Michael Avon Oeming

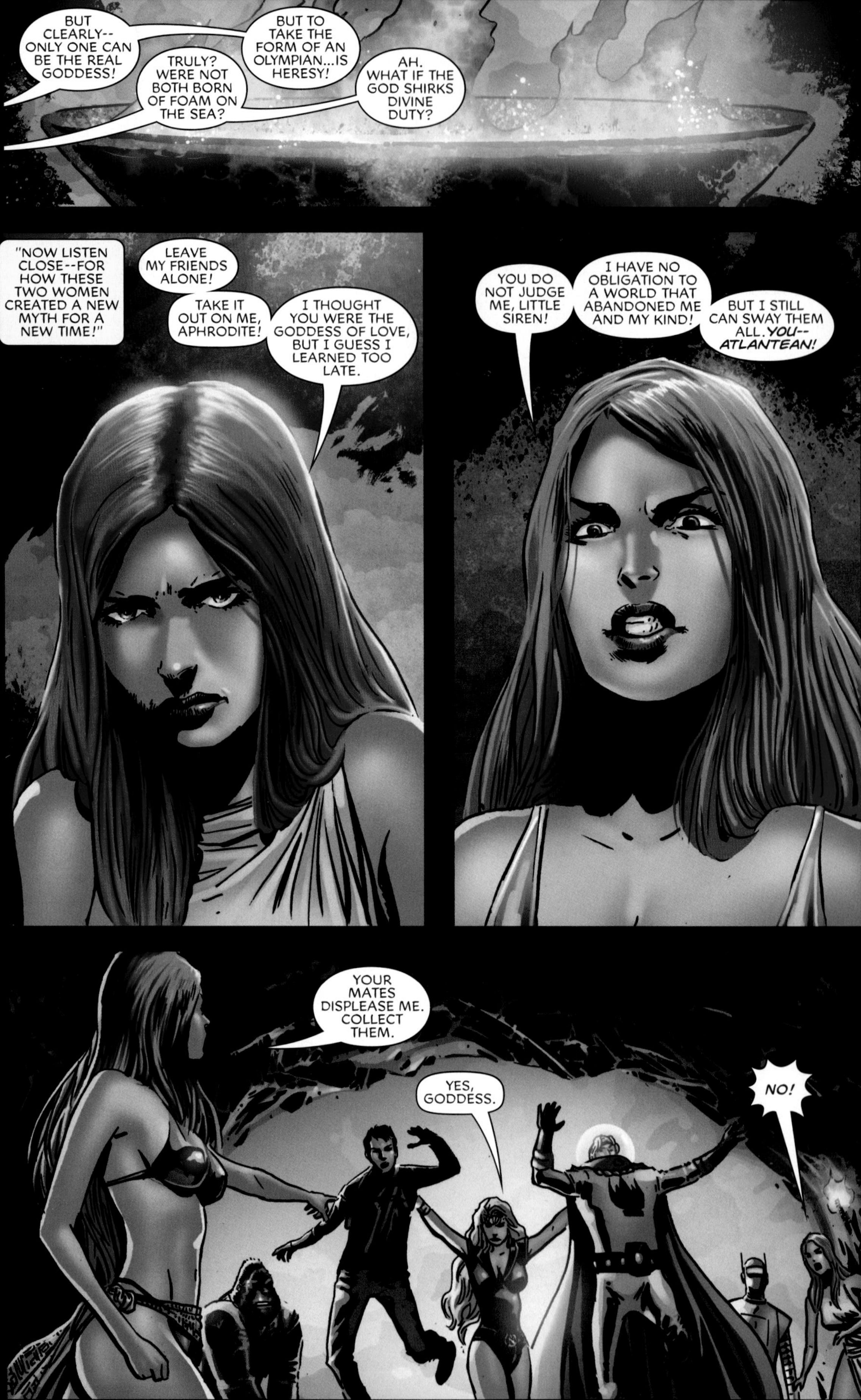
BUT CLEARLY--ONLY ONE CAN BE THE REAL GODDESS!
TRULY? WERE NOT BOTH BORN OF FOAM ON THE SEA?
BUT TO TAKE THE FORM OF AN OLYMPIAN...IS HERESY!
AH. WHAT IF THE GOD SHIRKS DIVINE DUTY?
"NOW LISTEN CLOSE--FOR HOW THESE TWO WOMEN CREATED A NEW MYTH FOR A NEW TIME!"
LEAVE MY FRIENDS ALONE!
TAKE IT OUT ON ME, APHRODITE!
I THOUGHT YOU WERE THE GODDESS OF LOVE, BUT I GUESS I LEARNED TOO LATE.
YOU DO NOT JUDGE ME, LITTLE SIREN!
I HAVE NO OBLIGATION TO A WORLD THAT ABANDONED ME AND MY KIND!
BUT I STILL CAN SWAY THEM ALL. YOU--ATLANTEAN!
YOUR MATES DISPLEASE ME. COLLECT THEM.
YES, GODDESS.
NO!

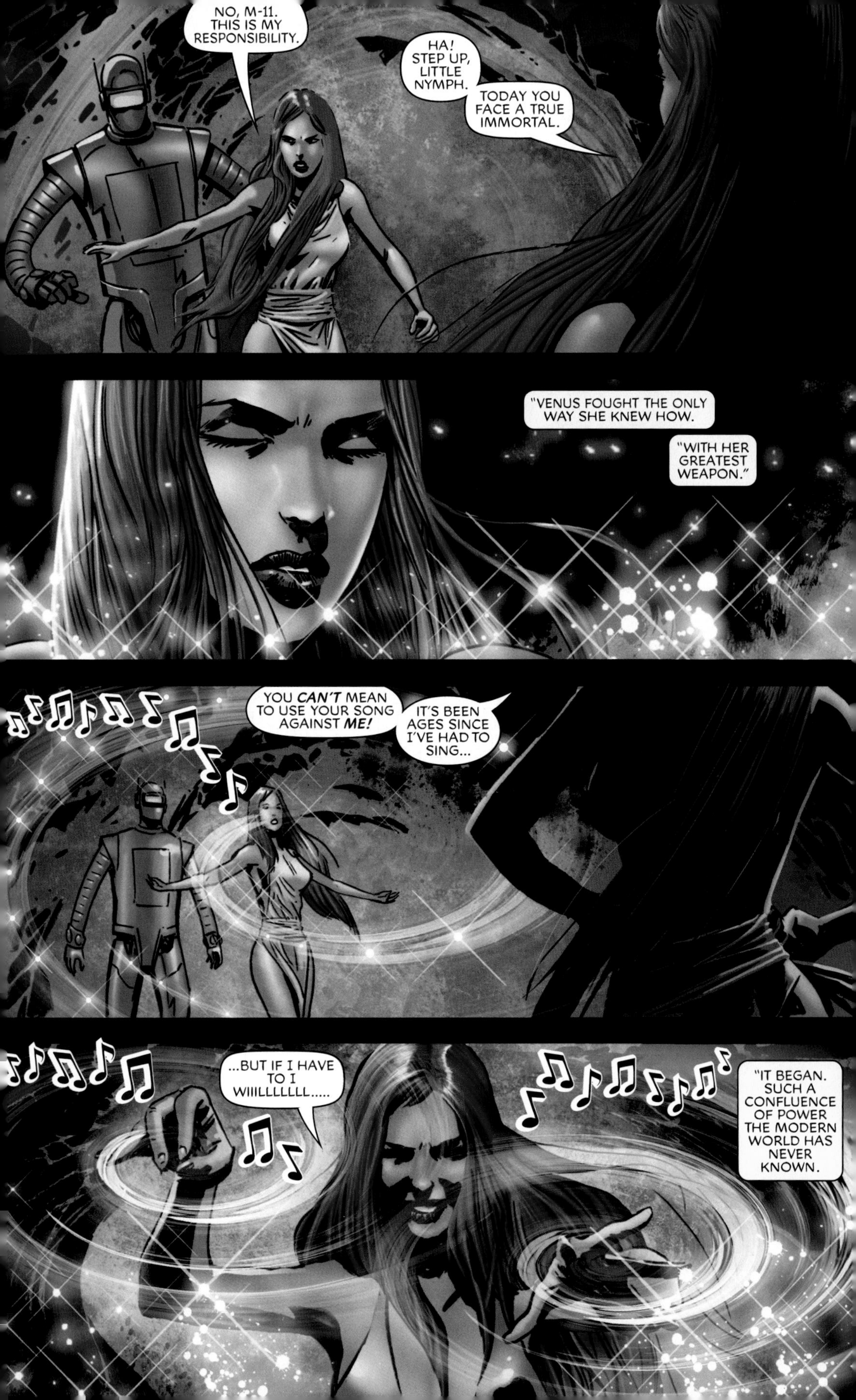
NO, M-11. THIS IS MY RESPONSIBILITY.
HA! STEP UP, LITTLE NYMPH.
TODAY YOU FACE A TRUE IMMORTAL.
"VENUS FOUGHT THE ONLY WAY SHE KNEW HOW.
"WITH HER GREATEST WEAPON."
YOU *CAN'T* MEAN TO USE YOUR SONG AGAINST *ME!*
IT'S BEEN AGES SINCE I'VE HAD TO SING...
...BUT IF I HAVE TO I WIIILLLLLLLL.....
"IT BEGAN. SUCH A CONFLUENCE OF POWER THE MODERN WORLD HAS NEVER KNOWN.

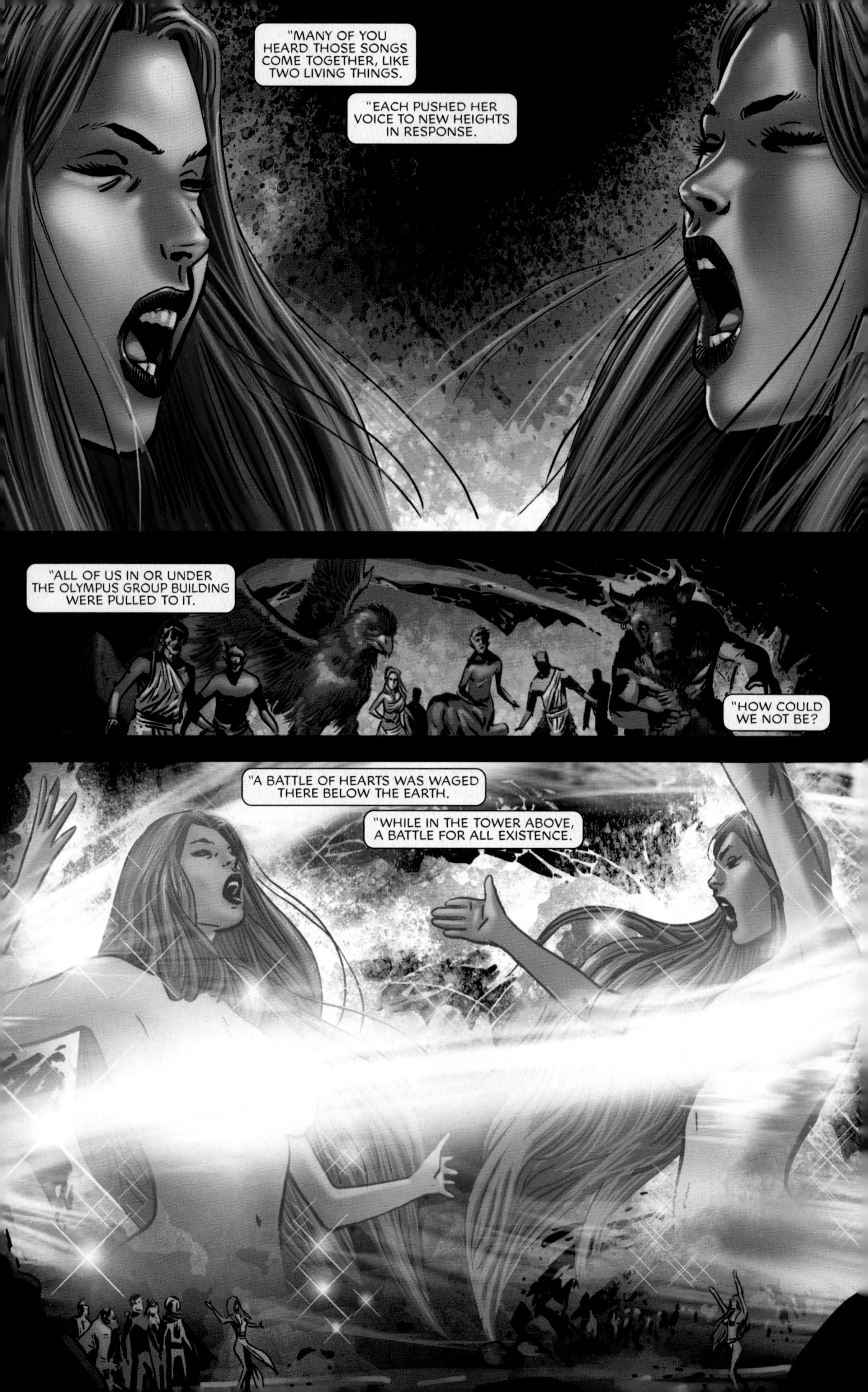
"MANY OF YOU HEARD THOSE SONGS COME TOGETHER, LIKE TWO LIVING THINGS.
"EACH PUSHED HER VOICE TO NEW HEIGHTS IN RESPONSE.
"ALL OF US IN OR UNDER THE OLYMPUS GROUP BUILDING WERE PULLED TO IT.
"HOW COULD WE NOT BE?
"A BATTLE OF HEARTS WAS WAGED THERE BELOW THE EARTH.
"WHILE IN THE TOWER ABOVE, A BATTLE FOR ALL EXISTENCE.

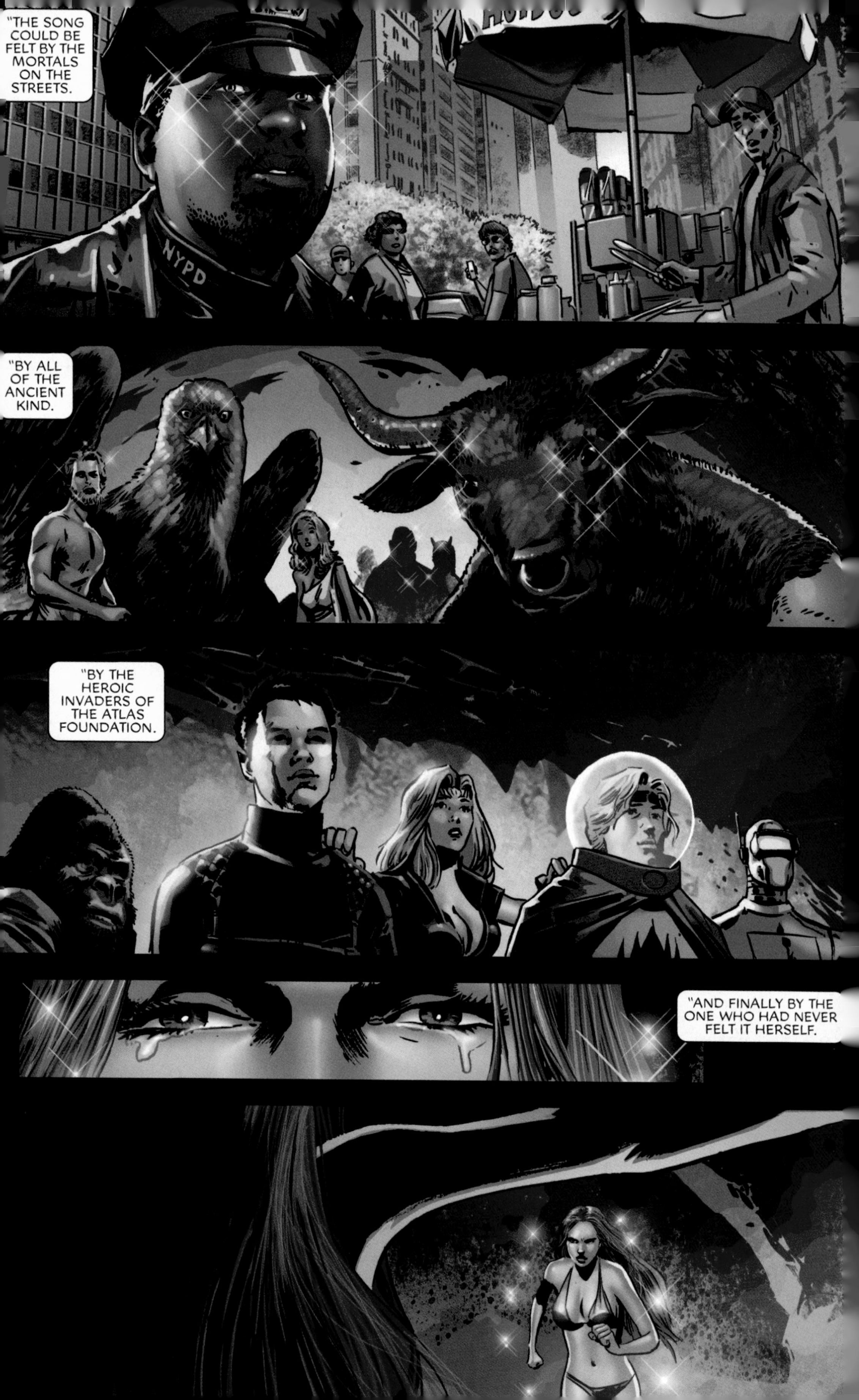
"THE SONG COULD BE FELT BY THE MORTALS ON THE STREETS.
NYPD
"BY ALL OF THE ANCIENT KIND.
"BY THE HEROIC INVADERS OF THE ATLAS FOUNDATION.
"AND FINALLY BY THE ONE WHO HAD NEVER FELT IT HERSELF.

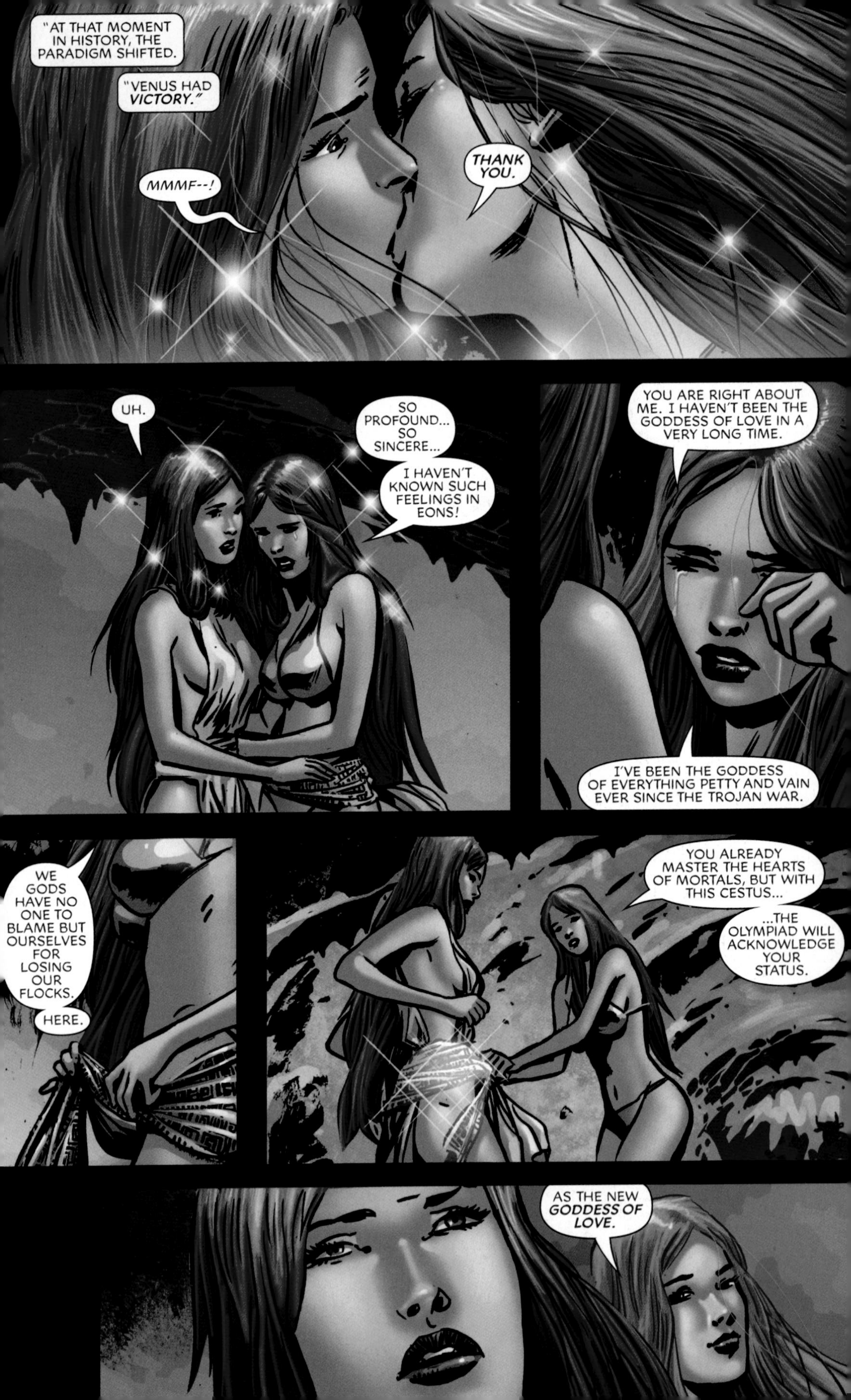
"AT THAT MOMENT IN HISTORY, THE PARADIGM SHIFTED.
"VENUS HAD *VICTORY*."
MMMF--!
THANK YOU.
UH.
SO PROFOUND... SO SINCERE...
I HAVEN'T KNOWN SUCH FEELINGS IN EONS!
YOU ARE RIGHT ABOUT ME. I HAVEN'T BEEN THE GODDESS OF LOVE IN A VERY LONG TIME.
I'VE BEEN THE GODDESS OF EVERYTHING PETTY AND VAIN EVER SINCE THE TROJAN WAR.
WE GODS HAVE NO ONE TO BLAME BUT OURSELVES FOR LOSING OUR FLOCKS.
HERE.
YOU ALREADY MASTER THE HEARTS OF MORTALS, BUT WITH THIS CESTUS...
...THE OLYMPIAD WILL ACKNOWLEDGE YOUR STATUS.
AS THE NEW *GODDESS OF LOVE.*

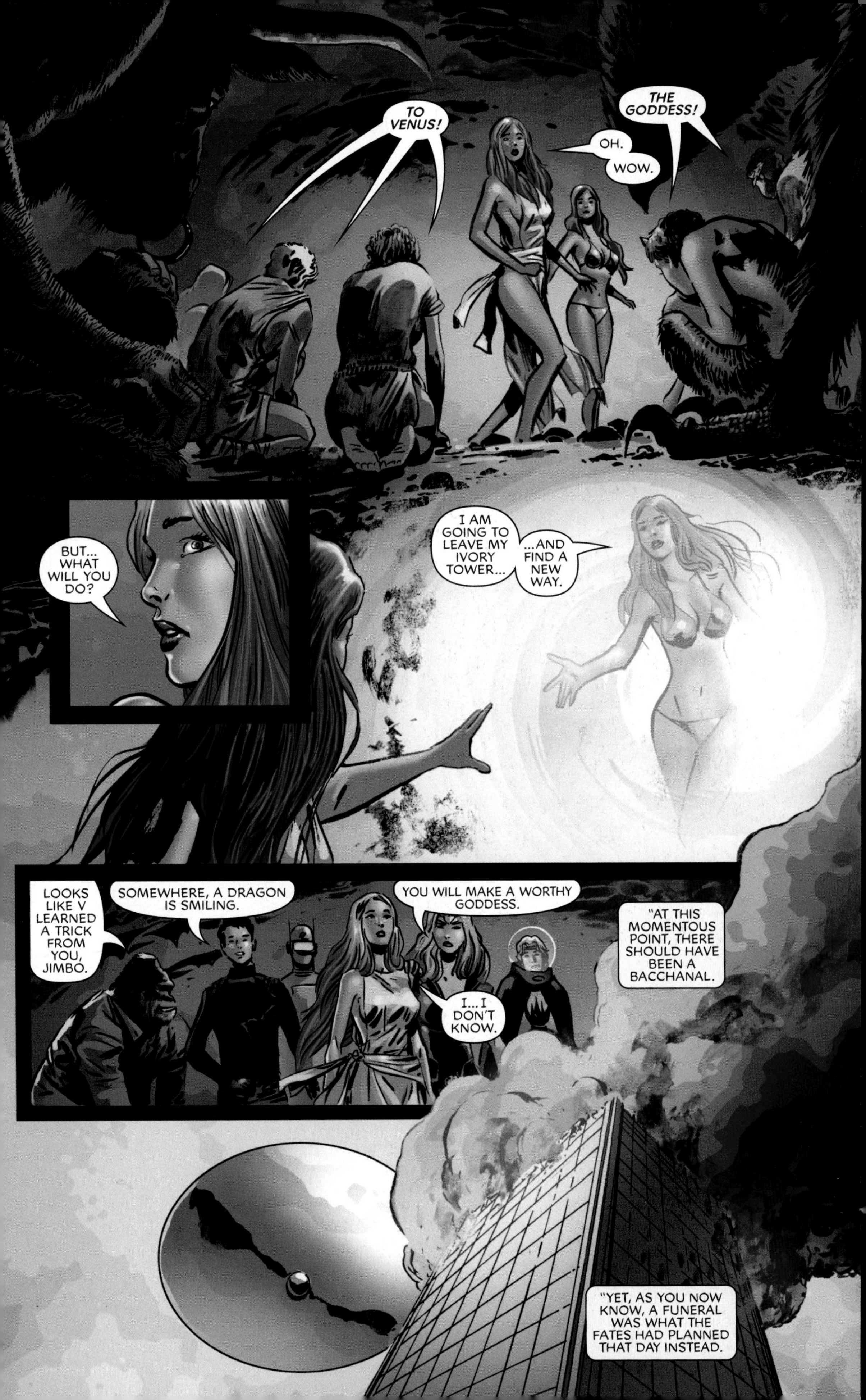
TO VENUS!
OH.
WOW.
THE GODDESS!
BUT... WHAT WILL YOU DO?
I AM GOING TO LEAVE MY IVORY TOWER...
...AND FIND A NEW WAY.
LOOKS LIKE V LEARNED A TRICK FROM YOU, JIMBO.
SOMEWHERE, A DRAGON IS SMILING.
YOU WILL MAKE A WORTHY GODDESS.
I...I DON'T KNOW.
"AT THIS MOMENTOUS POINT, THERE SHOULD HAVE BEEN A BACCHANAL.
"YET, AS YOU NOW KNOW, A FUNERAL WAS WHAT THE FATES HAD PLANNED THAT DAY INSTEAD.

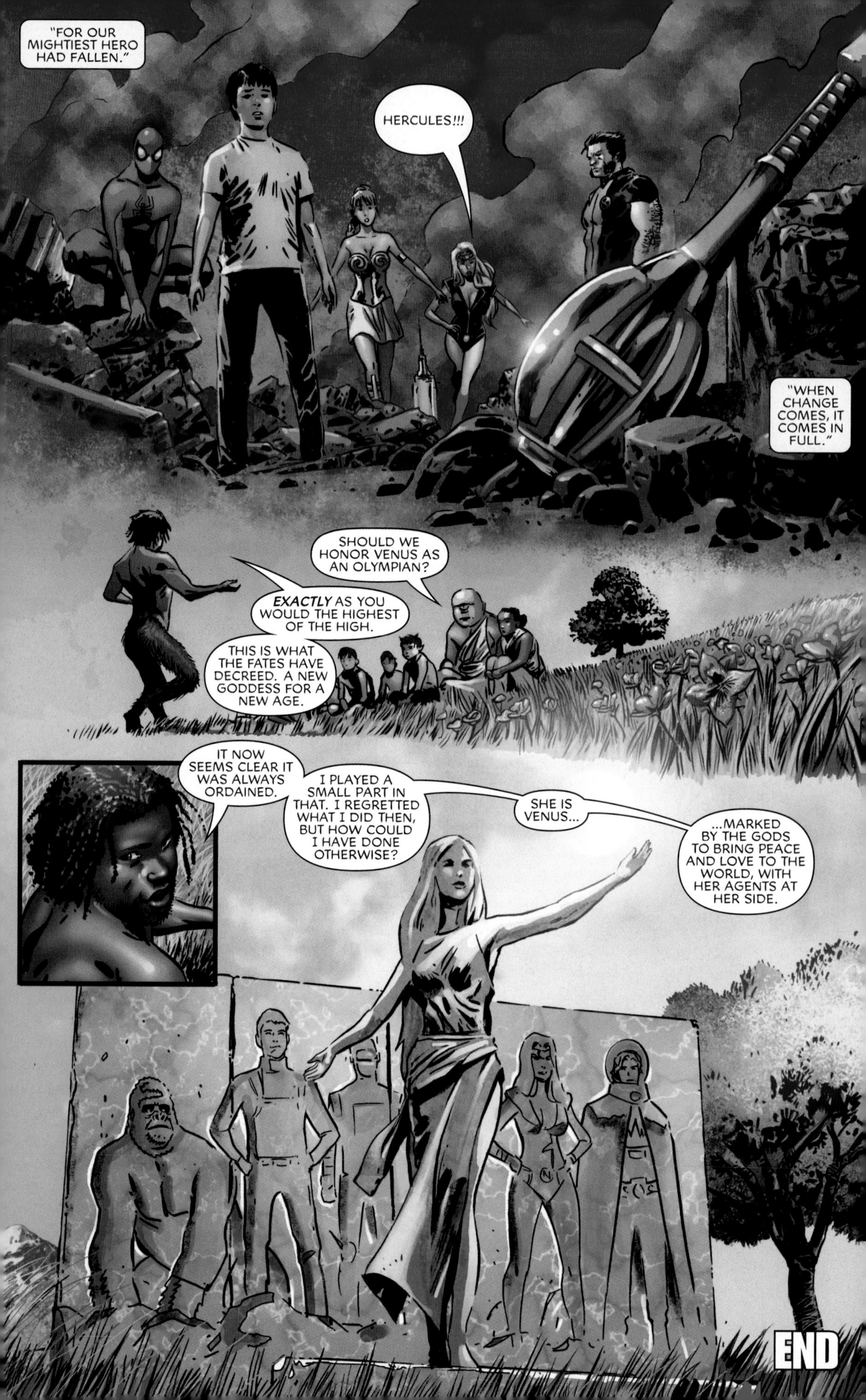
"FOR OUR MIGHTIEST HERO HAD FALLEN."
HERCULES!!!
"WHEN CHANGE COMES, IT COMES IN FULL."
SHOULD WE HONOR VENUS AS AN OLYMPIAN?
EXACTLY AS YOU WOULD THE HIGHEST OF THE HIGH.
THIS IS WHAT THE FATES HAVE DECREED. A NEW GODDESS FOR A NEW AGE.
IT NOW SEEMS CLEAR IT WAS ALWAYS ORDAINED.
I PLAYED A SMALL PART IN THAT. I REGRETTED WHAT I DID THEN, BUT HOW COULD I HAVE DONE OTHERWISE?
SHE IS VENUS...
...MARKED BY THE GODS TO BRING PEACE AND LOVE TO THE WORLD, WITH HER AGENTS AT HER SIDE.
END

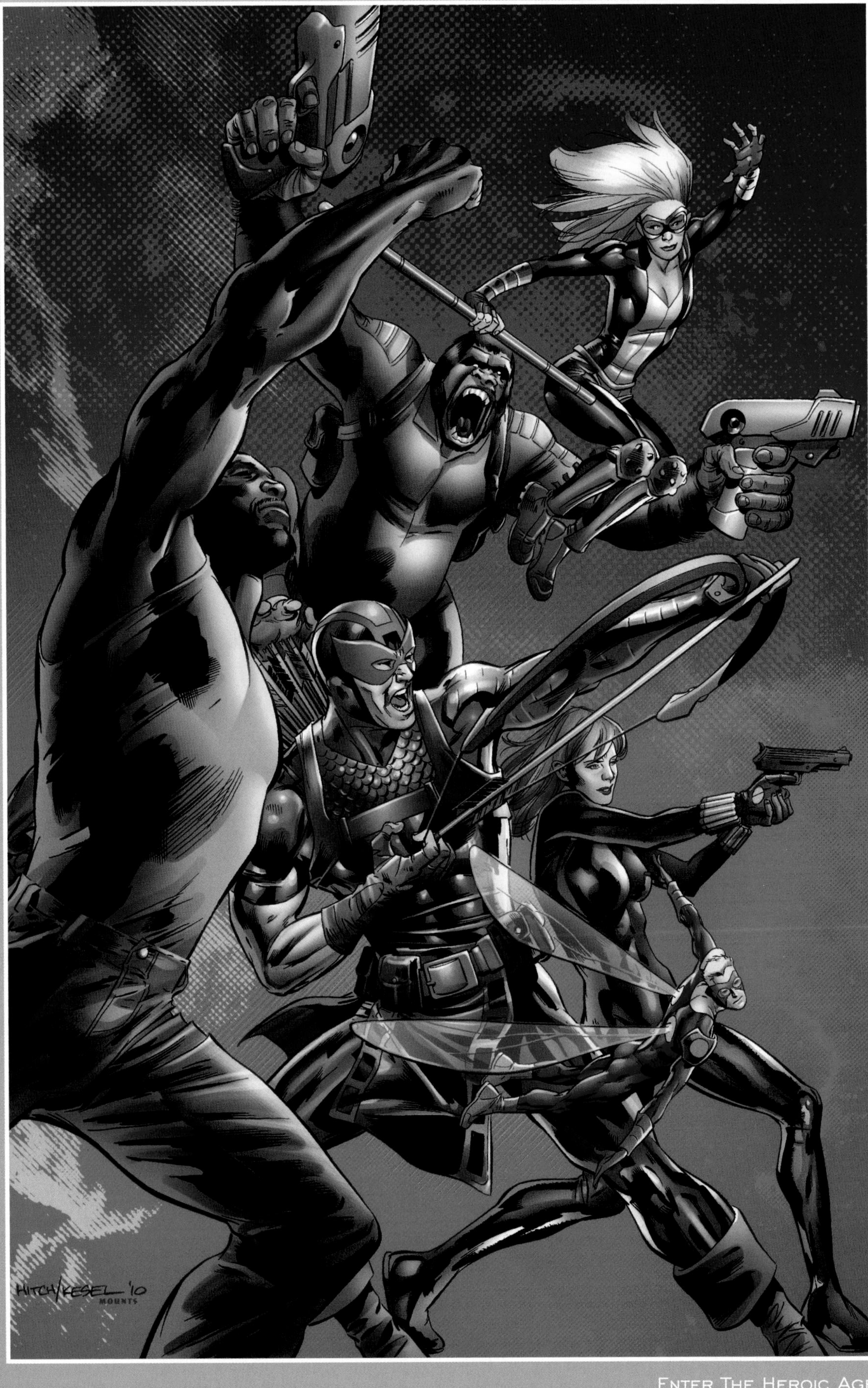
HITCH/KESEL '10
MOUNTS

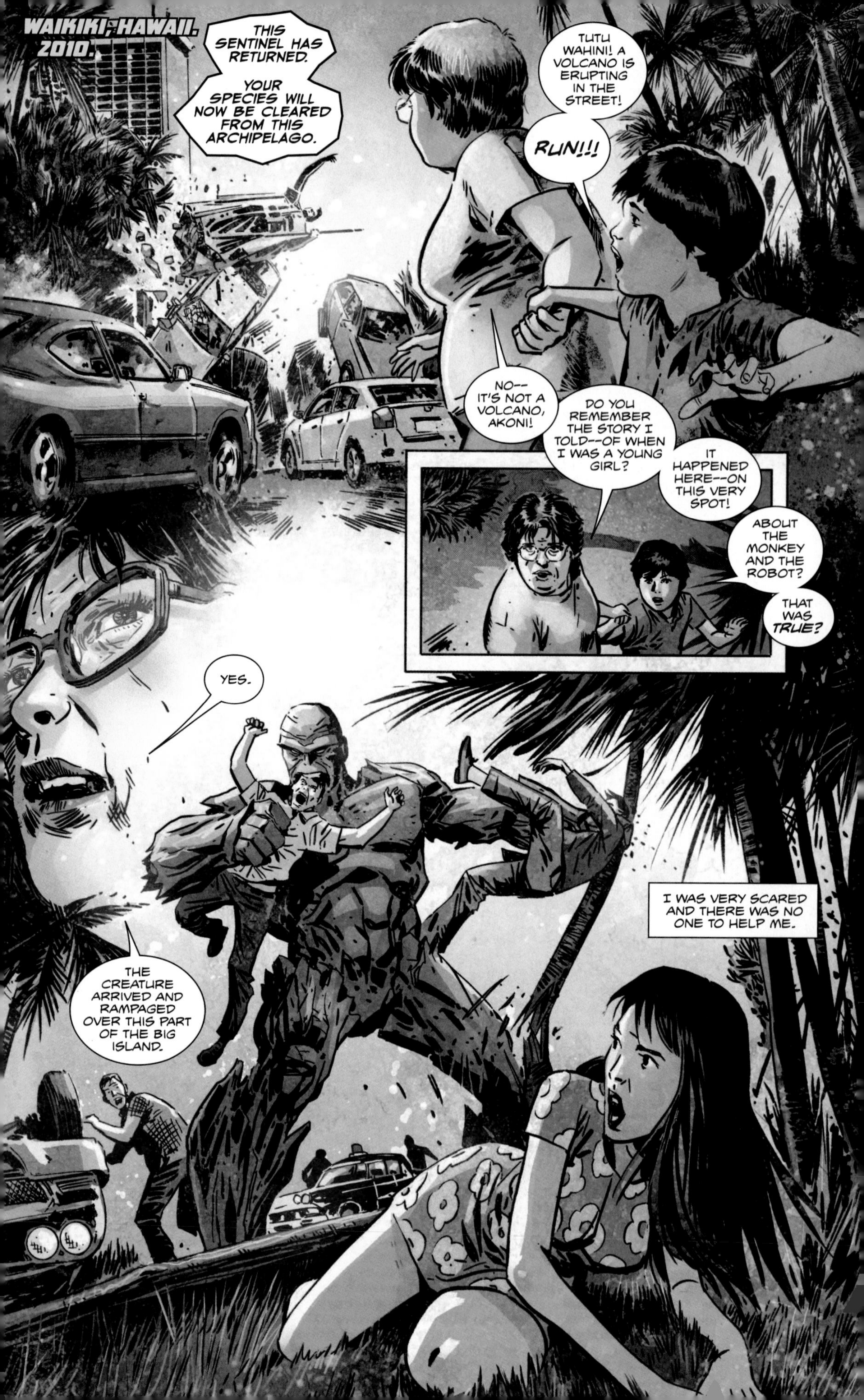
WAIKIKI, HAWAII. 2010.
THIS SENTINEL HAS RETURNED.
YOUR SPECIES WILL NOW BE CLEARED FROM THIS ARCHIPELAGO.
TUTU WAHINI! A VOLCANO IS ERUPTING IN THE STREET!
RUN!!!
NO-- IT'S NOT A VOLCANO, AKONI!
DO YOU REMEMBER THE STORY I TOLD--OF WHEN I WAS A YOUNG GIRL?
IT HAPPENED HERE--ON THIS VERY SPOT!
ABOUT THE MONKEY AND THE ROBOT?
THAT WAS TRUE?
YES.
THE CREATURE ARRIVED AND RAMPAGED OVER THIS PART OF THE BIG ISLAND.
I WAS VERY SCARED AND THERE WAS NO ONE TO HELP ME.

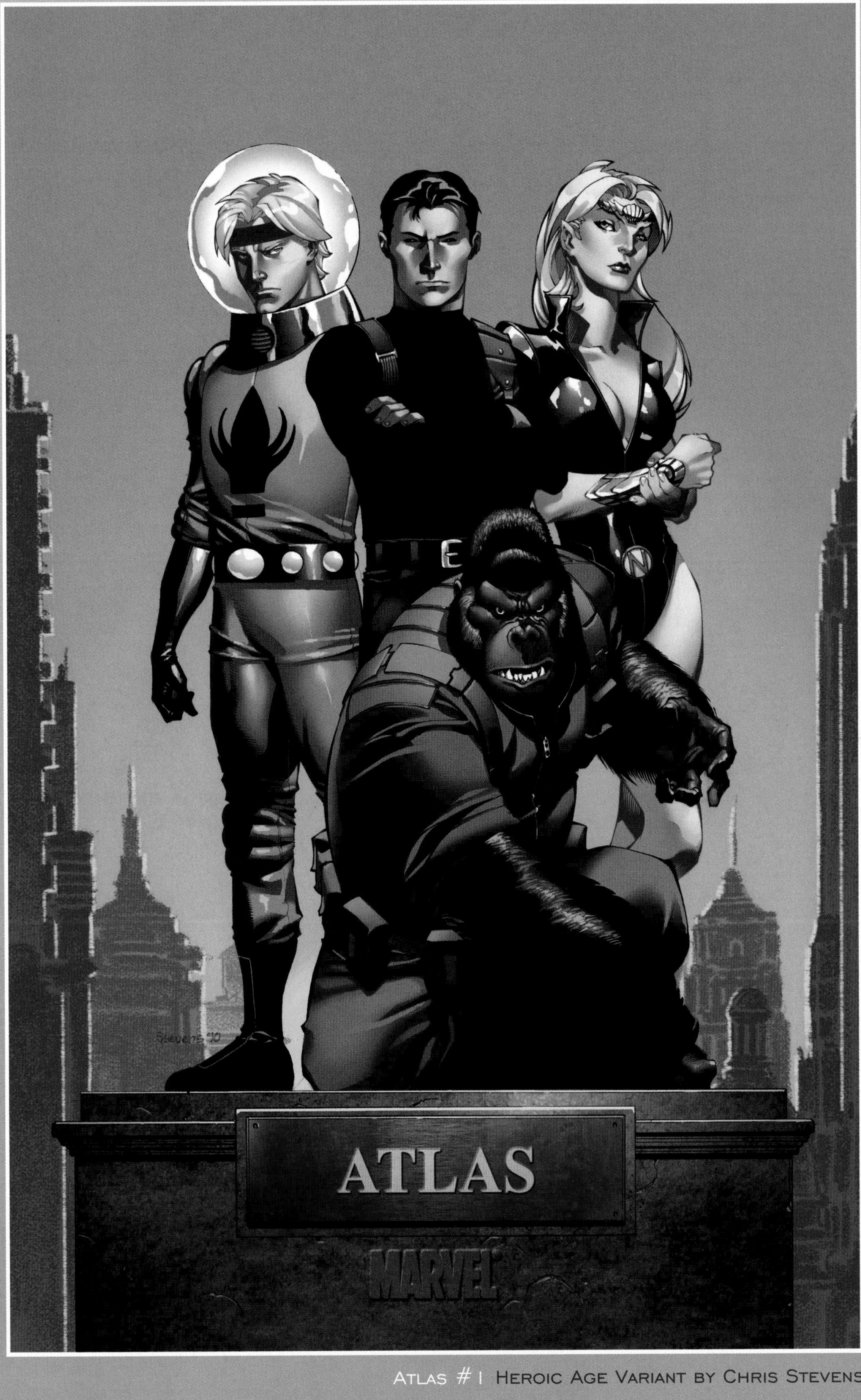
STEVENS '10
ATLAS
MARVEL
ATLAS #1 HEROIC AGE VARIANT BY CHRIS STEVENS

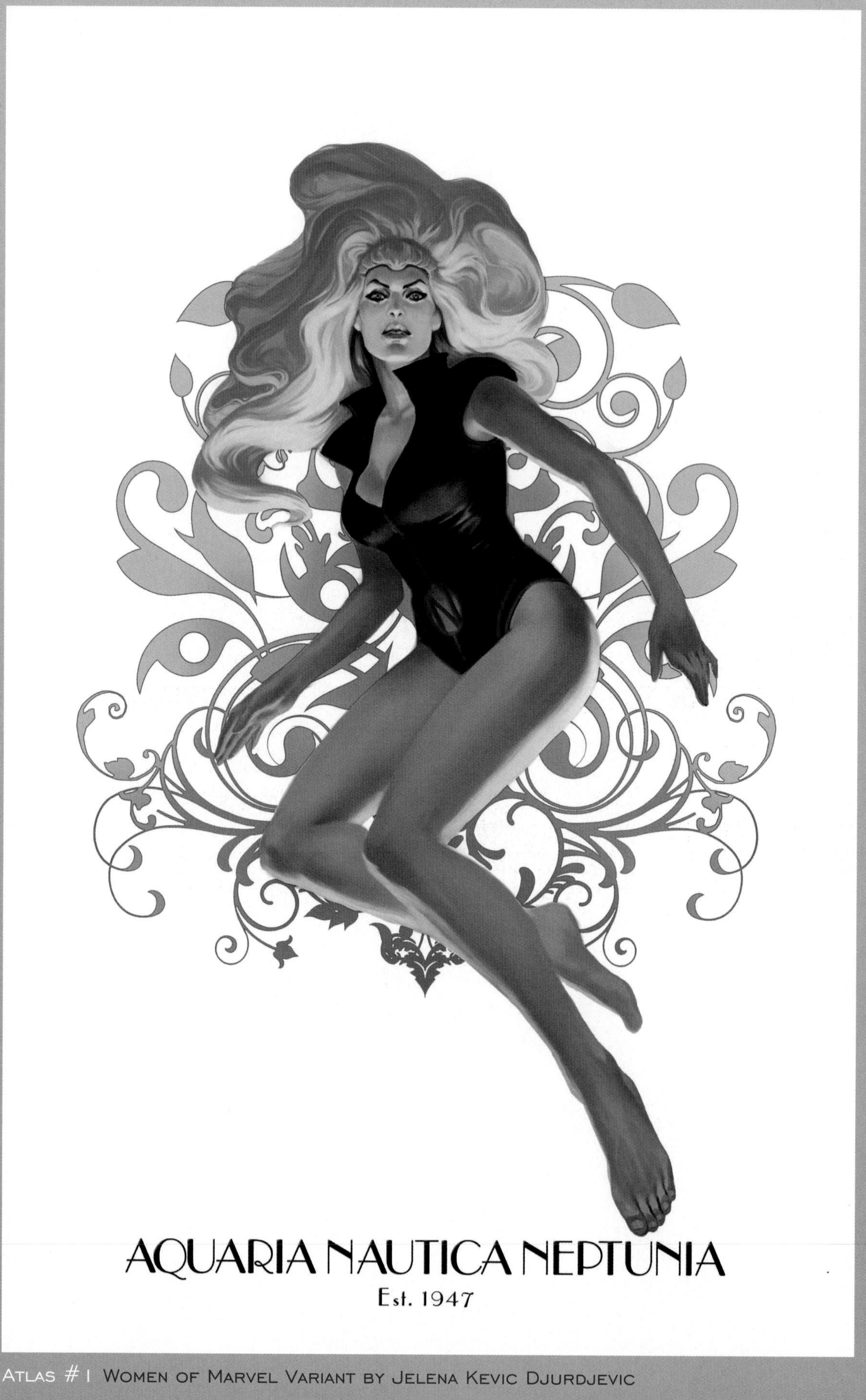
AQUARIA NAUTICA NEPTUNIA
Est. 1947

Atlas #1 Women of Marvel Variant by Jelena Kevic Djurdjevic

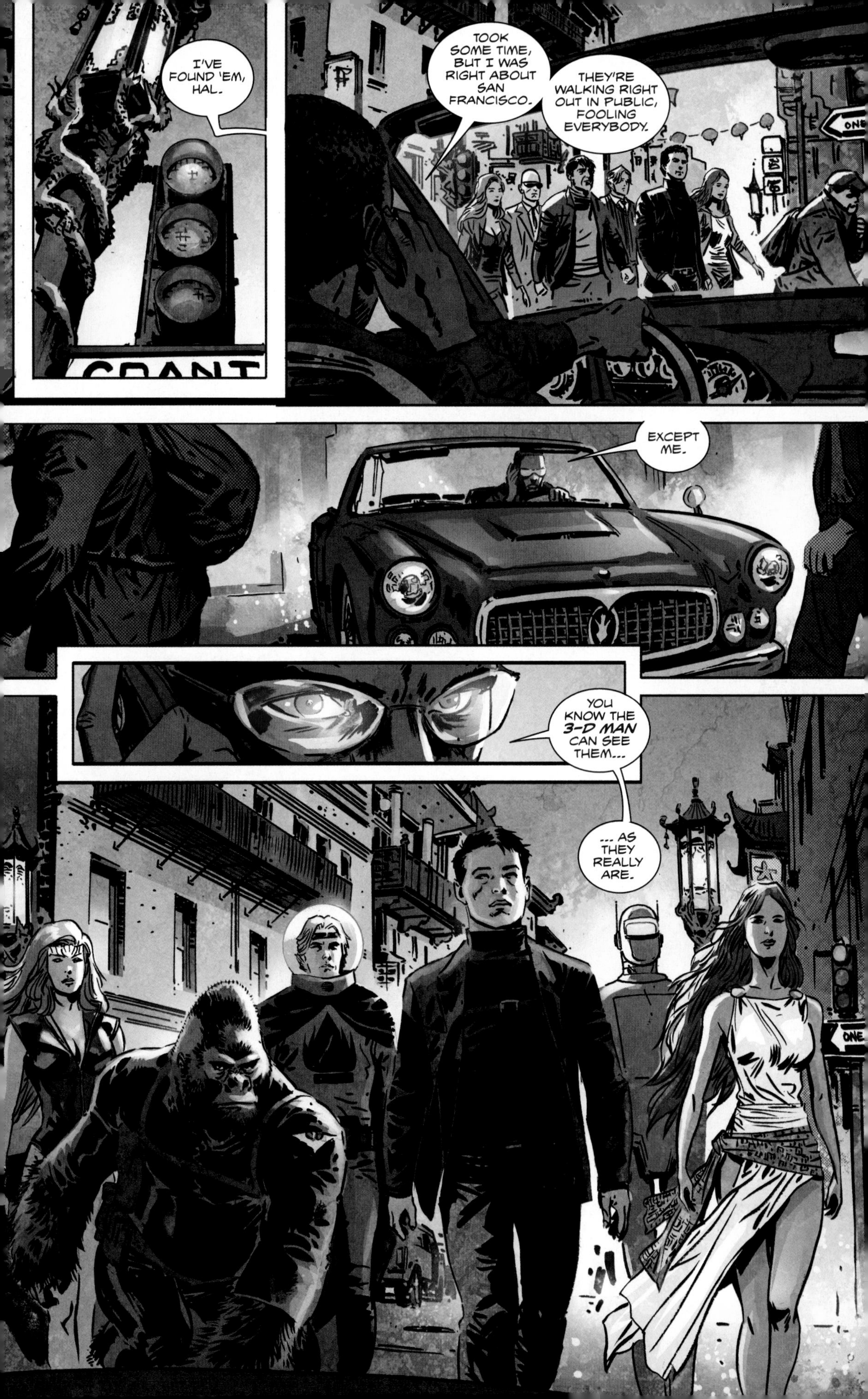
I'VE FOUND 'EM, HAL.
GRANT
TOOK SOME TIME, BUT I WAS RIGHT ABOUT SAN FRANCISCO.
THEY'RE WALKING RIGHT OUT IN PUBLIC, FOOLING EVERYBODY.
EXCEPT ME.
YOU KNOW THE ***3-D MAN*** CAN SEE THEM...
...AS THEY REALLY ARE.
ONE

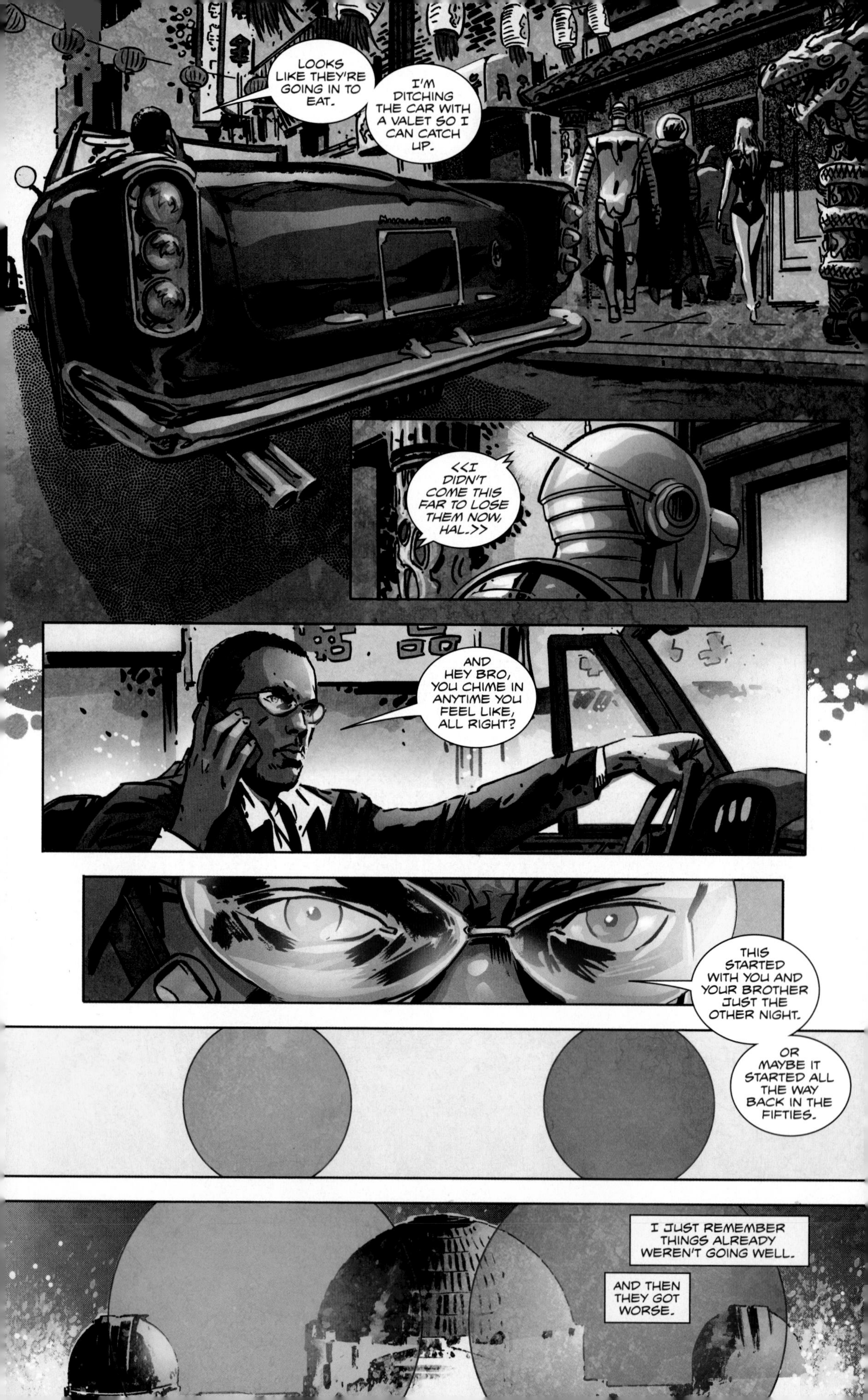

LOOKS LIKE THEY'RE GOING IN TO EAT.
I'M DITCHING THE CAR WITH A VALET SO I CAN CATCH UP.
<<I DIDN'T COME THIS FAR TO LOSE THEM NOW, HAL.>>
AND HEY BRO, YOU CHIME IN ANYTIME YOU FEEL LIKE, ALL RIGHT?
THIS STARTED WITH YOU AND YOUR BROTHER JUST THE OTHER NIGHT.
OR MAYBE IT STARTED ALL THE WAY BACK IN THE FIFTIES.
I JUST REMEMBER THINGS ALREADY WEREN'T GOING WELL.
AND THEN THEY GOT WORSE.

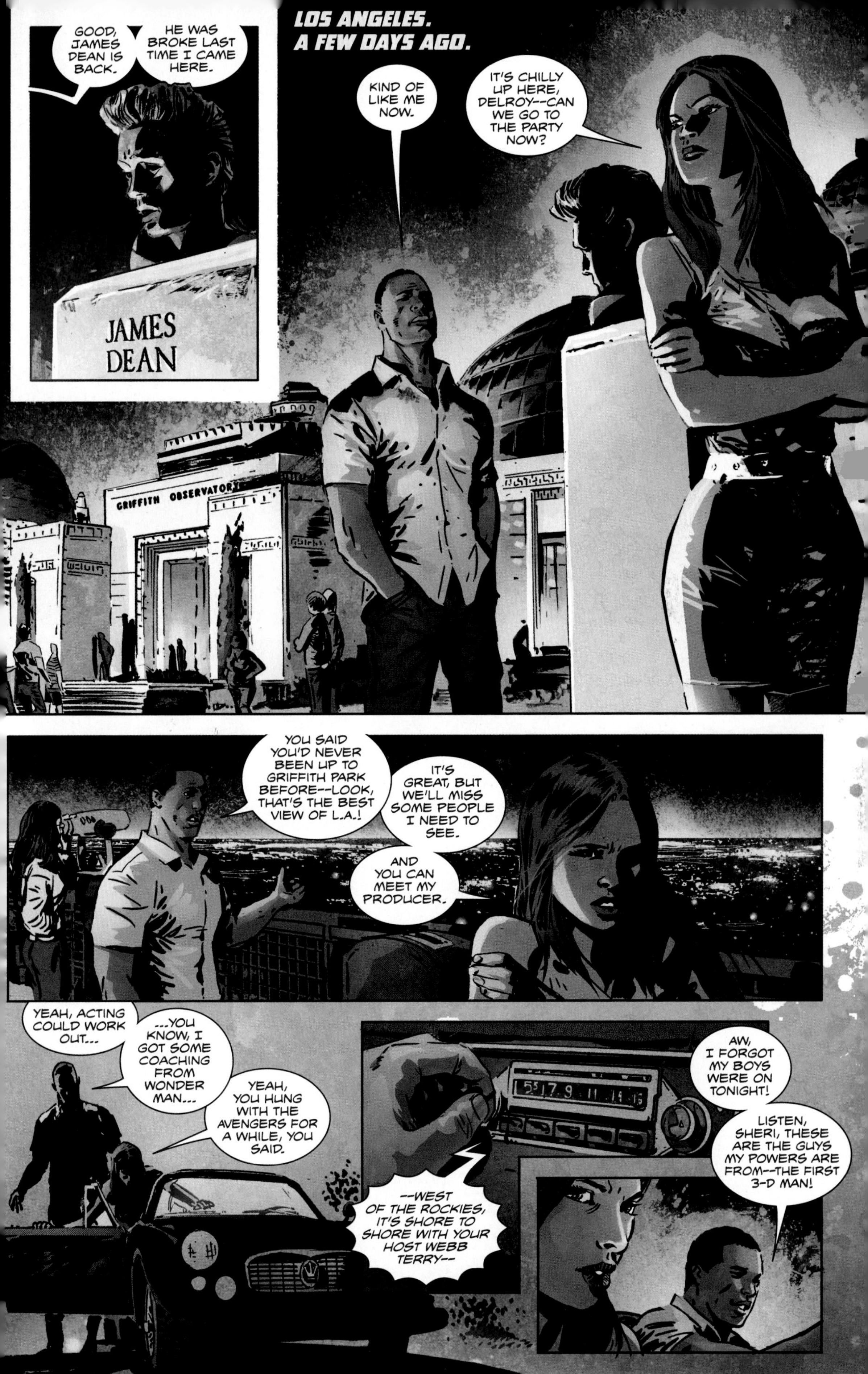
LOS ANGELES.
A FEW DAYS AGO.
GOOD, JAMES DEAN IS BACK.
HE WAS BROKE LAST TIME I CAME HERE.
JAMES DEAN
KIND OF LIKE ME NOW.
IT'S CHILLY UP HERE, DELROY--CAN WE GO TO THE PARTY NOW?
GRIFFITH OBSERVATORY
YOU SAID YOU'D NEVER BEEN UP TO GRIFFITH PARK BEFORE--LOOK, THAT'S THE BEST VIEW OF L.A.!
IT'S GREAT, BUT WE'LL MISS SOME PEOPLE I NEED TO SEE.
AND YOU CAN MEET MY PRODUCER.
YEAH, ACTING COULD WORK OUT...
...YOU KNOW, I GOT SOME COACHING FROM WONDER MAN...
YEAH, YOU HUNG WITH THE AVENGERS FOR A WHILE, YOU SAID.
--WEST OF THE ROCKIES, IT'S SHORE TO SHORE WITH YOUR HOST WEBB TERRY--
AW, I FORGOT MY BOYS WERE ON TONIGHT!
LISTEN, SHERI, THESE ARE THE GUYS MY POWERS ARE FROM--THE FIRST 3-D MAN!

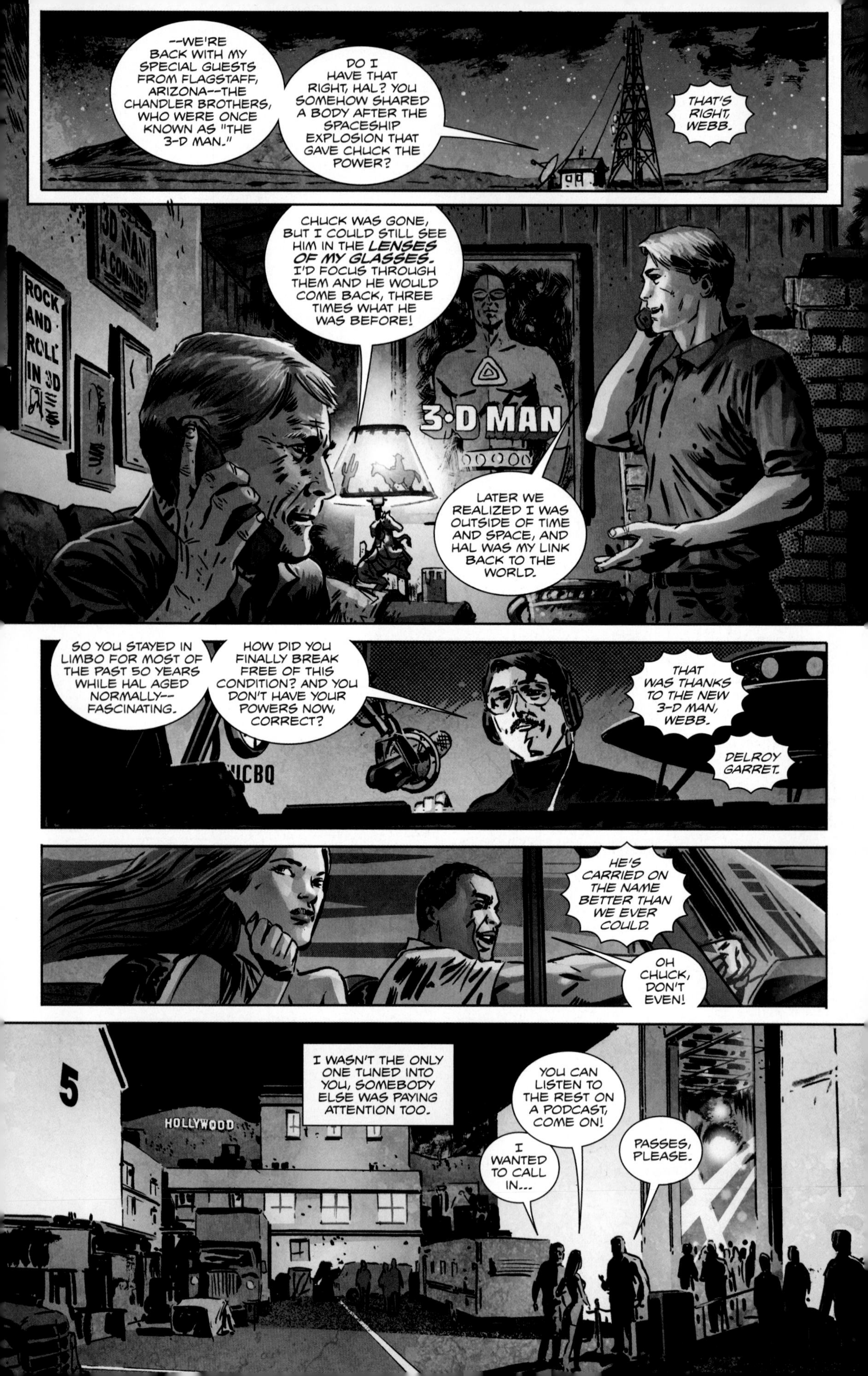
--WE'RE BACK WITH MY SPECIAL GUESTS FROM FLAGSTAFF, ARIZONA--THE CHANDLER BROTHERS, WHO WERE ONCE KNOWN AS "THE 3-D MAN."
DO I HAVE THAT RIGHT, HAL? YOU SOMEHOW SHARED A BODY AFTER THE SPACESHIP EXPLOSION THAT GAVE CHUCK THE POWER?
THAT'S RIGHT, WEBB.
3D MAN A COMIN'?
ROCK AND ROLL IN 3D
CHUCK WAS GONE, BUT I COULD STILL SEE HIM IN THE LENSES OF MY GLASSES. I'D FOCUS THROUGH THEM AND HE WOULD COME BACK, THREE TIMES WHAT HE WAS BEFORE!
3·D MAN
LATER WE REALIZED I WAS OUTSIDE OF TIME AND SPACE, AND HAL WAS MY LINK BACK TO THE WORLD.
SO YOU STAYED IN LIMBO FOR MOST OF THE PAST 50 YEARS WHILE HAL AGED NORMALLY--FASCINATING.
HOW DID YOU FINALLY BREAK FREE OF THIS CONDITION? AND YOU DON'T HAVE YOUR POWERS NOW, CORRECT?
THAT WAS THANKS TO THE NEW 3-D MAN, WEBB.
DELROY GARRET.
HE'S CARRIED ON THE NAME BETTER THAN WE EVER COULD.
OH CHUCK, DON'T EVEN!
5
HOLLYWOOD
I WASN'T THE ONLY ONE TUNED INTO YOU, SOMEBODY ELSE WAS PAYING ATTENTION TOO.
I WANTED TO CALL IN...
YOU CAN LISTEN TO THE REST ON A PODCAST, COME ON!
PASSES, PLEASE.

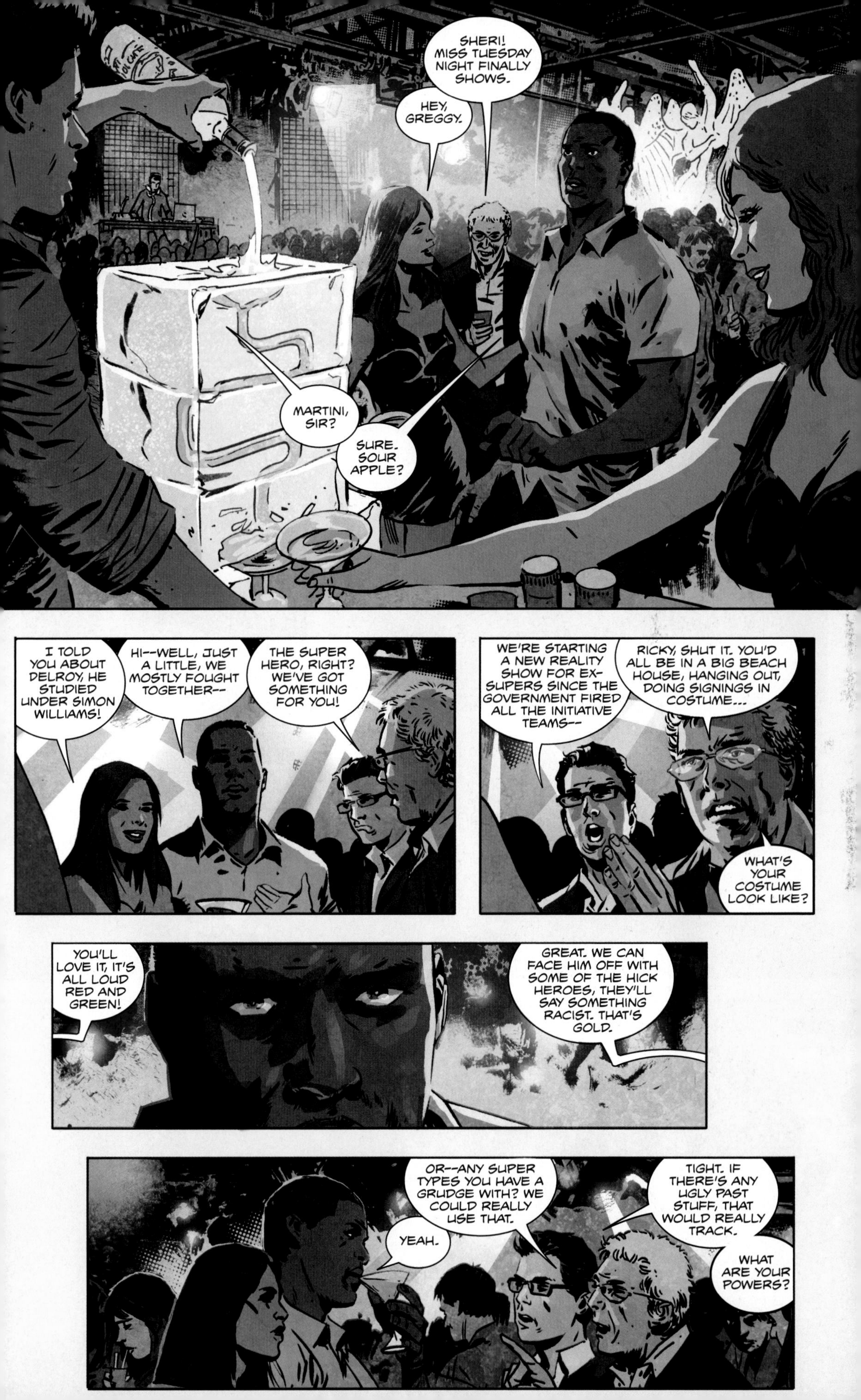
HEY, GREGGY.
SHERI! MISS TUESDAY NIGHT FINALLY SHOWS.
MARTINI, SIR?
SURE. SOUR APPLE?
I TOLD YOU ABOUT DELROY, HE STUDIED UNDER SIMON WILLIAMS!
HI--WELL, JUST A LITTLE, WE MOSTLY FOUGHT TOGETHER--
THE SUPER HERO, RIGHT? WE'VE GOT SOMETHING FOR YOU!
WE'RE STARTING A NEW REALITY SHOW FOR EX-SUPERS SINCE THE GOVERNMENT FIRED ALL THE INITIATIVE TEAMS--
RICKY, SHUT IT. YOU'D ALL BE IN A BIG BEACH HOUSE, HANGING OUT, DOING SIGNINGS IN COSTUME...
WHAT'S YOUR COSTUME LOOK LIKE?
YOU'LL LOVE IT, IT'S ALL LOUD RED AND GREEN!
GREAT. WE CAN FACE HIM OFF WITH SOME OF THE HICK HEROES, THEY'LL SAY SOMETHING RACIST. THAT'S GOLD.
OR--ANY SUPER TYPES YOU HAVE A GRUDGE WITH? WE COULD REALLY USE THAT.
YEAH.
TIGHT. IF THERE'S ANY UGLY PAST STUFF, THAT WOULD REALLY TRACK.
WHAT ARE YOUR POWERS?

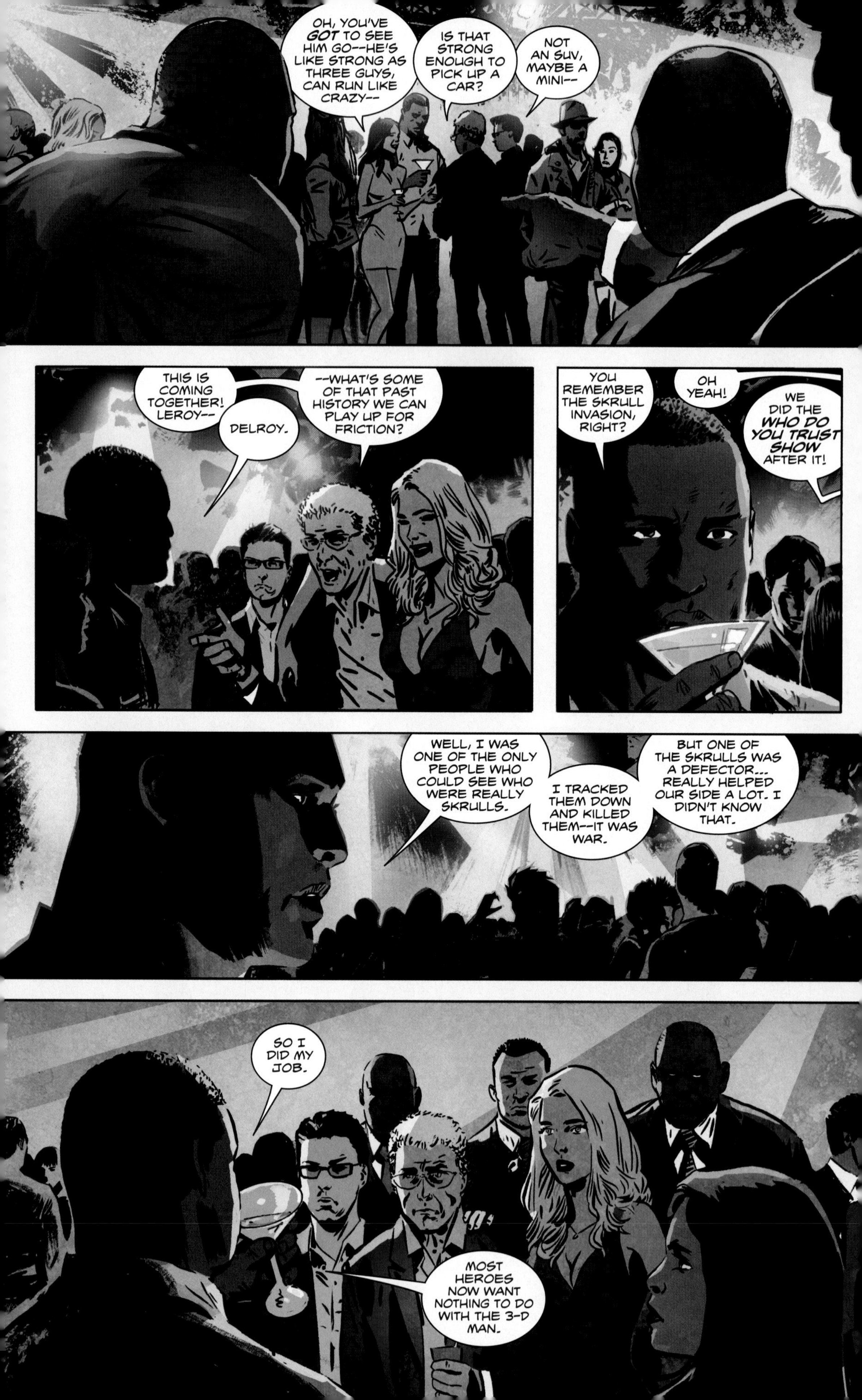
OH, YOU'VE GOT TO SEE HIM GO--HE'S LIKE STRONG AS THREE GUYS, CAN RUN LIKE CRAZY--
IS THAT STRONG ENOUGH TO PICK UP A CAR?
NOT AN SUV, MAYBE A MINI--
THIS IS COMING TOGETHER! LEROY--
DELROY.
--WHAT'S SOME OF THAT PAST HISTORY WE CAN PLAY UP FOR FRICTION?
YOU REMEMBER THE SKRULL INVASION, RIGHT?
OH YEAH!
WE DID THE WHO DO YOU TRUST SHOW AFTER IT!
WELL, I WAS ONE OF THE ONLY PEOPLE WHO COULD SEE WHO WERE REALLY SKRULLS.
I TRACKED THEM DOWN AND KILLED THEM--IT WAS WAR.
BUT ONE OF THE SKRULLS WAS A DEFECTOR... REALLY HELPED OUR SIDE A LOT. I DIDN'T KNOW THAT.
SO I DID MY JOB.
MOST HEROES NOW WANT NOTHING TO DO WITH THE 3-D MAN.

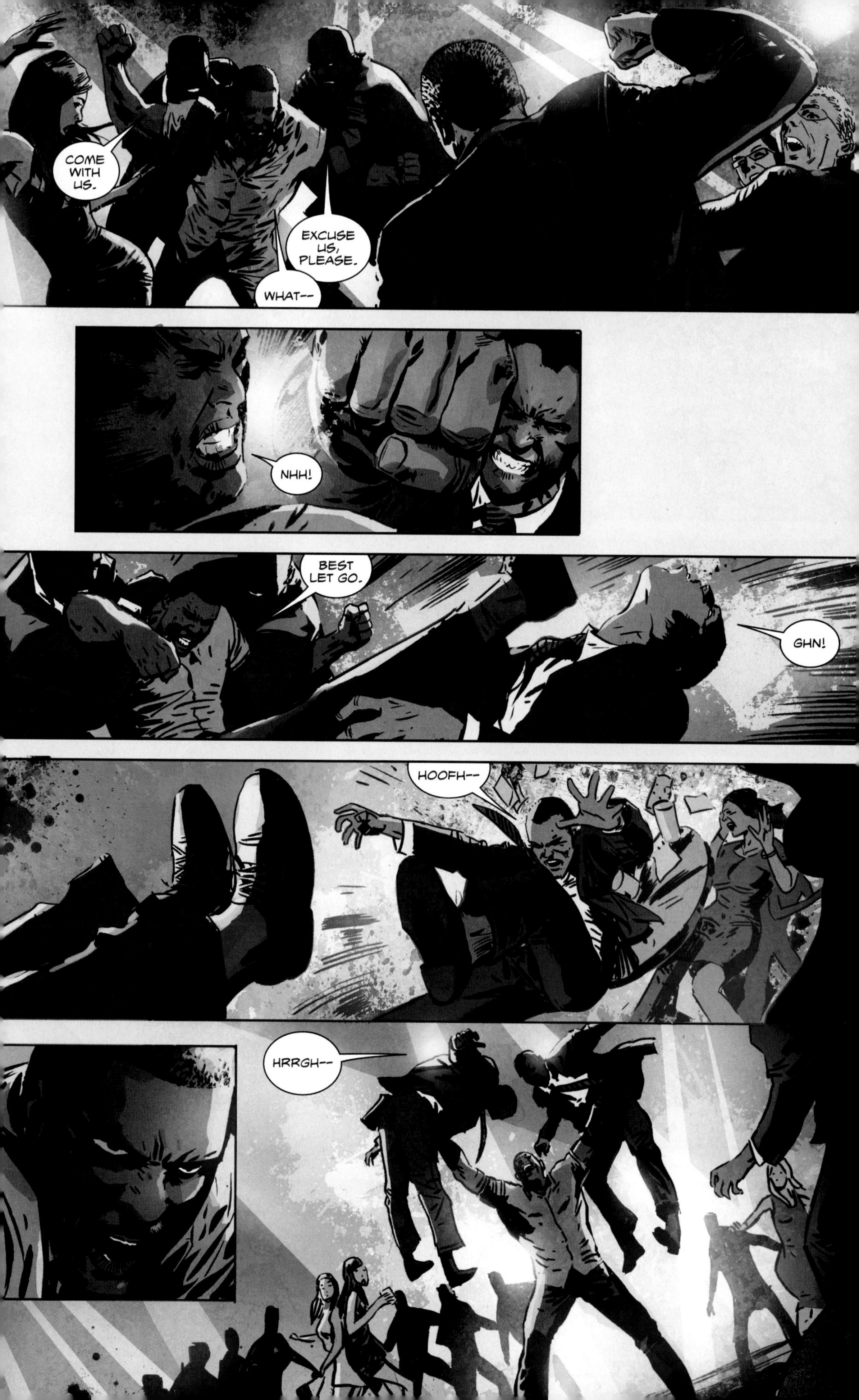
COME WITH US.
EXCUSE US, PLEASE.
WHAT--
NHH!
BEST LET GO.
GHN!
HOOFH--
HRRGH--

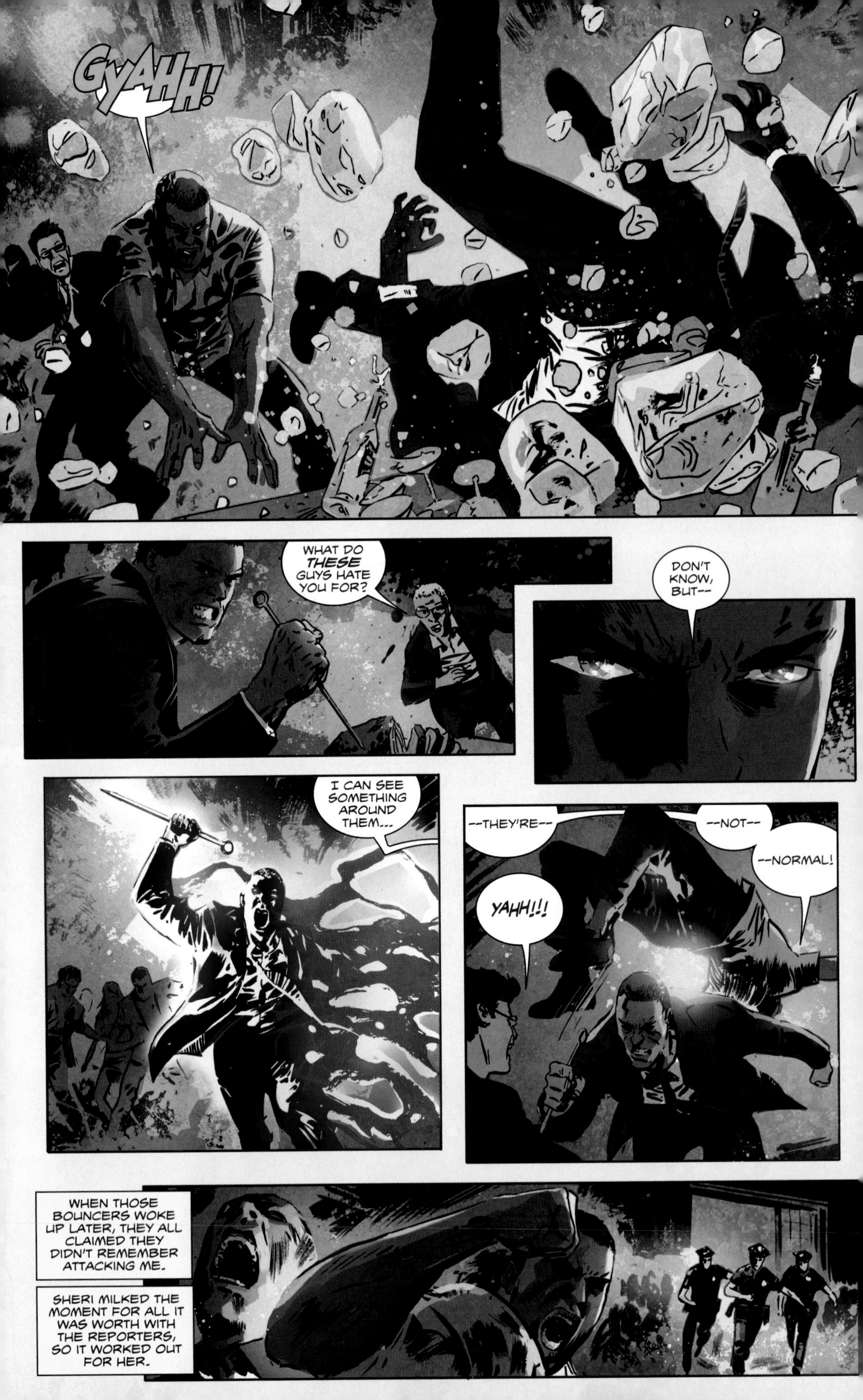
GYAHH!
WHAT DO *THESE* GUYS HATE YOU FOR?
DON'T KNOW, BUT--
I CAN SEE SOMETHING AROUND THEM...
--THEY'RE--
--NOT--
--NORMAL!
YAHH!!!
WHEN THOSE BOUNCERS WOKE UP LATER, THEY ALL CLAIMED THEY DIDN'T REMEMBER ATTACKING ME.
SHERI MILKED THE MOMENT FOR ALL IT WAS WORTH WITH THE REPORTERS, SO IT WORKED OUT FOR HER.

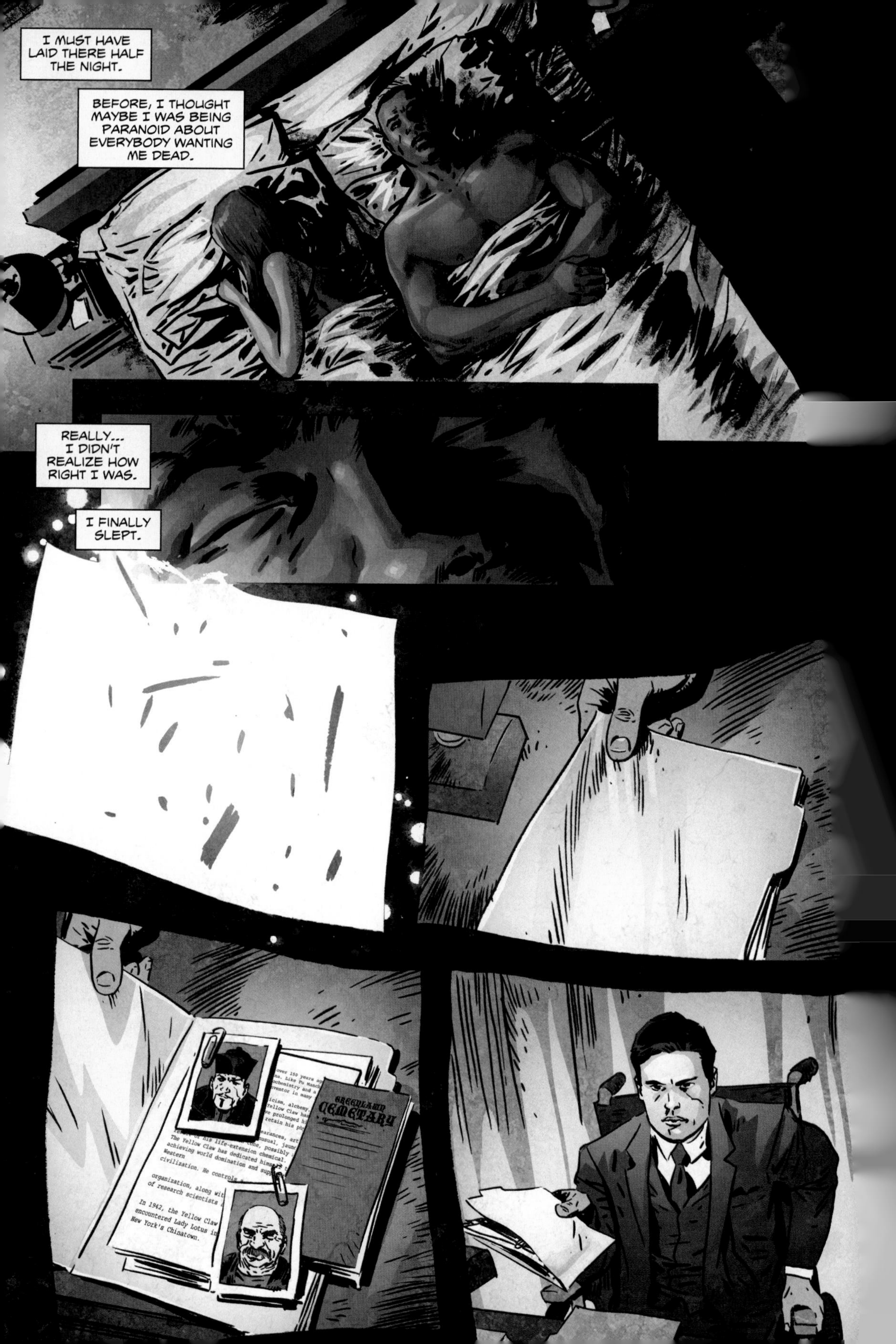
I MUST HAVE LAID THERE HALF THE NIGHT.
BEFORE, I THOUGHT MAYBE I WAS BEING PARANOID ABOUT EVERYBODY WANTING ME DEAD.
REALLY... I DIDN'T REALIZE HOW RIGHT I WAS.
I FINALLY SLEPT.
GREENLAWN CEMETARY
In 1942, the Yellow Claw encountered Lady Lotus in New York's Chinatown.

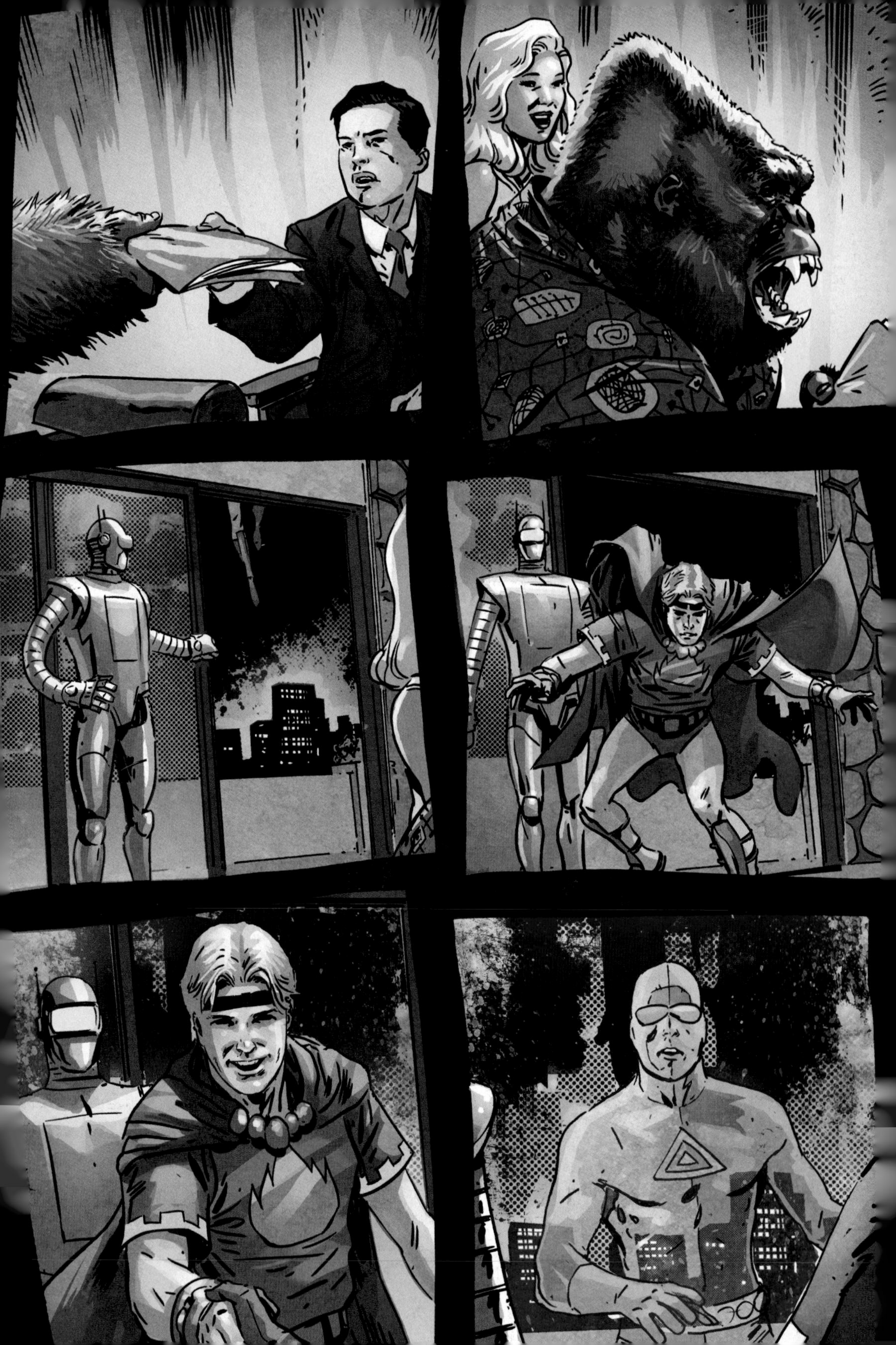

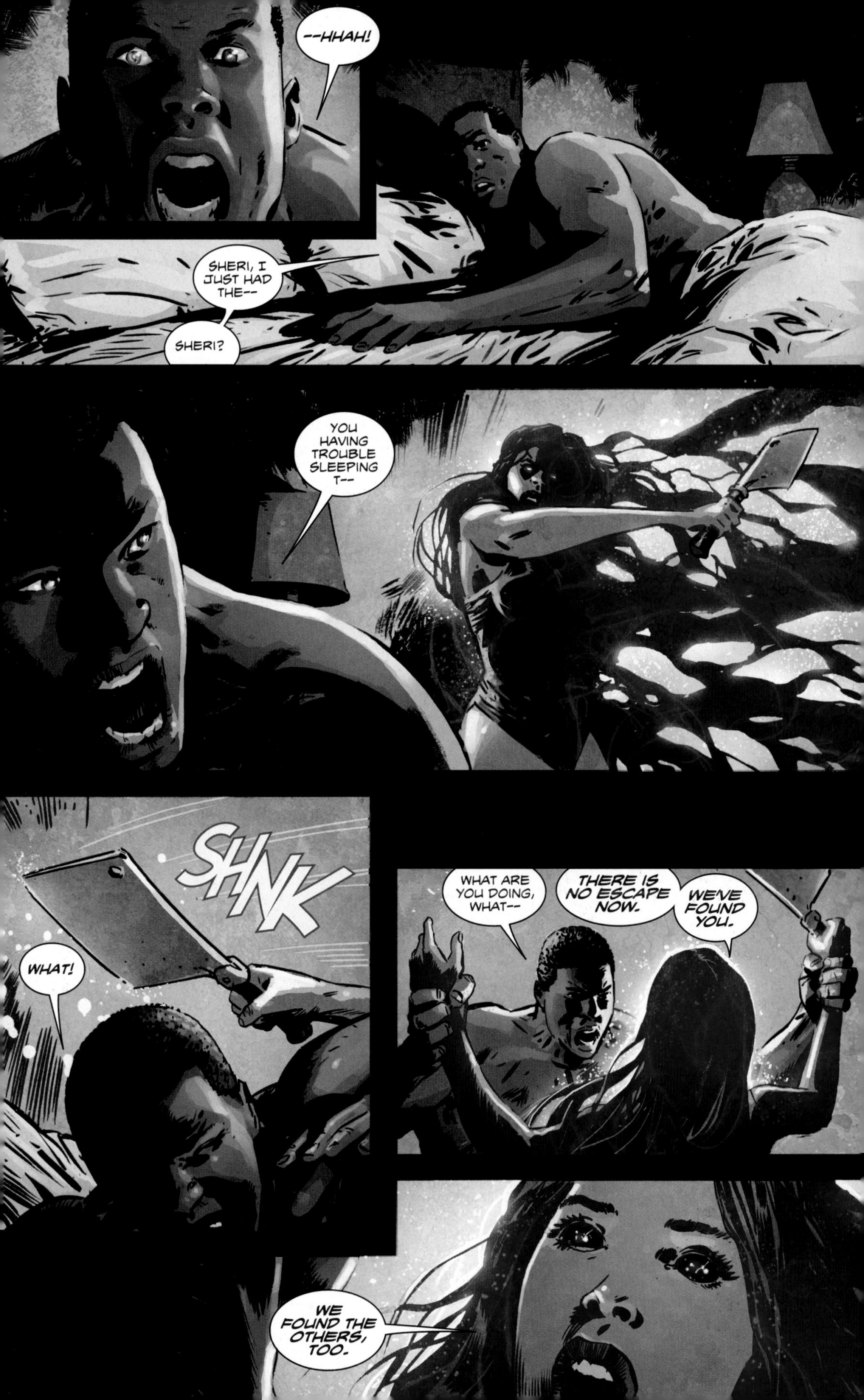
--HHAH!
SHERI, I JUST HAD THE--
SHERI?
YOU HAVING TROUBLE SLEEPING T--
SHNK
WHAT!
WHAT ARE YOU DOING, WHAT--
THERE IS NO ESCAPE NOW.
WE'VE FOUND YOU.
WE FOUND THE OTHERS, TOO.

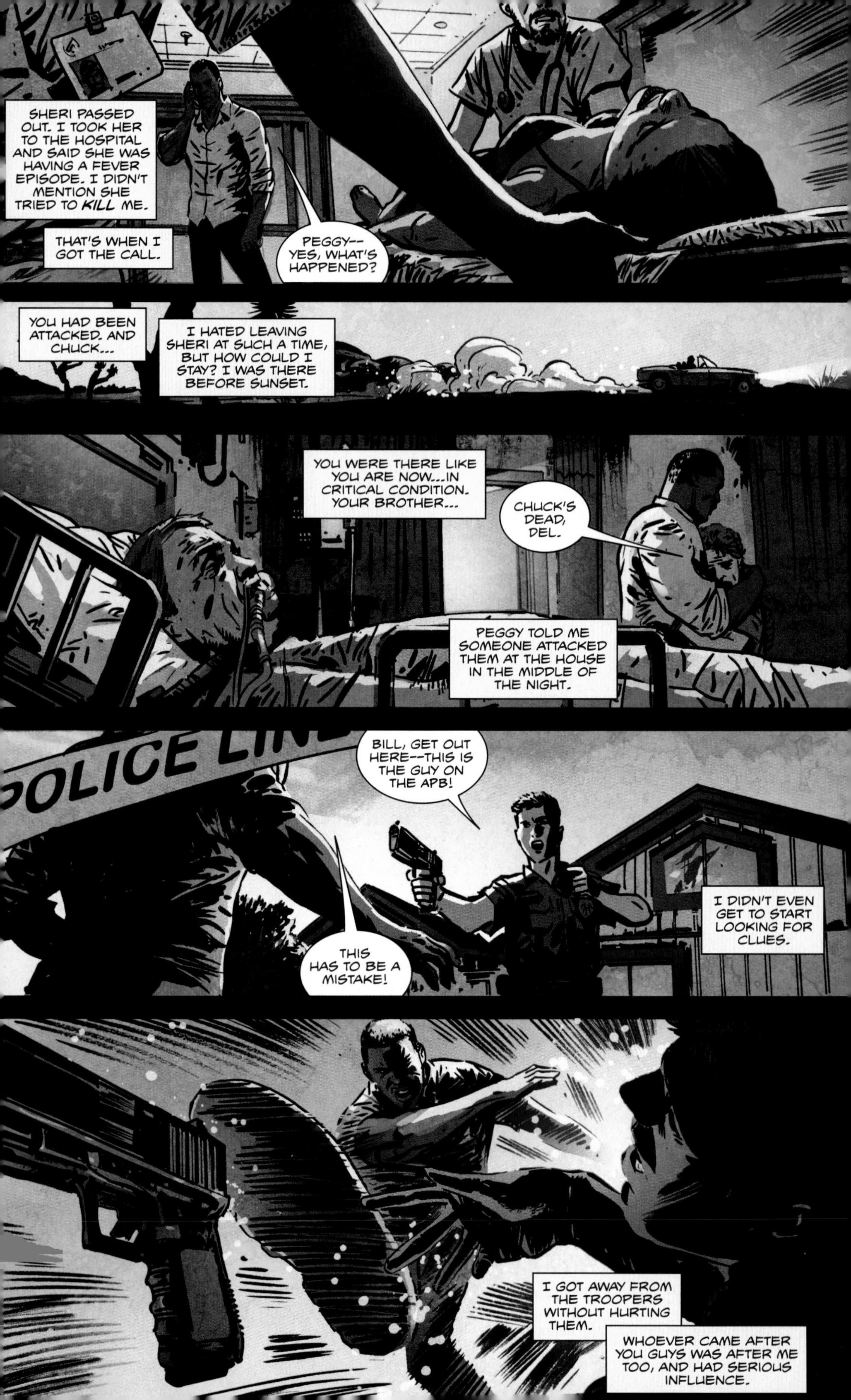
SHERI PASSED OUT. I TOOK HER TO THE HOSPITAL AND SAID SHE WAS HAVING A FEVER EPISODE. I DIDN'T MENTION SHE TRIED TO *KILL* ME.
THAT'S WHEN I GOT THE CALL.
PEGGY-- YES, WHAT'S HAPPENED?
YOU HAD BEEN ATTACKED. AND CHUCK...
I HATED LEAVING SHERI AT SUCH A TIME, BUT HOW COULD I STAY? I WAS THERE BEFORE SUNSET.
YOU WERE THERE LIKE YOU ARE NOW...IN CRITICAL CONDITION. YOUR BROTHER...
CHUCK'S DEAD, DEL.
PEGGY TOLD ME SOMEONE ATTACKED THEM AT THE HOUSE IN THE MIDDLE OF THE NIGHT.
POLICE LINE
BILL, GET OUT HERE--THIS IS THE GUY ON THE APB!
THIS HAS TO BE A MISTAKE!
I DIDN'T EVEN GET TO START LOOKING FOR CLUES.
I GOT AWAY FROM THE TROOPERS WITHOUT HURTING THEM.
WHOEVER CAME AFTER YOU GUYS WAS AFTER ME TOO, AND HAD SERIOUS INFLUENCE.

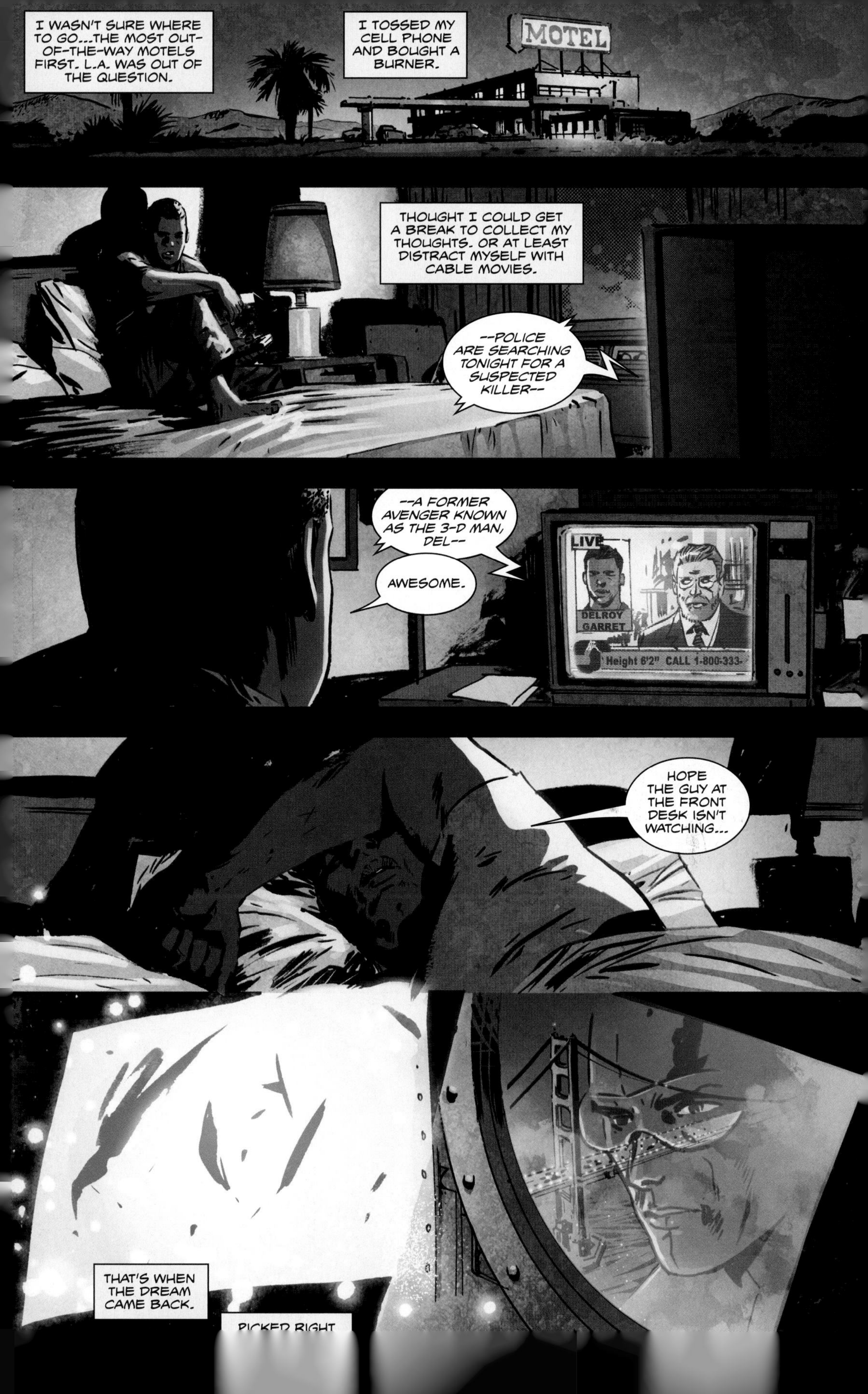
I WASN'T SURE WHERE TO GO...THE MOST OUT-OF-THE-WAY MOTELS FIRST. L.A. WAS OUT OF THE QUESTION.
I TOSSED MY CELL PHONE AND BOUGHT A BURNER.
MOTEL
THOUGHT I COULD GET A BREAK TO COLLECT MY THOUGHTS. OR AT LEAST DISTRACT MYSELF WITH CABLE MOVIES.
--POLICE ARE SEARCHING TONIGHT FOR A SUSPECTED KILLER--
--A FORMER AVENGER KNOWN AS THE 3-D MAN, DEL--
LIVE
DELROY GARRET
Height 6'2" CALL 1-800-333-
AWESOME.
HOPE THE GUY AT THE FRONT DESK ISN'T WATCHING...
THAT'S WHEN THE DREAM CAME BACK.
PICKED RIGHT

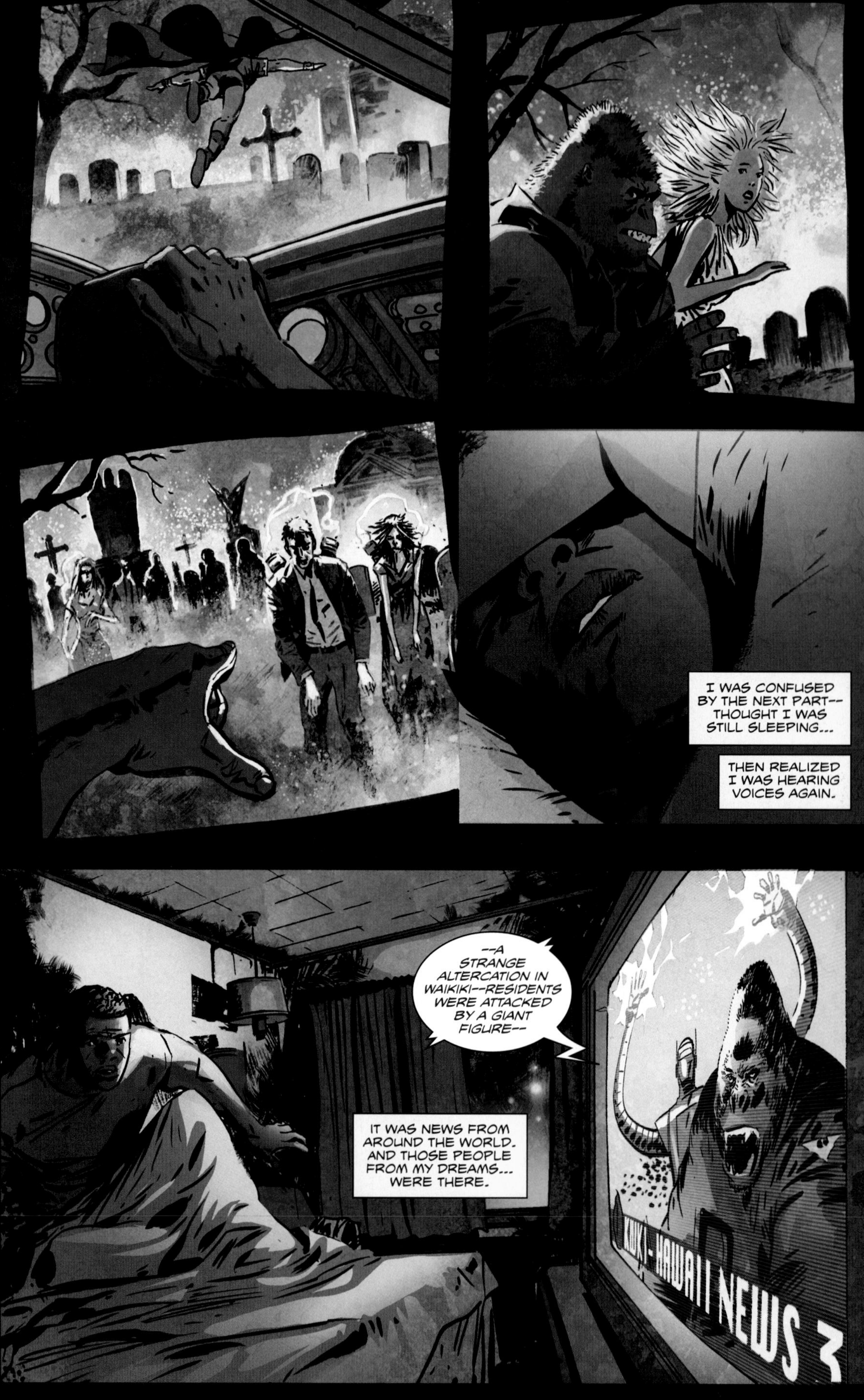
I WAS CONFUSED BY THE NEXT PART--THOUGHT I WAS STILL SLEEPING...
THEN REALIZED I WAS HEARING VOICES AGAIN.
--A STRANGE ALTERCATION IN WAIKIKI--RESIDENTS WERE ATTACKED BY A GIANT FIGURE--
IT WAS NEWS FROM AROUND THE WORLD. AND THOSE PEOPLE FROM MY DREAMS... WERE THERE.
KWKI - HAWAII NEWS 3

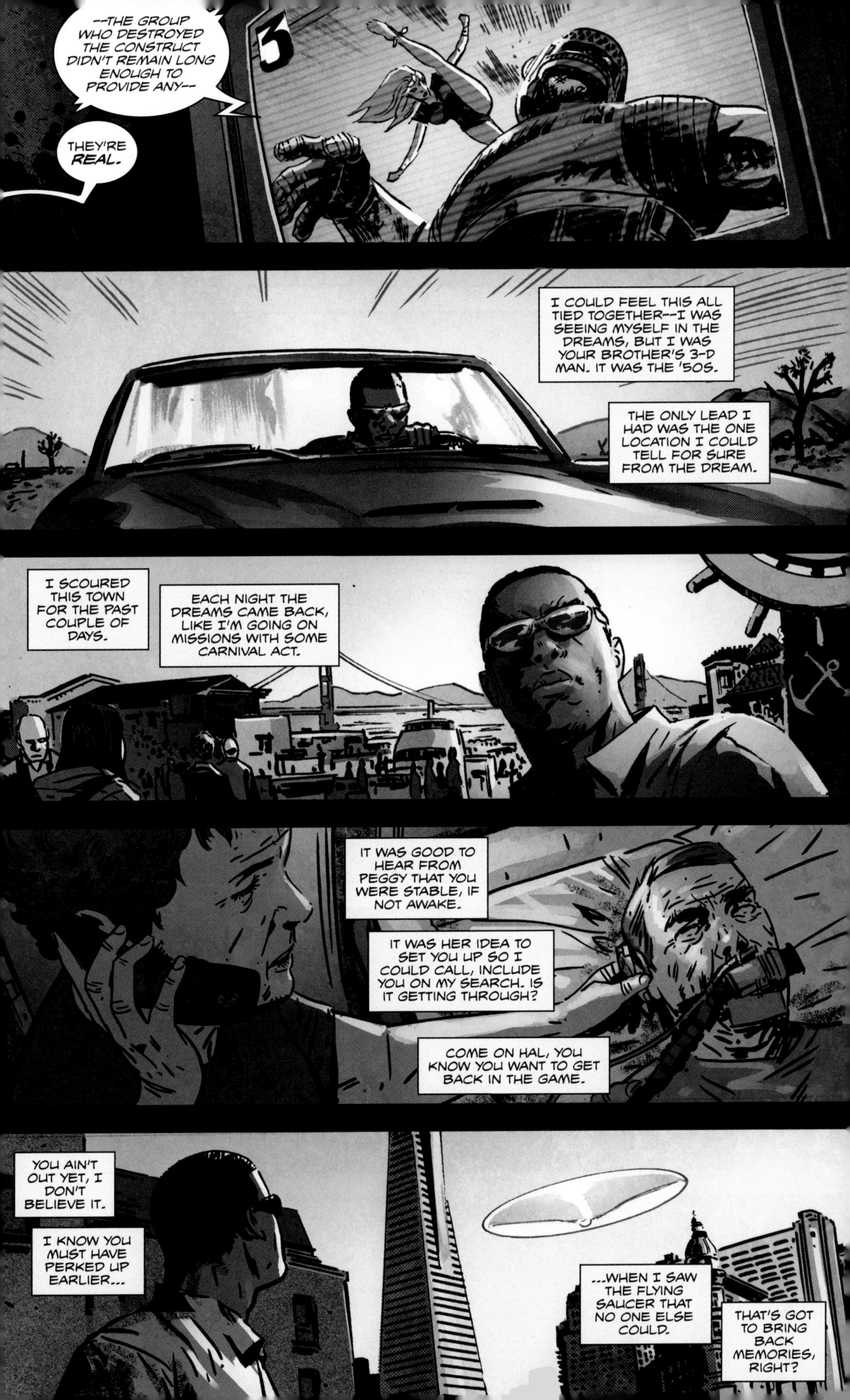
--THE GROUP WHO DESTROYED THE CONSTRUCT DIDN'T REMAIN LONG ENOUGH TO PROVIDE ANY--
THEY'RE REAL.
I COULD FEEL THIS ALL TIED TOGETHER--I WAS SEEING MYSELF IN THE DREAMS, BUT I WAS YOUR BROTHER'S 3-D MAN. IT WAS THE '50S.
THE ONLY LEAD I HAD WAS THE ONE LOCATION I COULD TELL FOR SURE FROM THE DREAM.
I SCOURED THIS TOWN FOR THE PAST COUPLE OF DAYS.
EACH NIGHT THE DREAMS CAME BACK, LIKE I'M GOING ON MISSIONS WITH SOME CARNIVAL ACT.
IT WAS GOOD TO HEAR FROM PEGGY THAT YOU WERE STABLE, IF NOT AWAKE.
IT WAS HER IDEA TO SET YOU UP SO I COULD CALL, INCLUDE YOU ON MY SEARCH. IS IT GETTING THROUGH?
COME ON HAL, YOU KNOW YOU WANT TO GET BACK IN THE GAME.
YOU AIN'T OUT YET, I DON'T BELIEVE IT.
I KNOW YOU MUST HAVE PERKED UP EARLIER...
...WHEN I SAW THE FLYING SAUCER THAT NO ONE ELSE COULD.
THAT'S GOT TO BRING BACK MEMORIES, RIGHT?

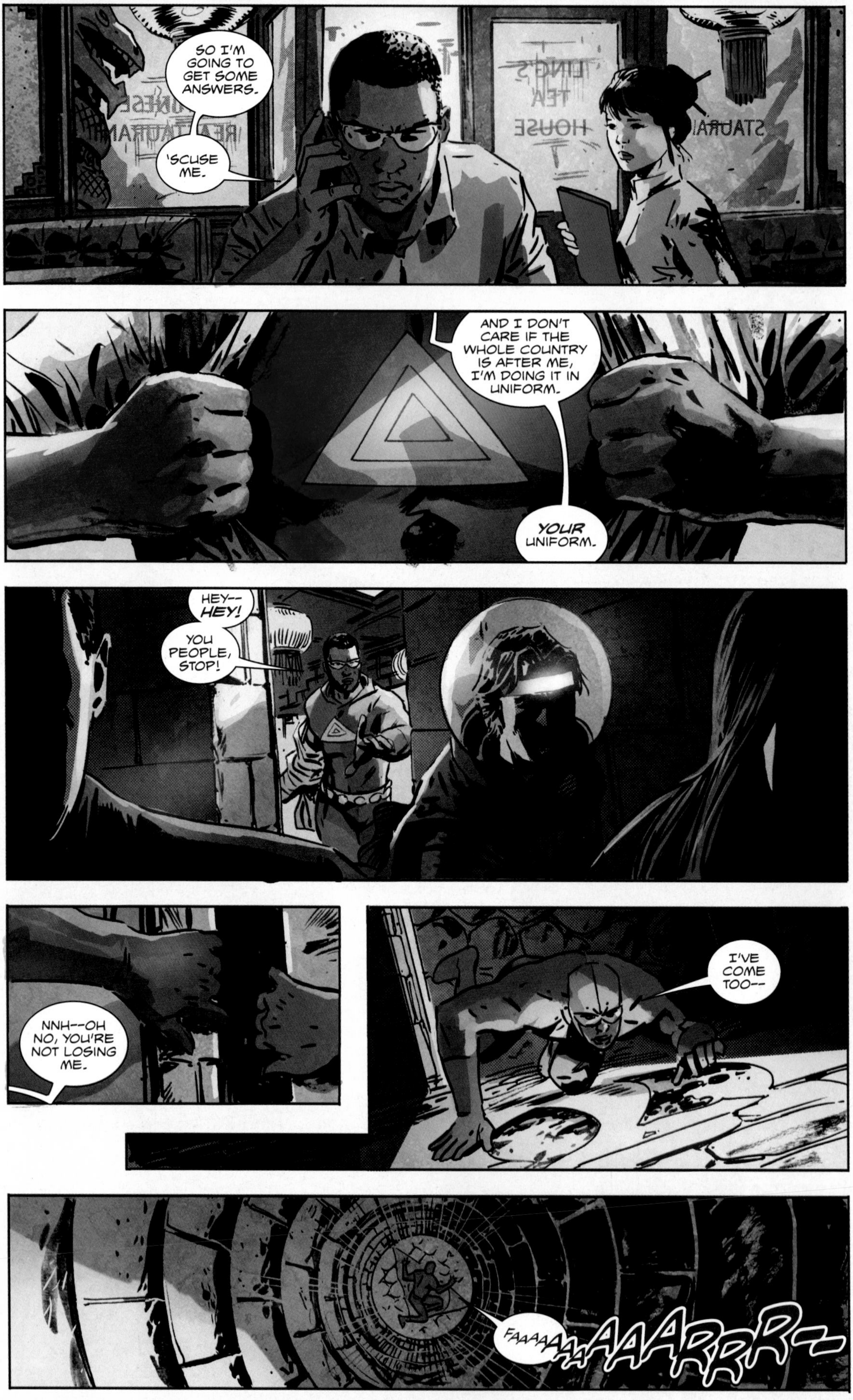
SO I'M GOING TO GET SOME ANSWERS.
'SCUSE ME.
LING'S TEA HOUSE
AND I DON'T CARE IF THE WHOLE COUNTRY IS AFTER ME, I'M DOING IT IN UNIFORM.
YOUR UNIFORM.
HEY--
HEY!
YOU PEOPLE, STOP!
NNH--OH NO, YOU'RE NOT LOSING ME.
I'VE COME TOO--
FAAAAAAAAAAARRRR--

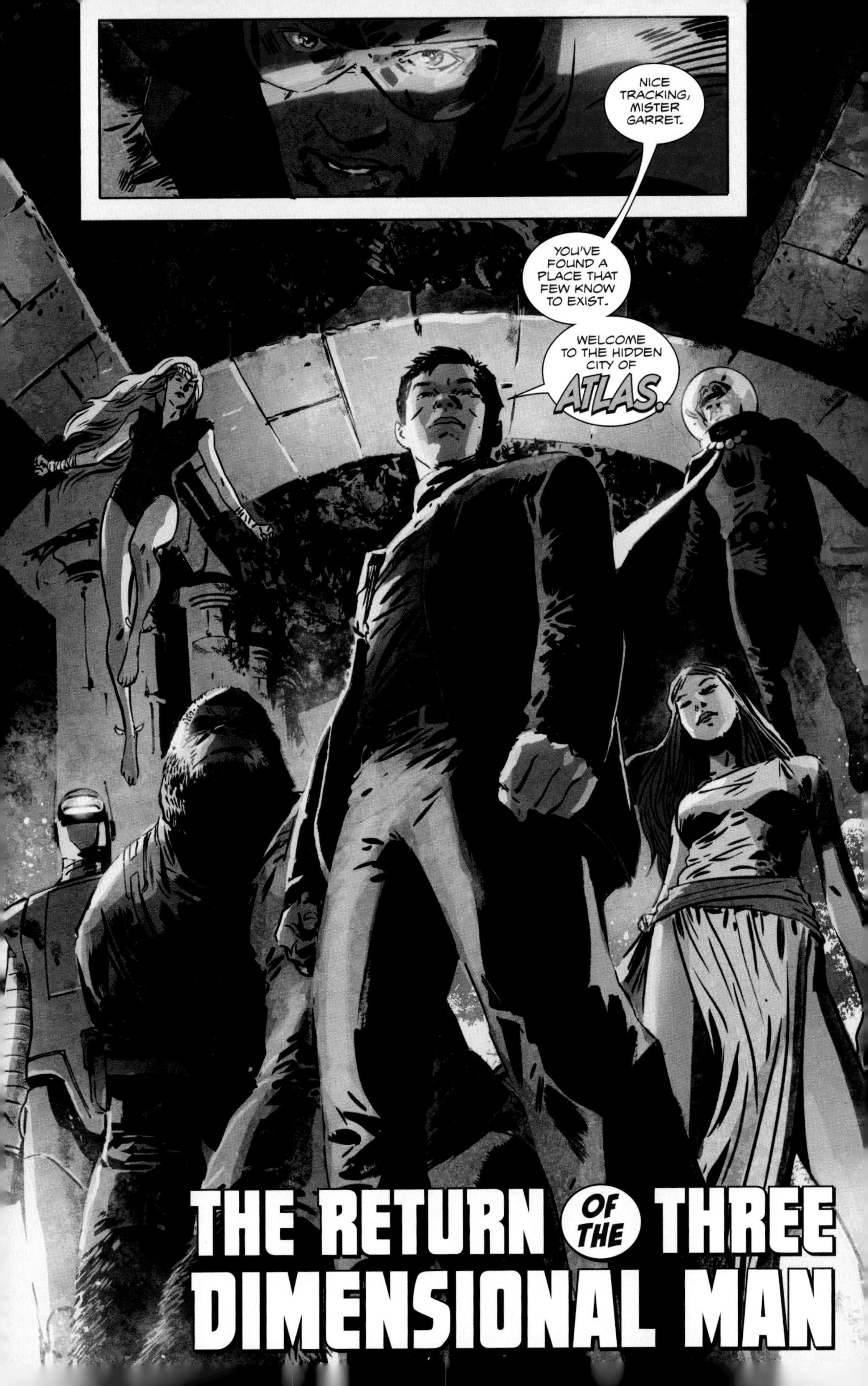
NICE TRACKING, MISTER GARRET.
YOU'VE FOUND A PLACE THAT FEW KNOW TO EXIST.
WELCOME TO THE HIDDEN CITY OF ATLAS.
THE RETURN OF THE THREE DIMENSIONAL MAN

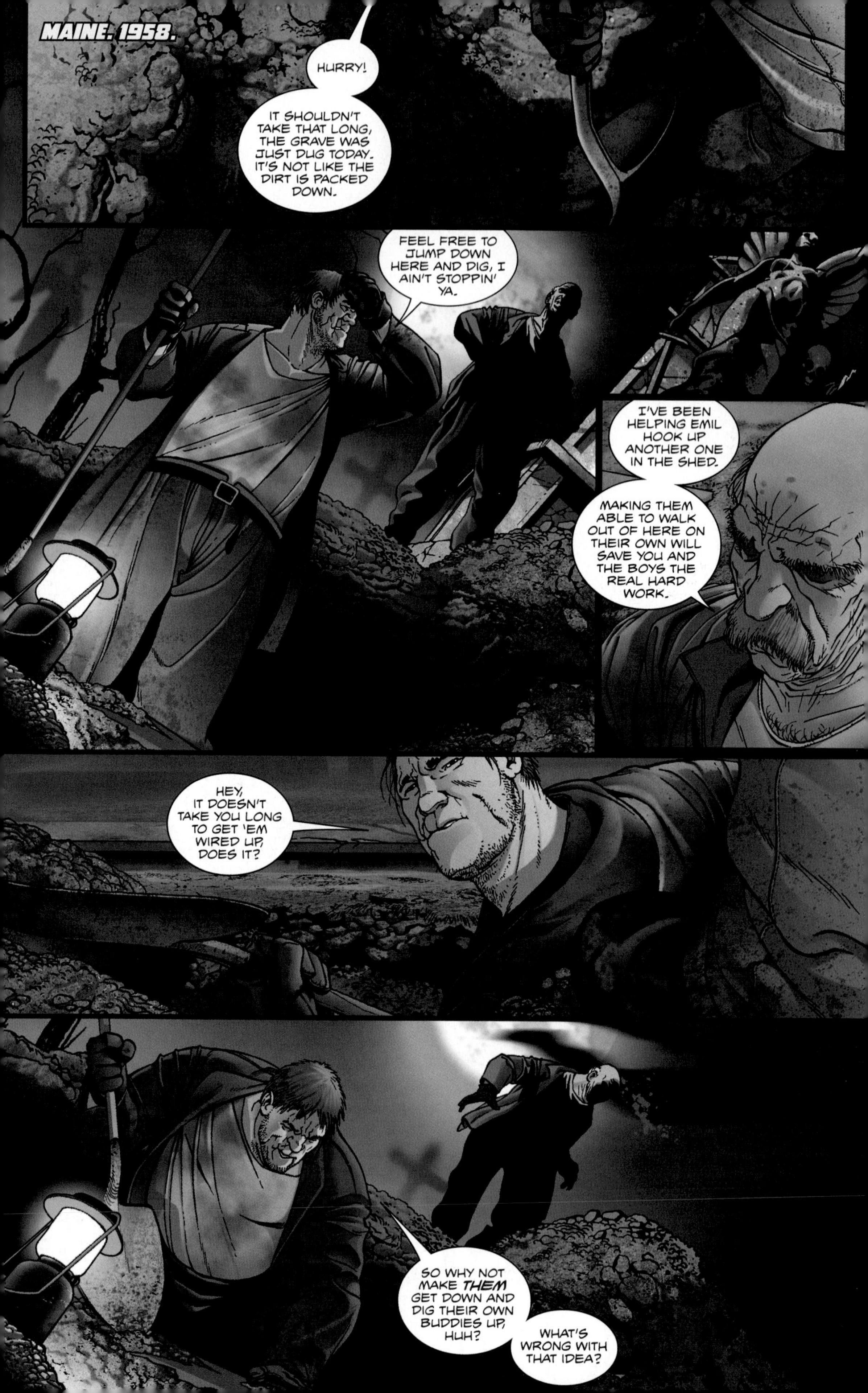
MAINE. 1958.
HURRY!
IT SHOULDN'T TAKE THAT LONG, THE GRAVE WAS JUST DUG TODAY. IT'S NOT LIKE THE DIRT IS PACKED DOWN.
FEEL FREE TO JUMP DOWN HERE AND DIG, I AIN'T STOPPIN' YA.
I'VE BEEN HELPING EMIL HOOK UP ANOTHER ONE IN THE SHED.
MAKING THEM ABLE TO WALK OUT OF HERE ON THEIR OWN WILL SAVE YOU AND THE BOYS THE REAL HARD WORK.
HEY, IT DOESN'T TAKE YOU LONG TO GET 'EM WIRED UP, DOES IT?
SO WHY NOT MAKE THEM GET DOWN AND DIG THEIR OWN BUDDIES UP, HUH?
WHAT'S WRONG WITH THAT IDEA?

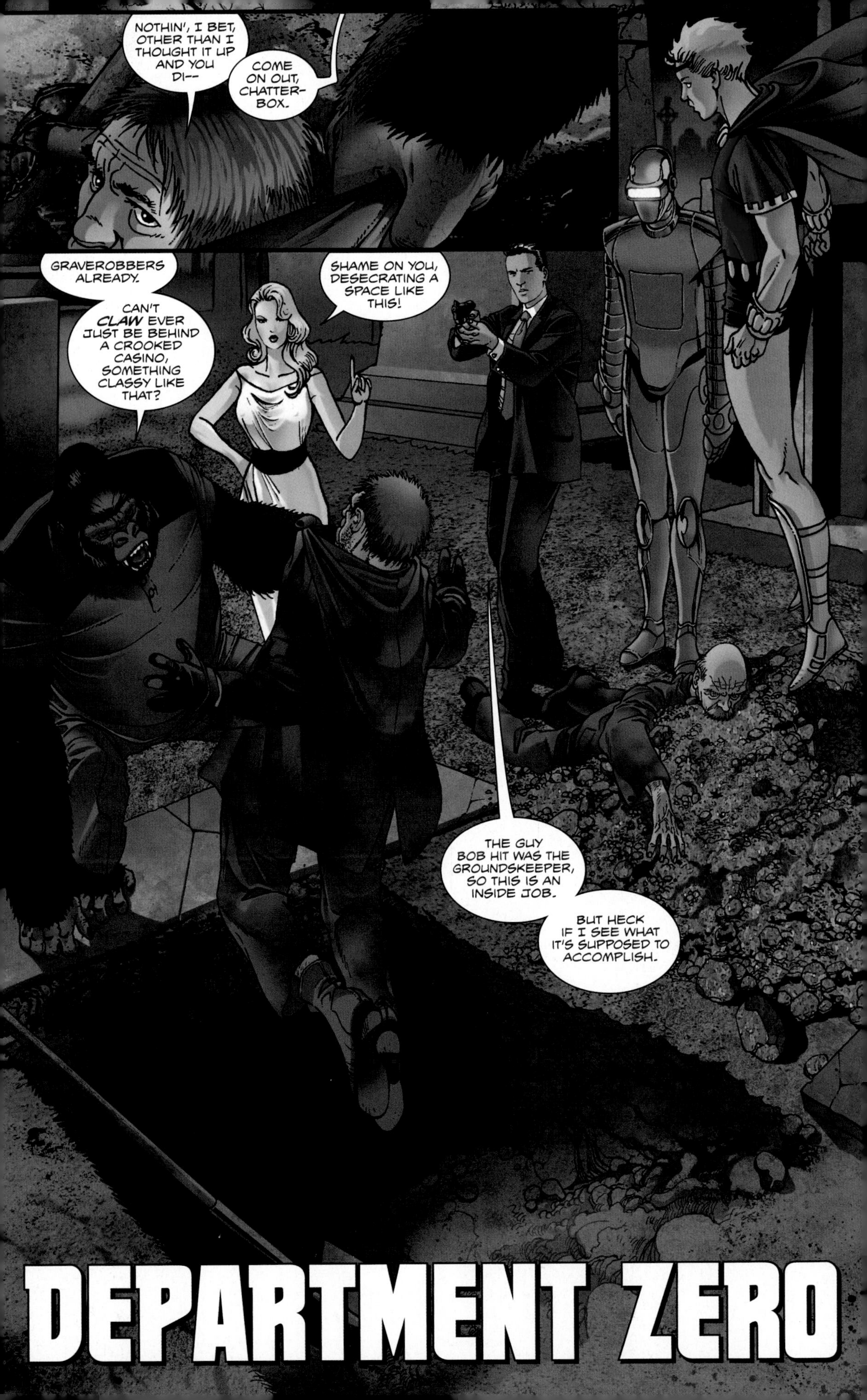
NOTHIN', I BET, OTHER THAN I THOUGHT IT UP AND YOU DI--
COME ON OUT, CHATTER-BOX.
GRAVEROBBERS ALREADY.
CAN'T *CLAW* EVER JUST BE BEHIND A CROOKED CASINO, SOMETHING CLASSY LIKE THAT?
SHAME ON YOU, DESECRATING A SPACE LIKE THIS!
THE GUY BOB HIT WAS THE GROUNDSKEEPER, SO THIS IS AN INSIDE JOB.
BUT HECK IF I SEE WHAT IT'S SUPPOSED TO ACCOMPLISH.
DEPARTMENT ZERO

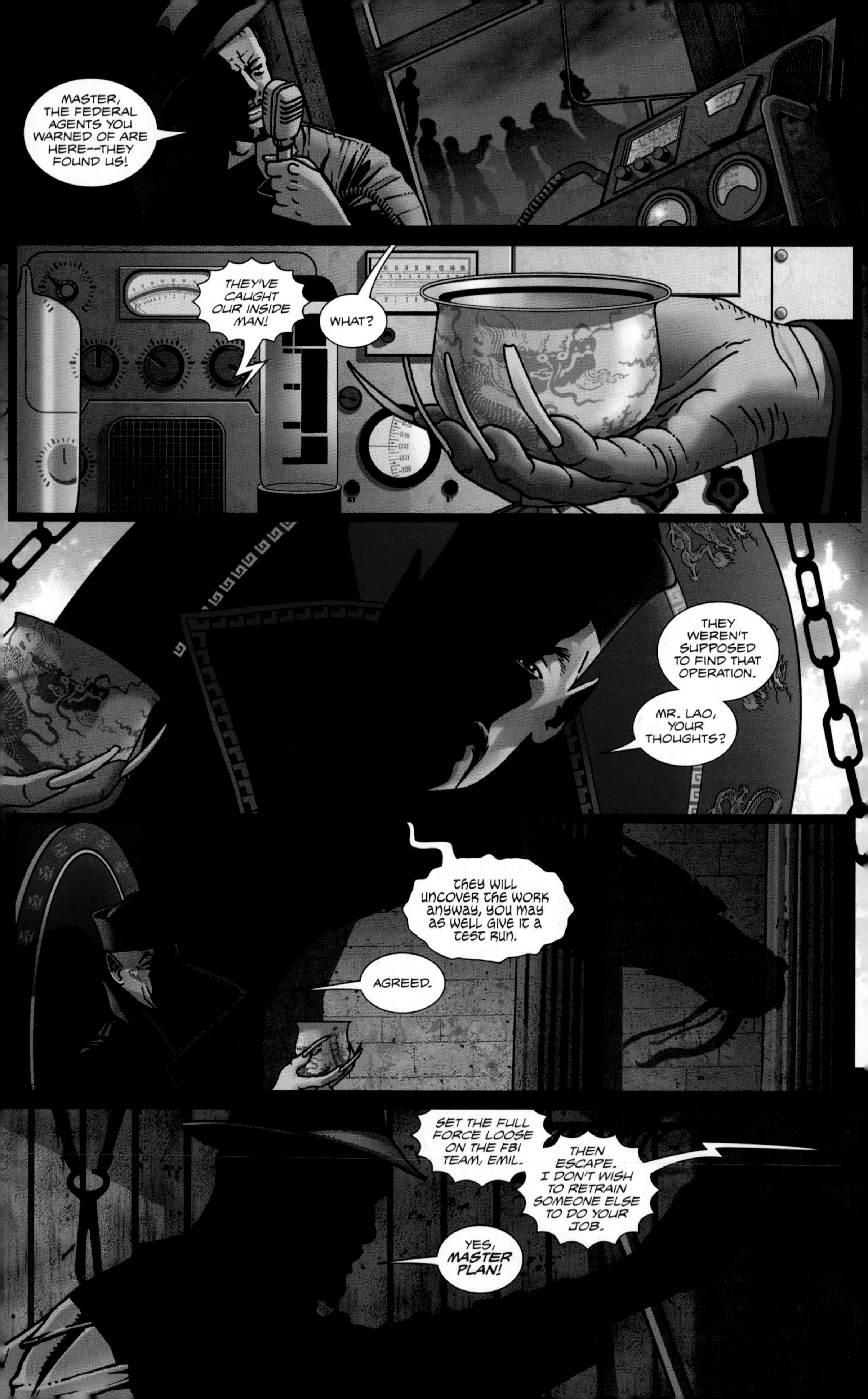
MASTER, THE FEDERAL AGENTS YOU WARNED OF ARE HERE--THEY FOUND US!
THEY'VE CAUGHT OUR INSIDE MAN!
WHAT?
THEY WEREN'T SUPPOSED TO FIND THAT OPERATION.
MR. LAO, YOUR THOUGHTS?
THEY WILL UNCOVER THE WORK ANYWAY, YOU MAY AS WELL GIVE IT A TEST RUN.
AGREED.
SET THE FULL FORCE LOOSE ON THE FBI TEAM, EMIL.
THEN ESCAPE. I DON'T WISH TO RETRAIN SOMEONE ELSE TO DO YOUR JOB.
YES, MASTER PLAN!

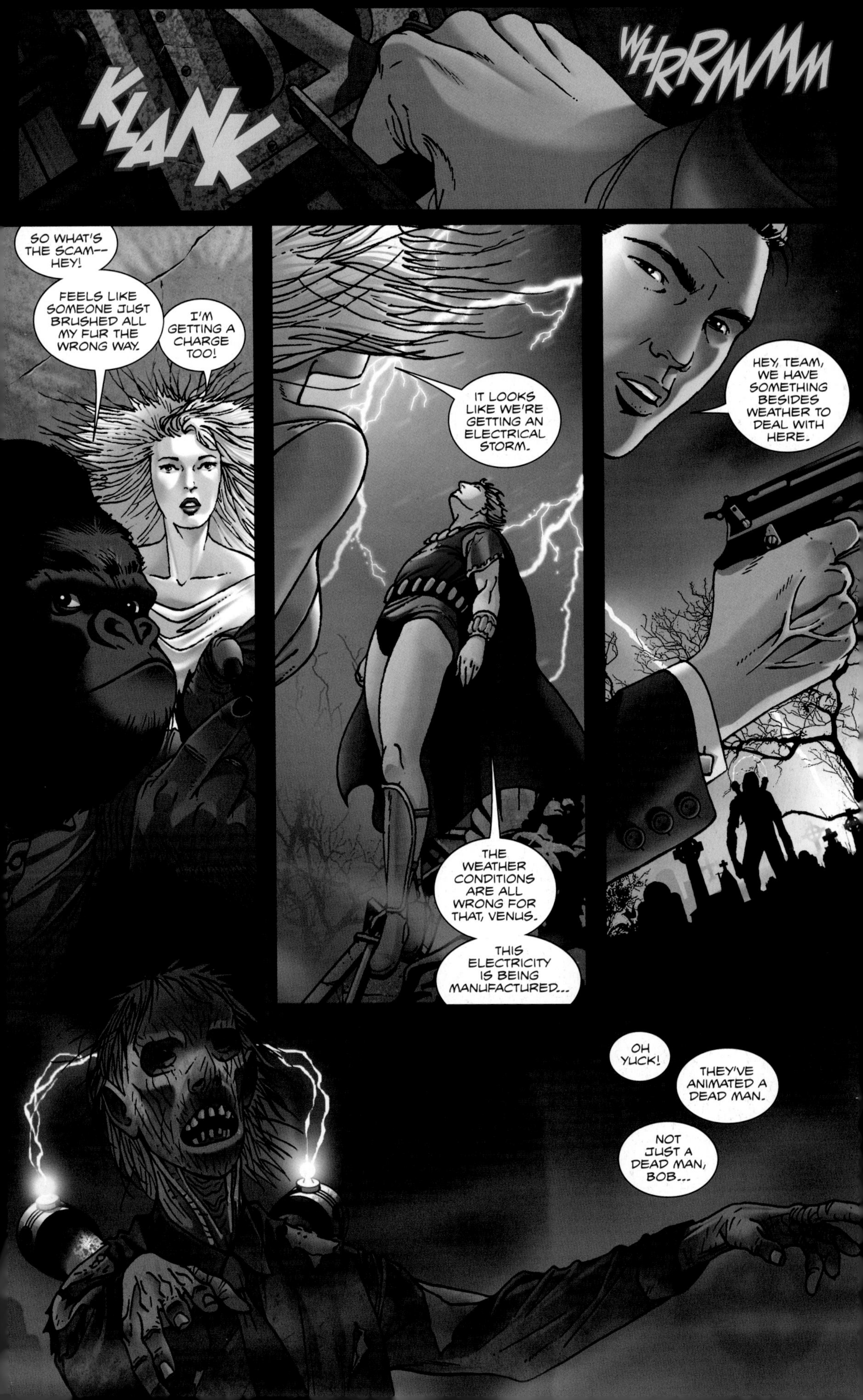

KLANK
WHRRMMM
SO WHAT'S THE SCAM-- HEY!
FEELS LIKE SOMEONE JUST BRUSHED ALL MY FUR THE WRONG WAY.
I'M GETTING A CHARGE TOO!
IT LOOKS LIKE WE'RE GETTING AN ELECTRICAL STORM.
THE WEATHER CONDITIONS ARE ALL WRONG FOR THAT, VENUS.
THIS ELECTRICITY IS BEING MANUFACTURED...
HEY, TEAM, WE HAVE SOMETHING BESIDES WEATHER TO DEAL WITH HERE.
OH YUCK!
THEY'VE ANIMATED A DEAD MAN.
NOT JUST A DEAD MAN, BOB...

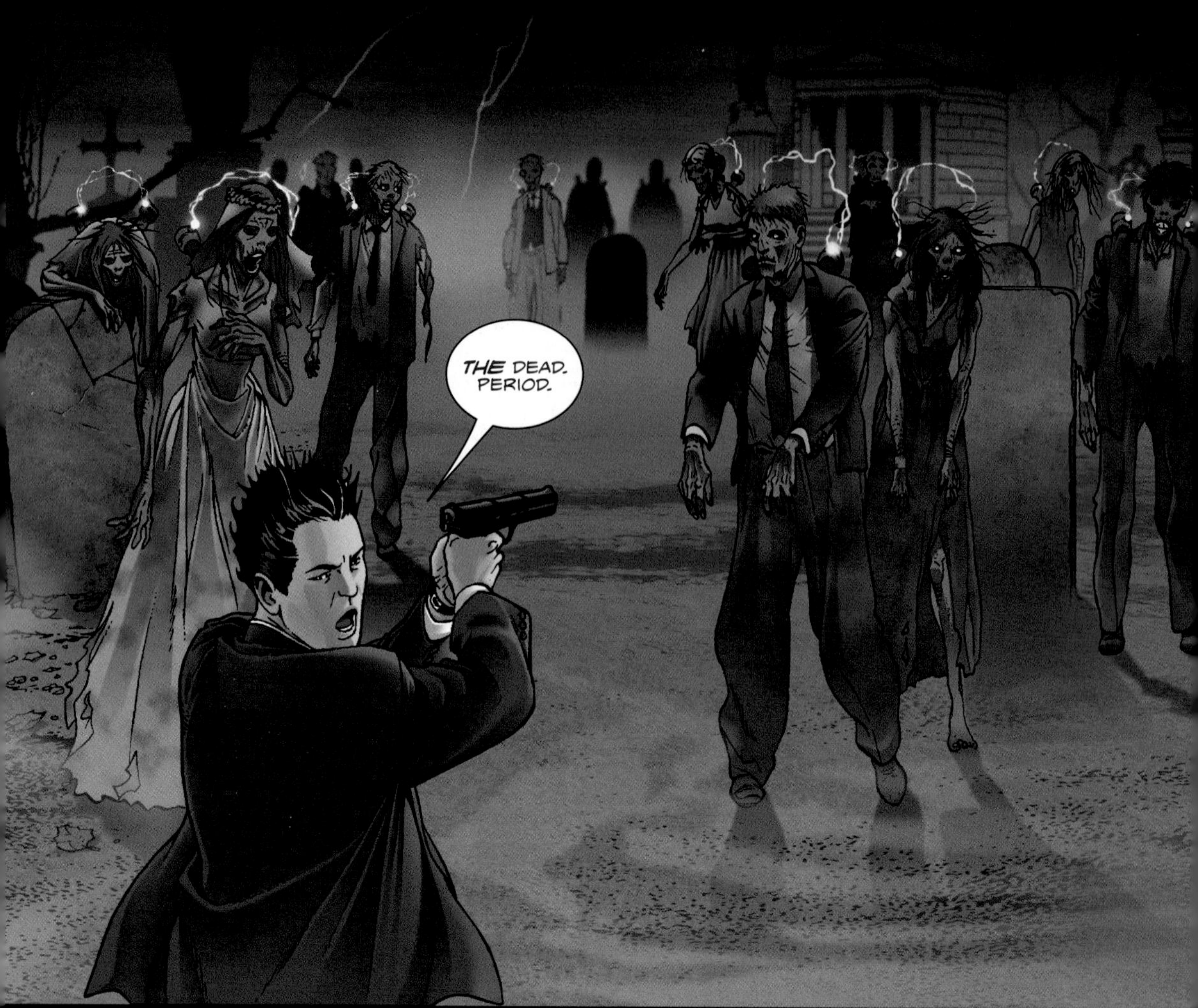
THE DEAD. PERIOD.

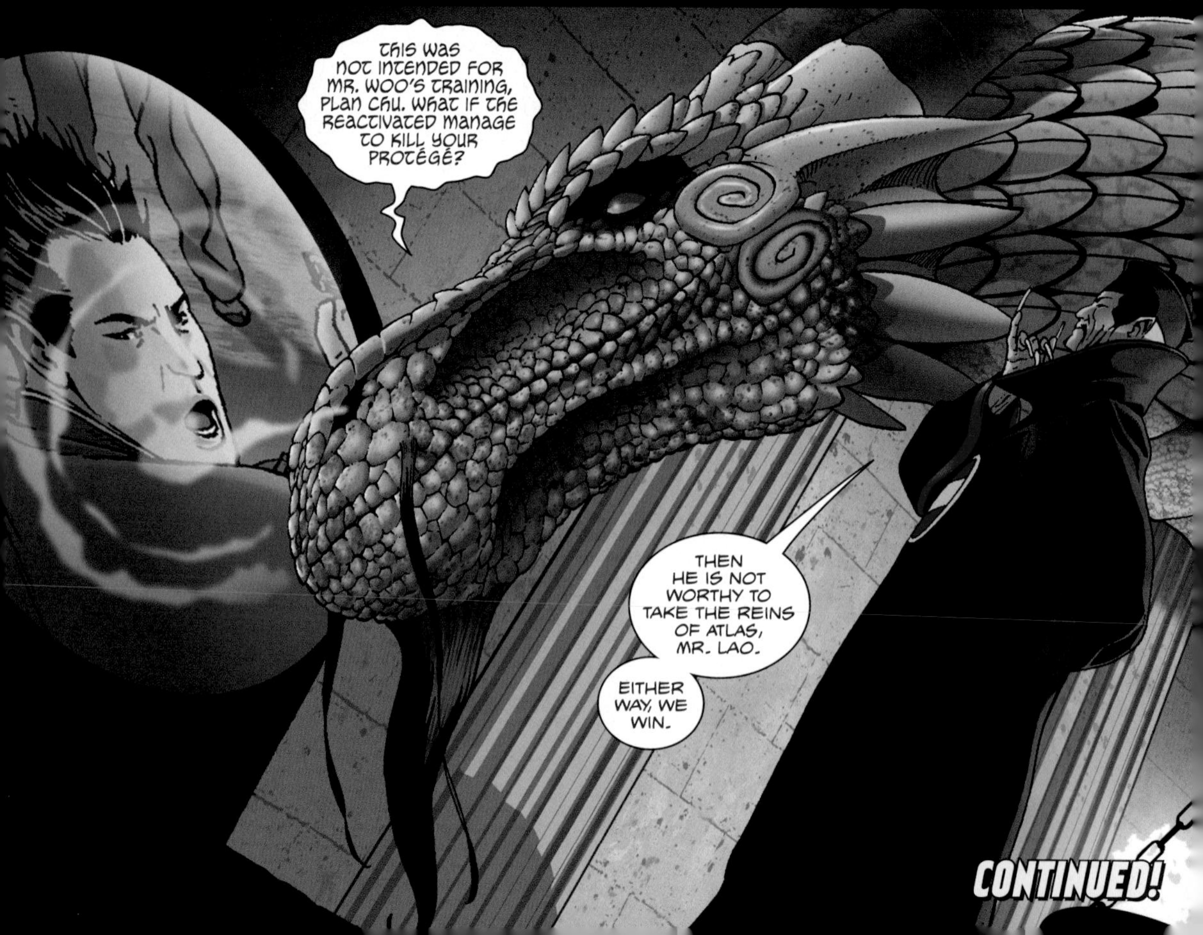
THIS WAS NOT INTENDED FOR MR. WOO'S TRAINING, PLAN CHU. WHAT IF THE REACTIVATED MANAGE TO KILL YOUR PROTÉGÉ?
THEN HE IS NOT WORTHY TO TAKE THE REINS OF ATLAS, MR. LAO.
EITHER WAY, WE WIN.
CONTINUED!

SHORE TO SHORE AM

WITH YOUR HOST WEBB TERRY
The Radio Call-In Show of The Unexplained

BROADCAST TRANSCRIPT: SHOW 6545 - "THE 3-D MEN"

WEBB: We're back in our second hour with guests Chuck and Hal Chandler, the men who shared the hero identity, the 3-D Man, back in the '50s.

Gentlemen, the 3-D Man was very little known in the '50s. In fact most thought he was a rumor or publicity stunt. Why do you think that was?

HAL: The public wasn't really open to the idea of costumed heroes at that time, Webb. As a country we won a world war by pulling together- I think the individualism of your super heroes weren't embraced until much later.

CHUCK: Also, some people got the idea we were Communist because of the red in the outfit! Can you believe that? (laughter)

WEBB: It was certainly a striking uniform. Did you apply red and green makeup to make it seem to cover your face that way?

CHUCK: Nope, my special flight suit was bonded to me and changed to those colors. And that was my actual face you see in the photos. It was strange, no doubt.

HAL: No doubt.

WEBB: What was the triangle emblem containing three triangles about? A lot of our listeners wrote in saying they think that symbol is familiar but can't place it.

CHUCK: You know, I never really questioned it. It was just part of my flight suit when I was testing out the XF-13 prototype. They always give you some mission badge or patch, you know?

HAL: Yeah, I never thought of it. Aren't the emblems usually eagles or rockets though, stuff like that?

CHUCK: I think they just made triangles 'cause it was easy. Who cares?

WEBB: Let's take a call. David in Chandler, Arizona, you're on.

DAVID: Hi Webb, thanks for taking my call. Did I hear right earlier that Hal married Chuck's girlfriend while he was stuck in some limbo dimension?

HAL: Uh...yeah.

CHUCK: I never had any hard feelings about that, Peggy couldn't wait for me forever. She and Hal have made a great family.

DAVID: So you weren't floating around like a ghost able to see it all going 'Nooo! Hands off my lady, bro!'

CHUCK: Ah, no. To me, no time passed. I didn't see anything.

HAL: whew

DAVID: Okay, that's cool. So they had kids?

HAL: Yes we did. They're grown now, in their forties.

DAVID: Whoa, so they're older than their uncle? How messed up is that! I'd be all like-
(disconnect)

WEBB: Thanks David. We're going to take a sponsor break and we'll be back.

END OF TRANSCRIPT

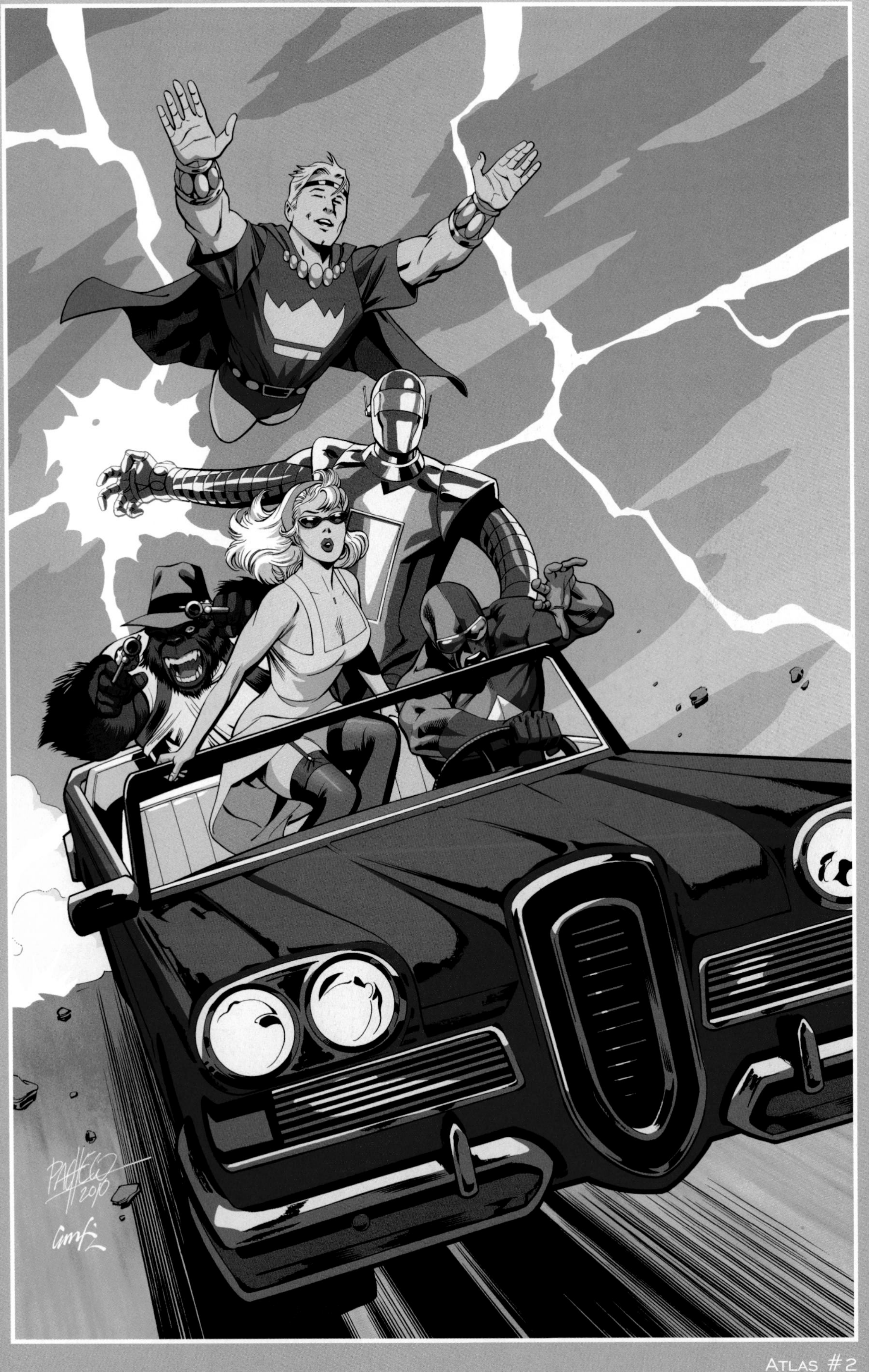
PACHECO 2010

ATLAS #2

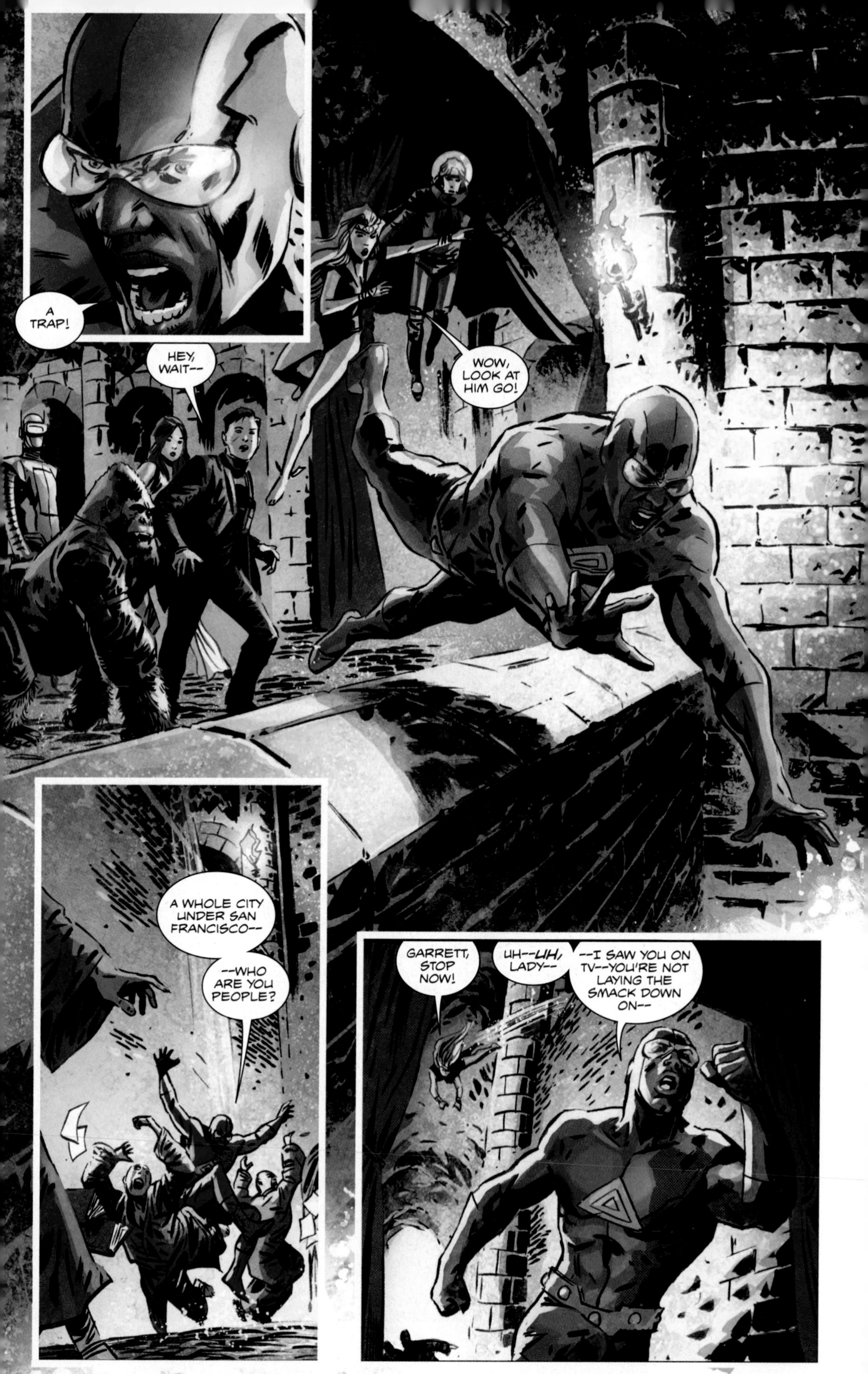
A TRAP!
HEY, WAIT--
WOW, LOOK AT HIM GO!
A WHOLE CITY UNDER SAN FRANCISCO--
--WHO ARE YOU PEOPLE?
GARRETT, STOP NOW!
UH--UH, LADY--
--I SAW YOU ON TV--YOU'RE NOT LAYING THE SMACK DOWN ON--

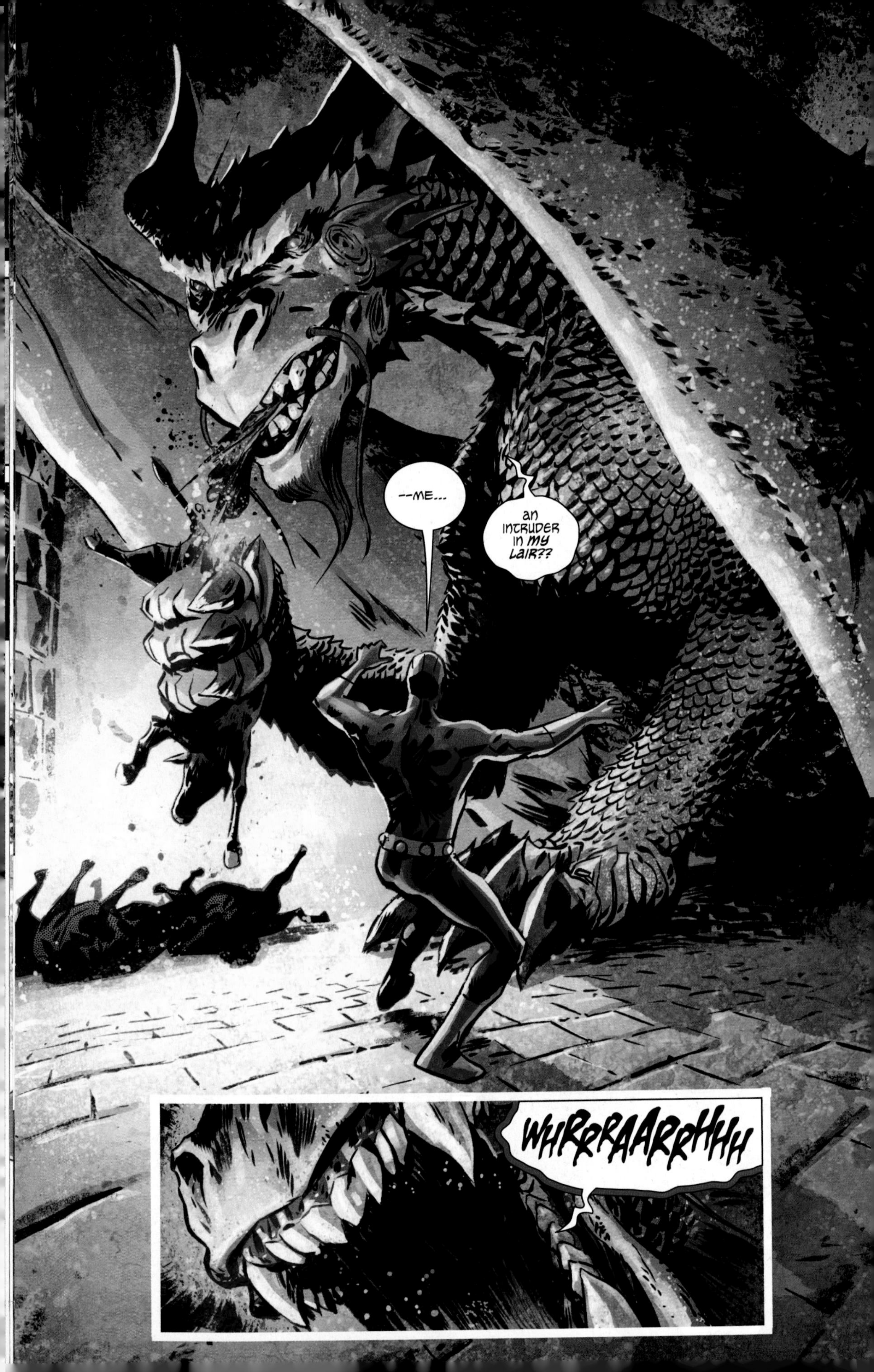
--ME...
AN INTRUDER IN MY LAIR??
WHRRRAARRHHH

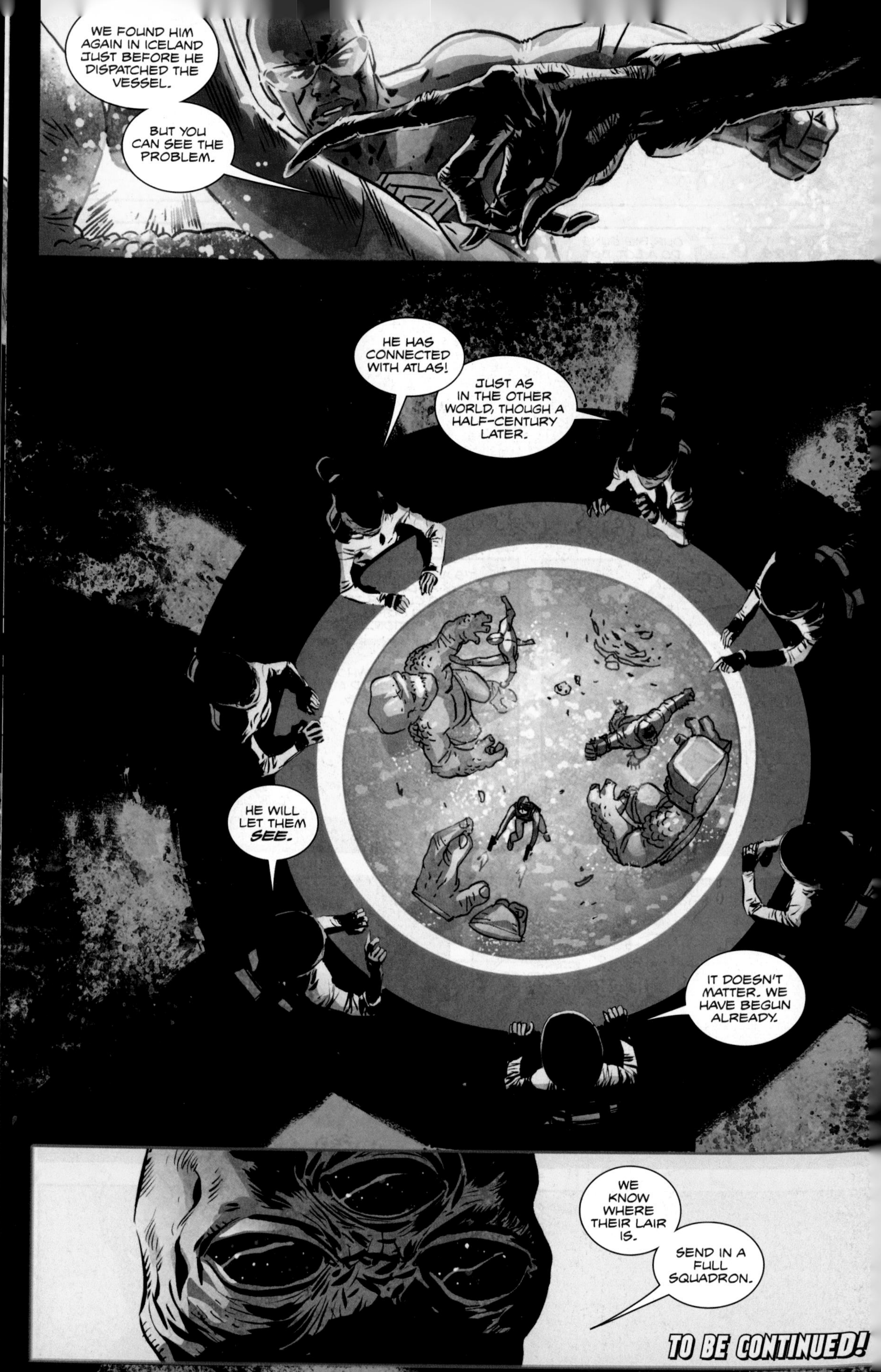
WE FOUND HIM AGAIN IN ICELAND JUST BEFORE HE DISPATCHED THE VESSEL.
BUT YOU CAN SEE THE PROBLEM.
HE HAS CONNECTED WITH ATLAS!
JUST AS IN THE OTHER WORLD, THOUGH A HALF-CENTURY LATER.
HE WILL LET THEM *SEE.*
IT DOESN'T MATTER. WE HAVE BEGUN ALREADY.
WE KNOW WHERE THEIR LAIR IS.
SEND IN A FULL SQUADRON.
TO BE CONTINUED!

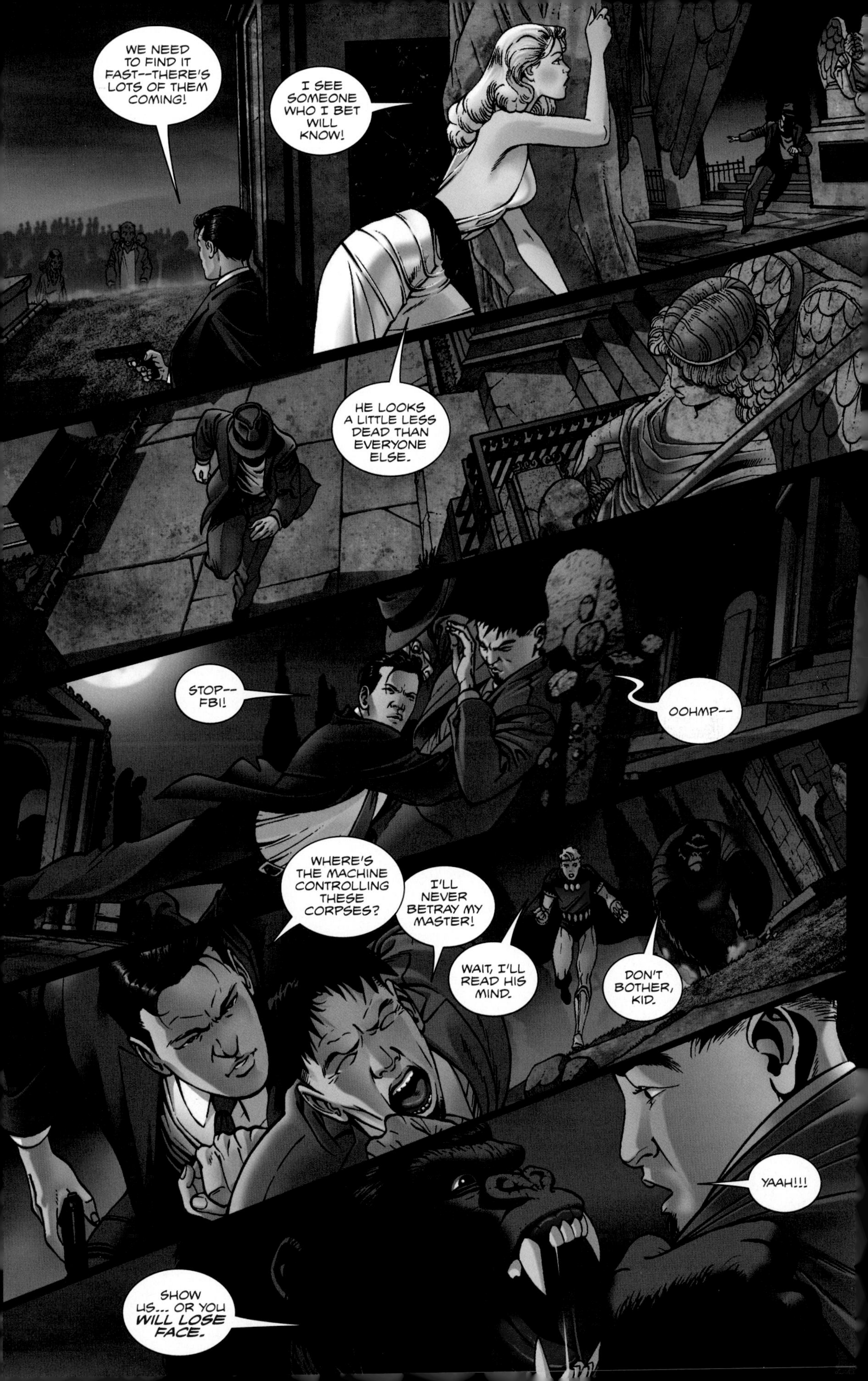
WE NEED TO FIND IT FAST--THERE'S LOTS OF THEM COMING!
I SEE SOMEONE WHO I BET WILL KNOW!
HE LOOKS A LITTLE LESS DEAD THAN EVERYONE ELSE.
STOP-- FBI!
OOHMP--
WHERE'S THE MACHINE CONTROLLING THESE CORPSES?
I'LL NEVER BETRAY MY MASTER!
WAIT, I'LL READ HIS MIND.
DON'T BOTHER, KID.
YAAH!!!
SHOW US... OR YOU *WILL LOSE FACE.*

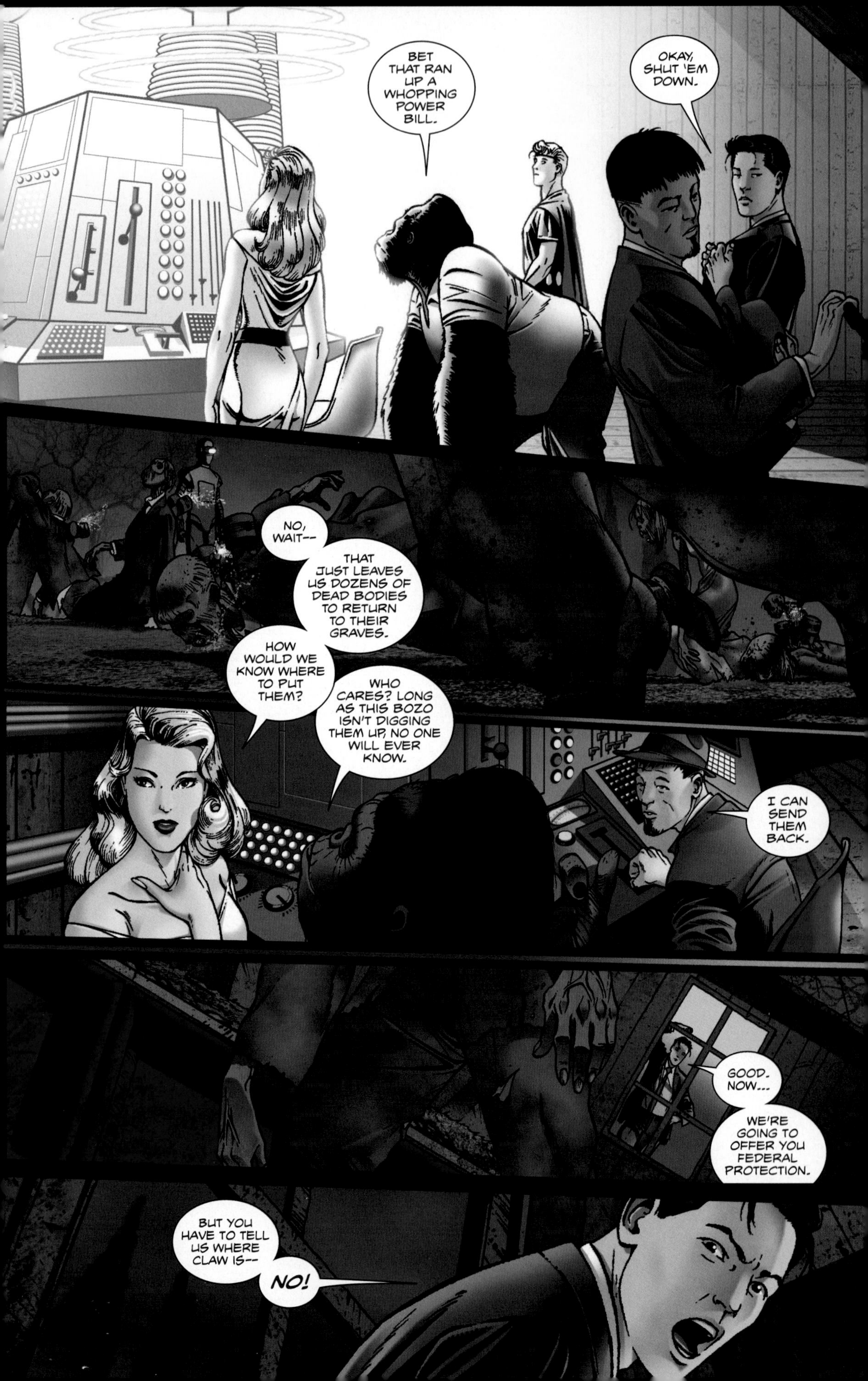
BET THAT RAN UP A WHOPPING POWER BILL.
OKAY, SHUT 'EM DOWN.
NO, WAIT--
THAT JUST LEAVES US DOZENS OF DEAD BODIES TO RETURN TO THEIR GRAVES.
HOW WOULD WE KNOW WHERE TO PUT THEM?
WHO CARES? LONG AS THIS BOZO ISN'T DIGGING THEM UP, NO ONE WILL EVER KNOW.
I CAN SEND THEM BACK.
GOOD. NOW...
WE'RE GOING TO OFFER YOU FEDERAL PROTECTION.
BUT YOU HAVE TO TELL US WHERE CLAW IS--
NO!

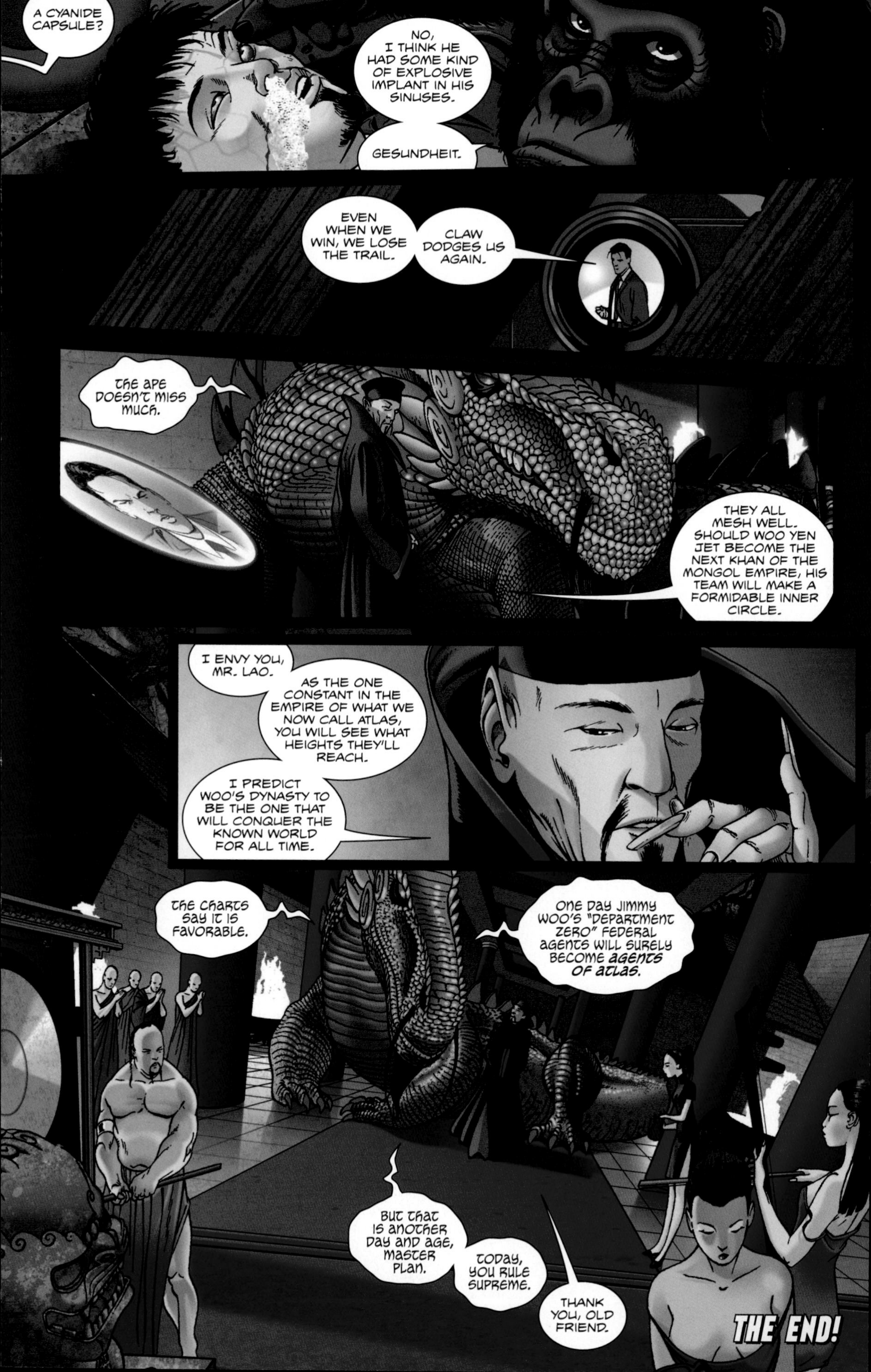
A CYANIDE CAPSULE?
NO, I THINK HE HAD SOME KIND OF EXPLOSIVE IMPLANT IN HIS SINUSES.
GESUNDHEIT.
EVEN WHEN WE WIN, WE LOSE THE TRAIL.
CLAW DODGES US AGAIN.
THE APE DOESN'T MISS MUCH.
THEY ALL MESH WELL. SHOULD WOO YEN JET BECOME THE NEXT KHAN OF THE MONGOL EMPIRE, HIS TEAM WILL MAKE A FORMIDABLE INNER CIRCLE.
I ENVY YOU, MR. LAO.
AS THE ONE CONSTANT IN THE EMPIRE OF WHAT WE NOW CALL ATLAS, YOU WILL SEE WHAT HEIGHTS THEY'LL REACH.
I PREDICT WOO'S DYNASTY TO BE THE ONE THAT WILL CONQUER THE KNOWN WORLD FOR ALL TIME.
THE CHARTS SAY IT IS FAVORABLE.
ONE DAY JIMMY WOO'S "DEPARTMENT ZERO" FEDERAL AGENTS WILL SURELY BECOME AGENTS OF ATLAS.
BUT THAT IS ANOTHER DAY AND AGE, MASTER PLAN.
TODAY, YOU RULE SUPREME.
THANK YOU, OLD FRIEND.
THE END!

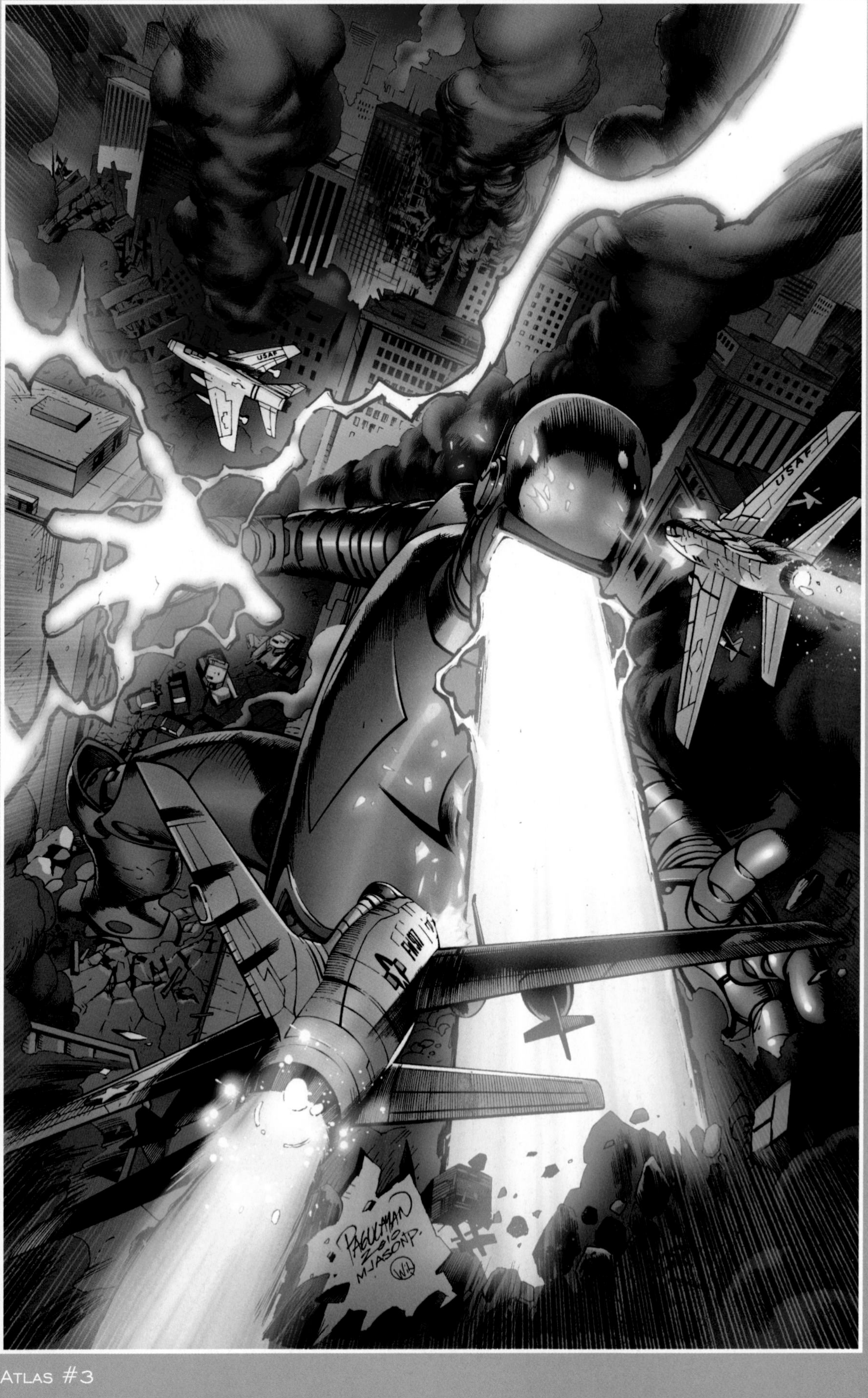
USAF
USAF

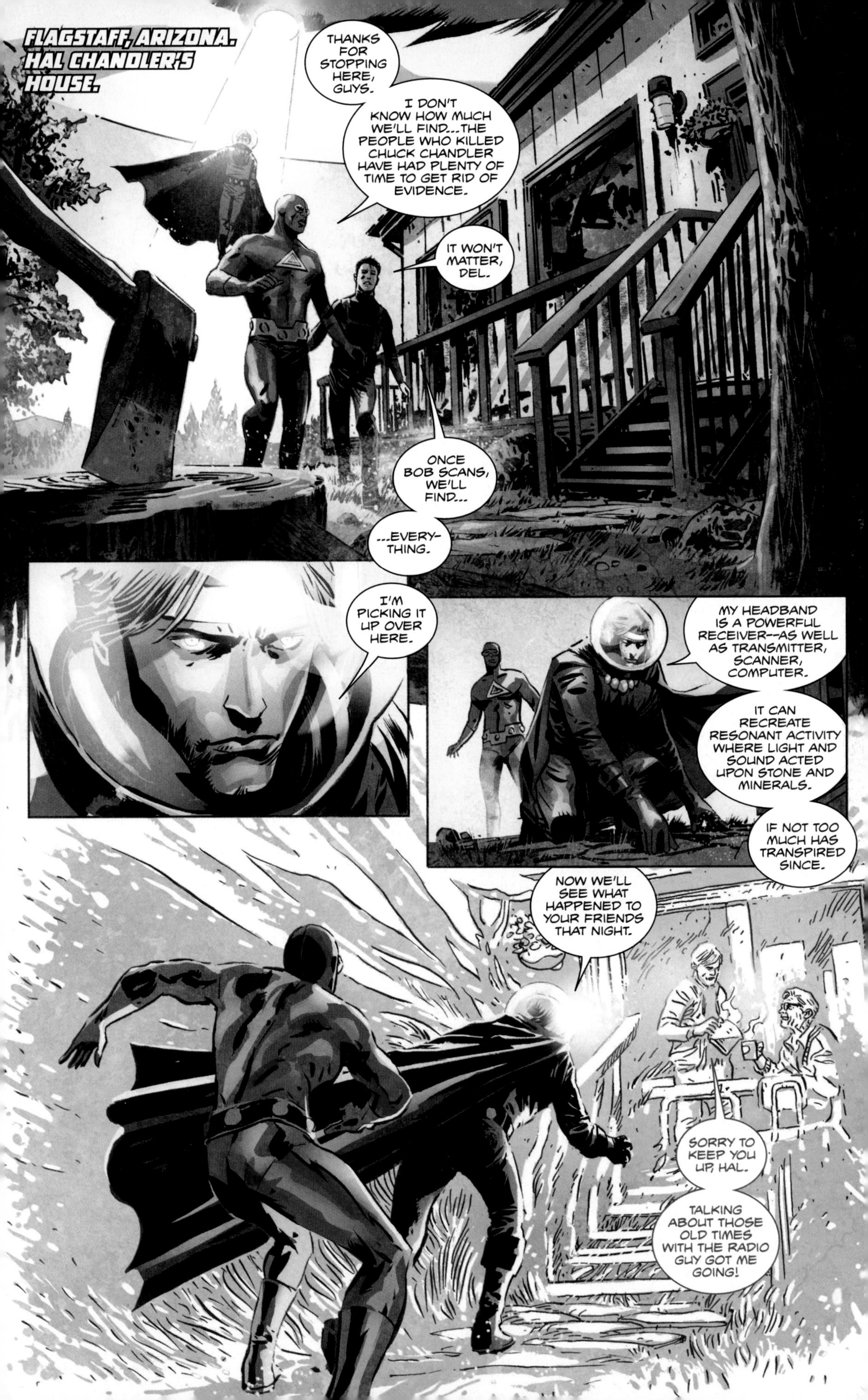
FLAGSTAFF, ARIZONA. HAL CHANDLER'S HOUSE.
THANKS FOR STOPPING HERE, GUYS.
I DON'T KNOW HOW MUCH WE'LL FIND... THE PEOPLE WHO KILLED CHUCK CHANDLER HAVE HAD PLENTY OF TIME TO GET RID OF EVIDENCE.
IT WON'T MATTER, DEL.
ONCE BOB SCANS, WE'LL FIND...
...EVERY-THING.
I'M PICKING IT UP OVER HERE.
MY HEADBAND IS A POWERFUL RECEIVER--AS WELL AS TRANSMITTER, SCANNER, COMPUTER.
IT CAN RECREATE RESONANT ACTIVITY WHERE LIGHT AND SOUND ACTED UPON STONE AND MINERALS.
IF NOT TOO MUCH HAS TRANSPIRED SINCE.
NOW WE'LL SEE WHAT HAPPENED TO YOUR FRIENDS THAT NIGHT.
SORRY TO KEEP YOU UP, HAL.
TALKING ABOUT THOSE OLD TIMES WITH THE RADIO GUY GOT ME GOING!

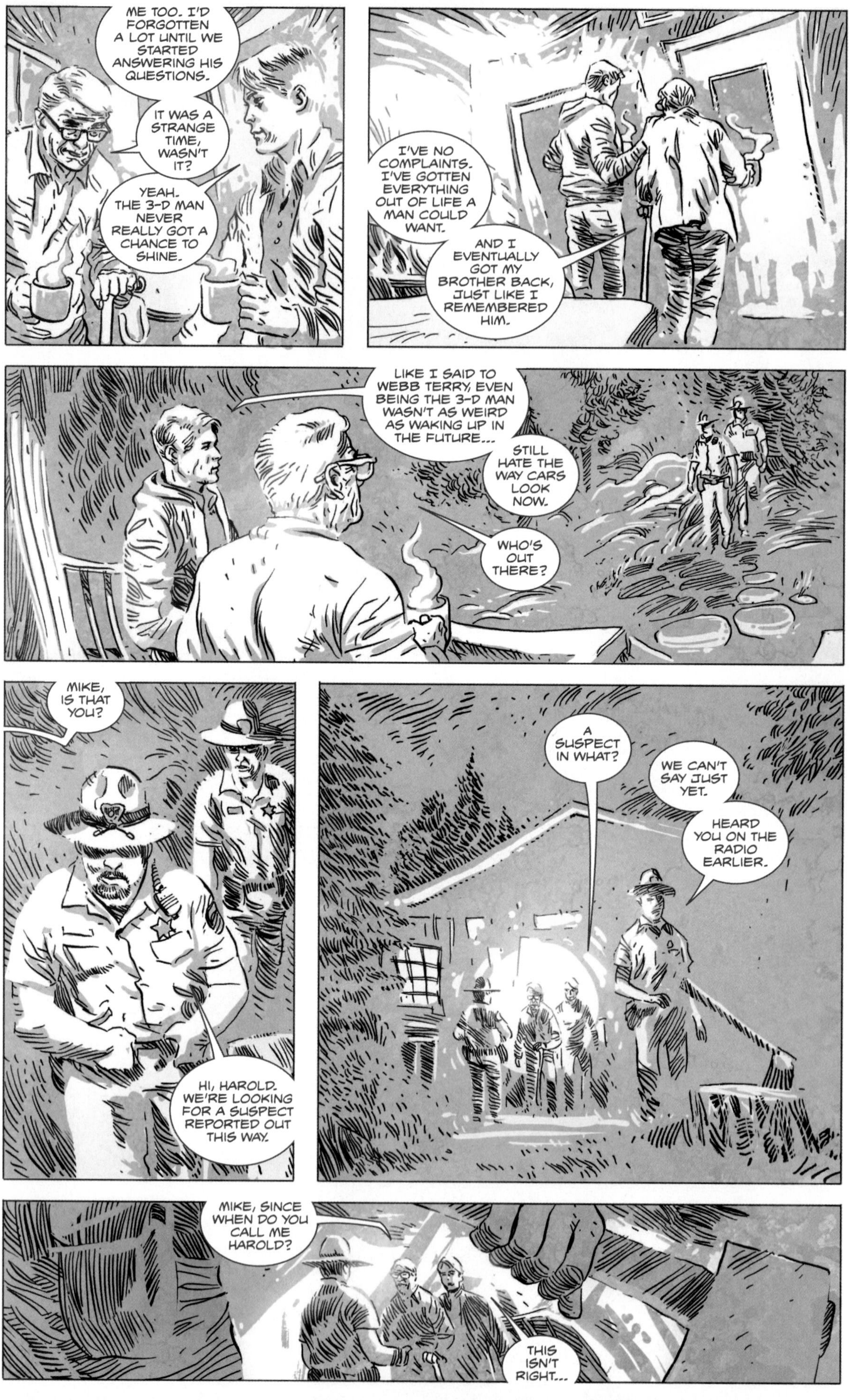
ME TOO. I'D FORGOTTEN A LOT UNTIL WE STARTED ANSWERING HIS QUESTIONS.
IT WAS A STRANGE TIME, WASN'T IT?
YEAH. THE 3-D MAN NEVER REALLY GOT A CHANCE TO SHINE.
I'VE NO COMPLAINTS. I'VE GOTTEN EVERYTHING OUT OF LIFE A MAN COULD WANT.
AND I EVENTUALLY GOT MY BROTHER BACK, JUST LIKE I REMEMBERED HIM.
LIKE I SAID TO WEBB TERRY, EVEN BEING THE 3-D MAN WASN'T AS WEIRD AS WAKING UP IN THE FUTURE...
STILL HATE THE WAY CARS LOOK NOW.
WHO'S OUT THERE?
MIKE, IS THAT YOU?
HI, HAROLD. WE'RE LOOKING FOR A SUSPECT REPORTED OUT THIS WAY.
A SUSPECT IN WHAT?
WE CAN'T SAY JUST YET.
HEARD YOU ON THE RADIO EARLIER.
MIKE, SINCE WHEN DO YOU CALL ME HAROLD?
THIS ISN'T RIGHT...

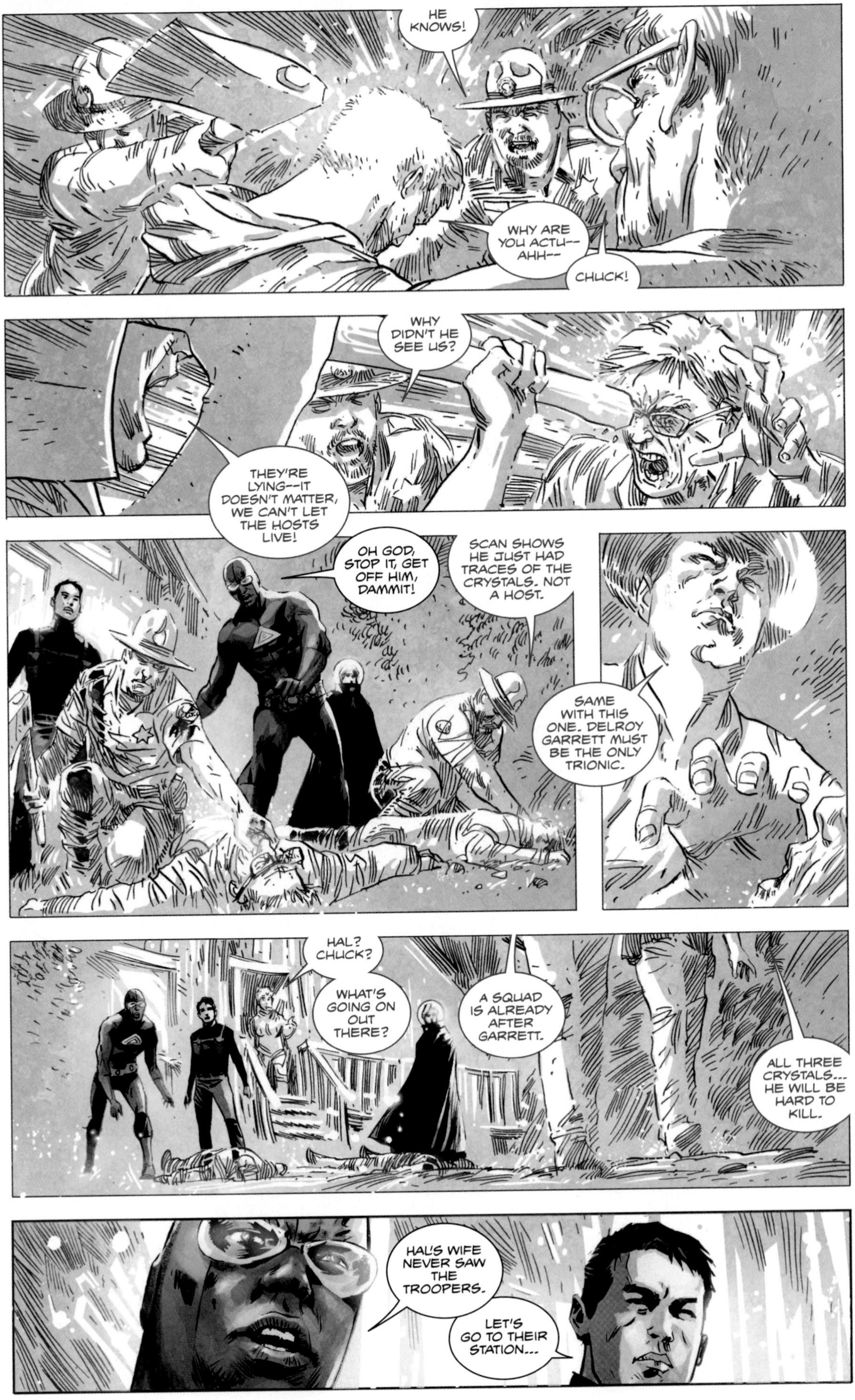
HE KNOWS!
WHY ARE YOU ACTU--AHH--
CHUCK!
WHY DIDN'T HE SEE US?
THEY'RE LYING--IT DOESN'T MATTER, WE CAN'T LET THE HOSTS LIVE!
OH GOD, STOP IT, GET OFF HIM, DAMMIT!
SCAN SHOWS HE JUST HAD TRACES OF THE CRYSTALS. NOT A HOST.
SAME WITH THIS ONE. DELROY GARRETT MUST BE THE ONLY TRIONIC.
HAL? CHUCK?
WHAT'S GOING ON OUT THERE?
A SQUAD IS ALREADY AFTER GARRETT.
ALL THREE CRYSTALS... HE WILL BE HARD TO KILL.
HAL'S WIFE NEVER SAW THE TROOPERS.
LET'S GO TO THEIR STATION...

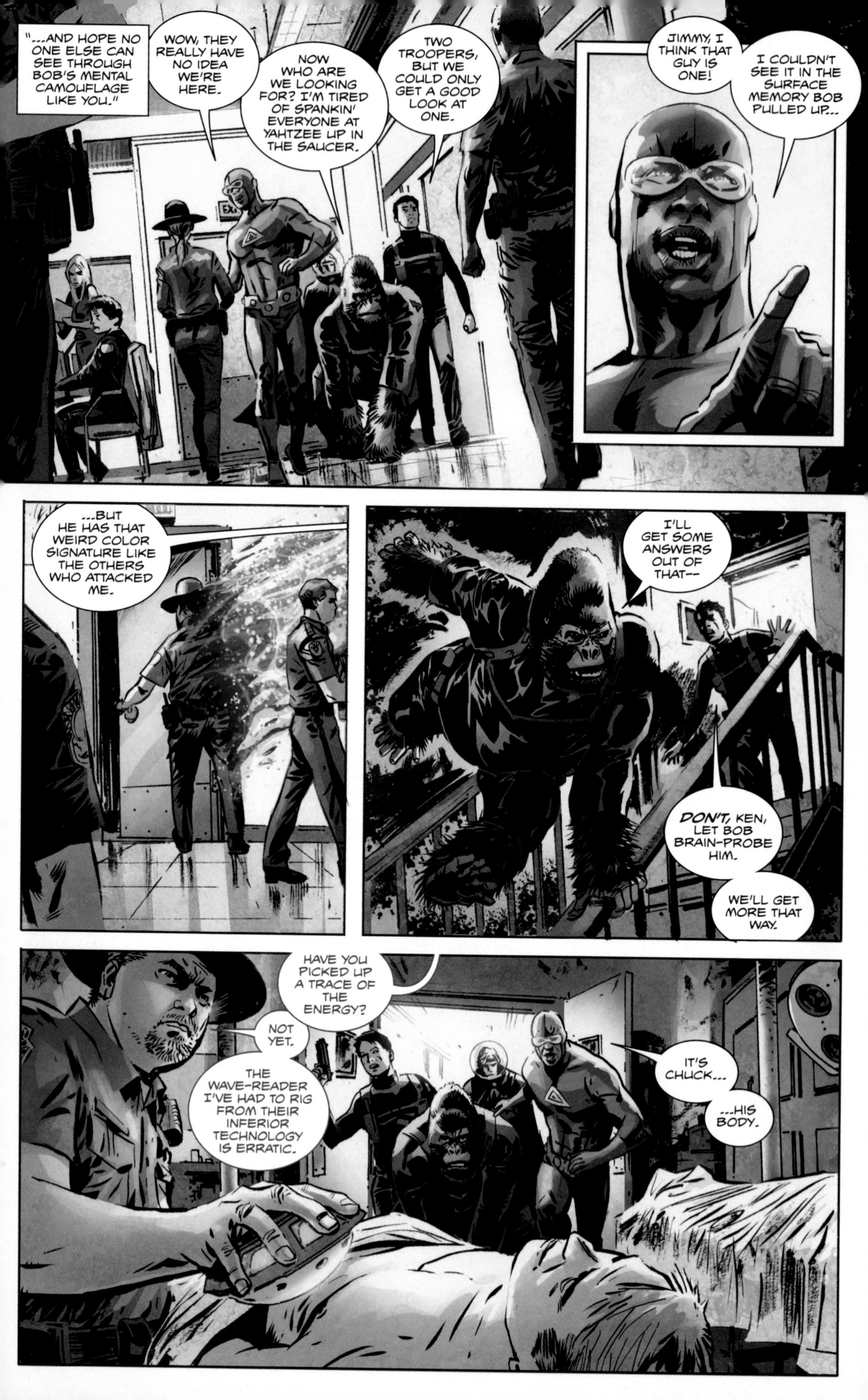
"...AND HOPE NO ONE ELSE CAN SEE THROUGH BOB'S MENTAL CAMOUFLAGE LIKE YOU."
WOW, THEY REALLY HAVE NO IDEA WE'RE HERE.
NOW WHO ARE WE LOOKING FOR? I'M TIRED OF SPANKIN' EVERYONE AT YAHTZEE UP IN THE SAUCER.
TWO TROOPERS, BUT WE COULD ONLY GET A GOOD LOOK AT ONE.
JIMMY, I THINK THAT GUY IS ONE!
I COULDN'T SEE IT IN THE SURFACE MEMORY BOB PULLED UP...
...BUT HE HAS THAT WEIRD COLOR SIGNATURE LIKE THE OTHERS WHO ATTACKED ME.
I'LL GET SOME ANSWERS OUT OF THAT--
DON'T, KEN, LET BOB BRAIN-PROBE HIM.
WE'LL GET MORE THAT WAY.
HAVE YOU PICKED UP A TRACE OF THE ENERGY?
NOT YET.
THE WAVE-READER I'VE HAD TO RIG FROM THEIR INFERIOR TECHNOLOGY IS ERRATIC.
IT'S CHUCK...
...HIS BODY.

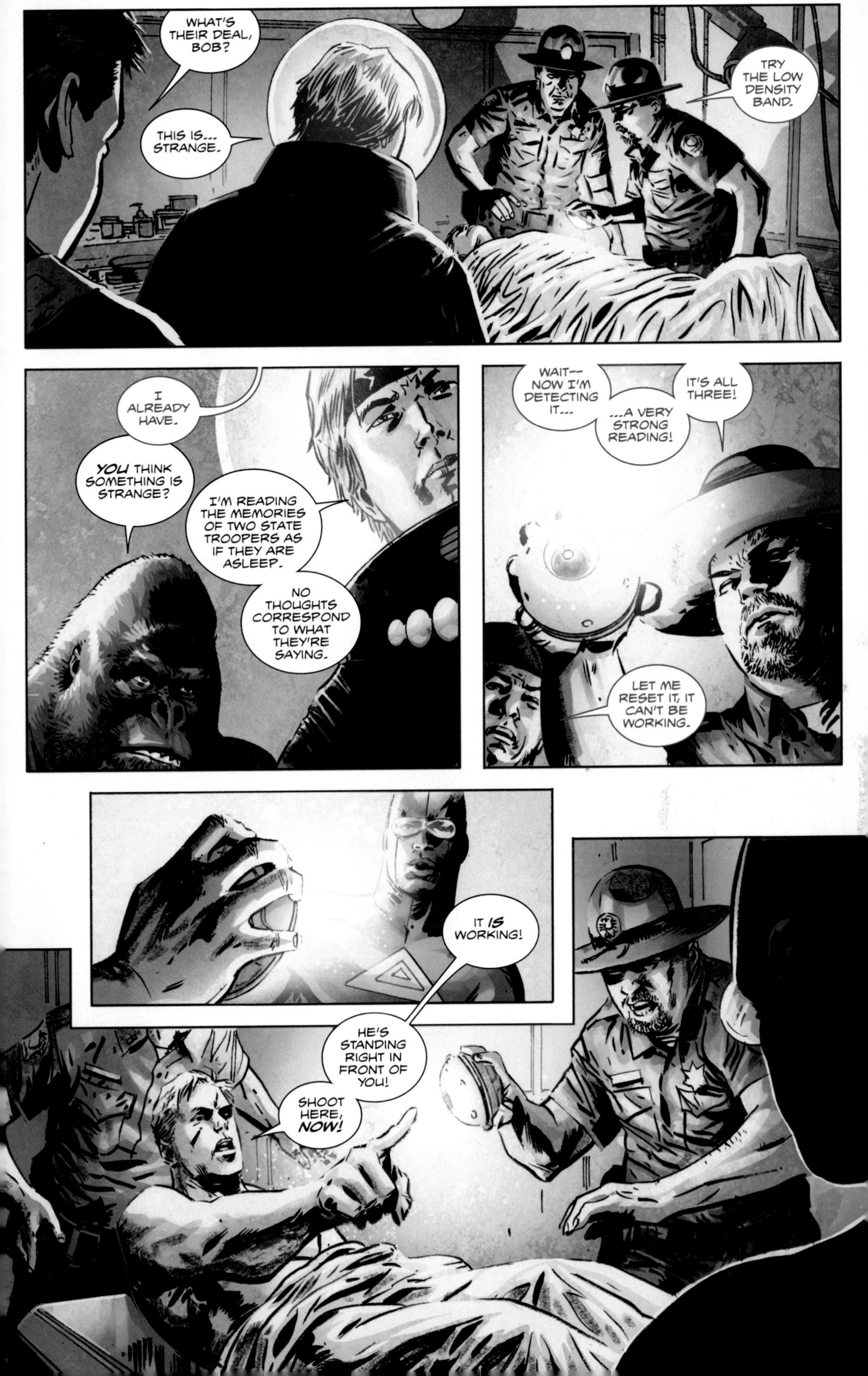
WHAT'S THEIR DEAL, BOB?
THIS IS... STRANGE.
TRY THE LOW DENSITY BAND.
I ALREADY HAVE.
YOU THINK SOMETHING IS STRANGE?
I'M READING THE MEMORIES OF TWO STATE TROOPERS AS IF THEY ARE ASLEEP.
NO THOUGHTS CORRESPOND TO WHAT THEY'RE SAYING.
WAIT-- NOW I'M DETECTING IT...
...A VERY STRONG READING!
IT'S ALL THREE!
LET ME RESET IT, IT CAN'T BE WORKING.
IT IS WORKING!
HE'S STANDING RIGHT IN FRONT OF YOU!
SHOOT HERE, NOW!

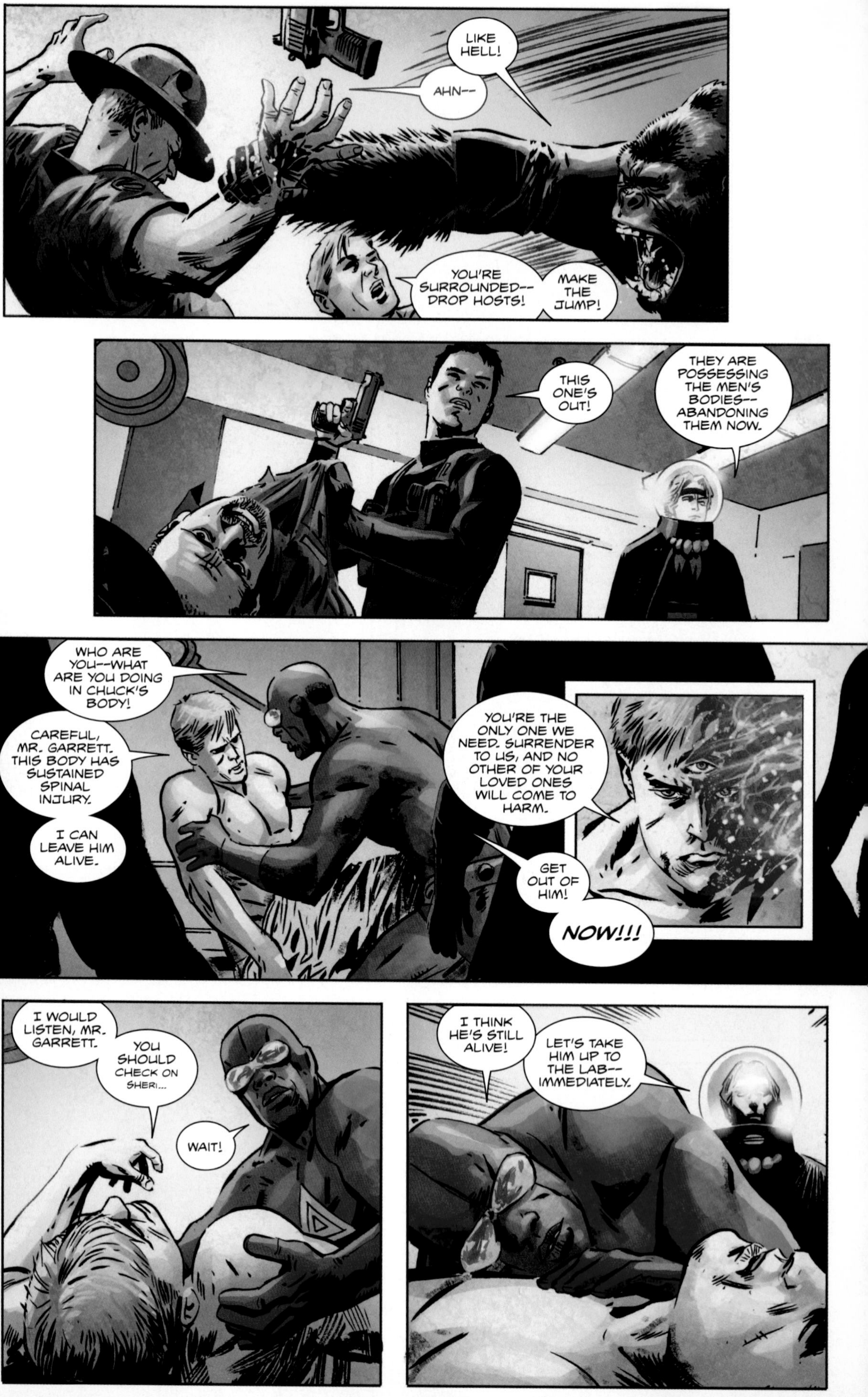
LIKE HELL!
AHN--
YOU'RE SURROUNDED-- DROP HOSTS!
MAKE THE JUMP!
THIS ONE'S OUT!
THEY ARE POSSESSING THE MEN'S BODIES-- ABANDONING THEM NOW.
WHO ARE YOU--WHAT ARE YOU DOING IN CHUCK'S BODY!
CAREFUL, MR. GARRETT. THIS BODY HAS SUSTAINED SPINAL INJURY.
I CAN LEAVE HIM ALIVE.
YOU'RE THE ONLY ONE WE NEED. SURRENDER TO US, AND NO OTHER OF YOUR LOVED ONES WILL COME TO HARM.
GET OUT OF HIM!
NOW!!!
I WOULD LISTEN, MR. GARRETT.
YOU SHOULD CHECK ON SHERI...
WAIT!
I THINK HE'S STILL ALIVE!
LET'S TAKE HIM UP TO THE LAB-- IMMEDIATELY.

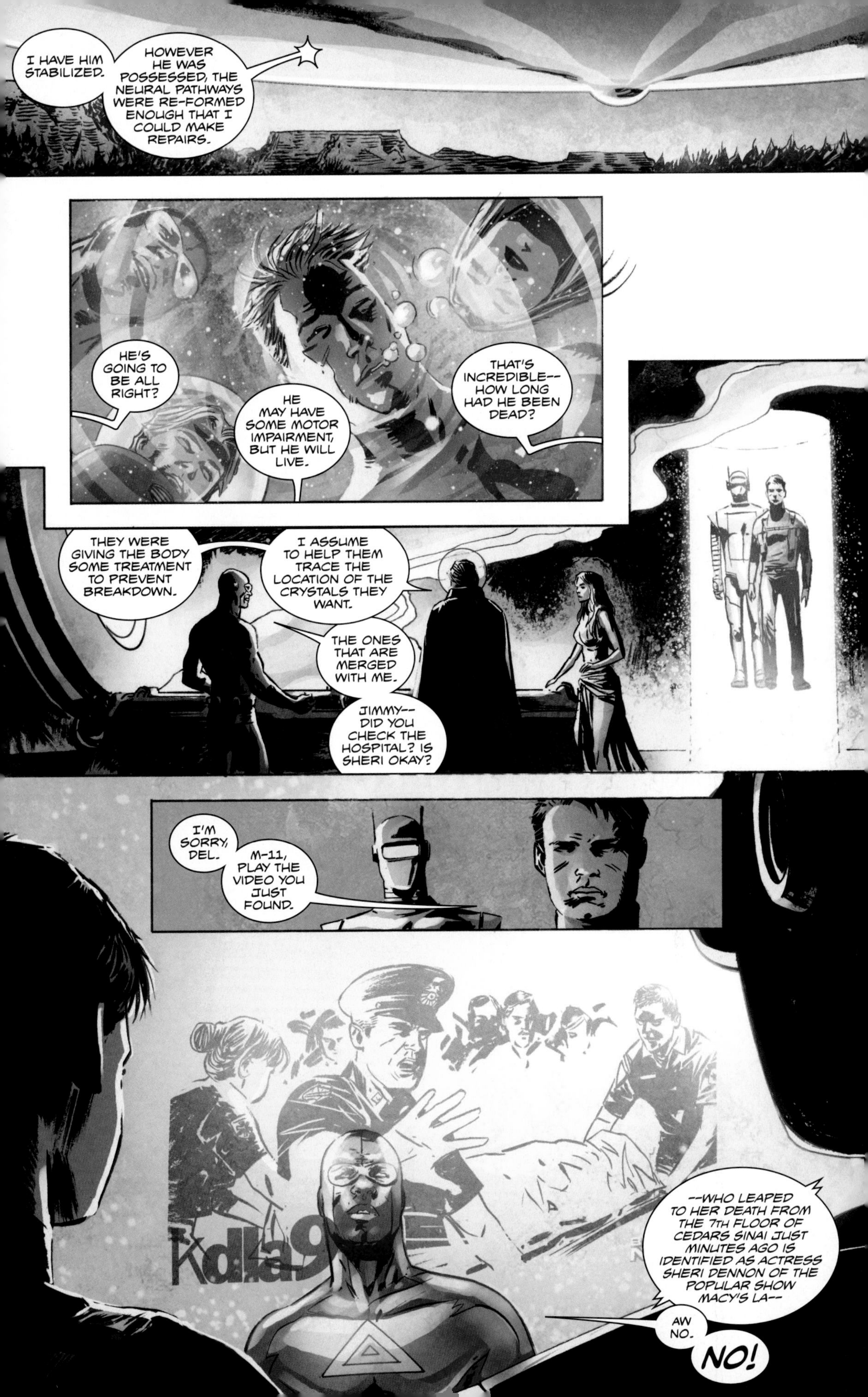
I HAVE HIM STABILIZED.
HOWEVER HE WAS POSSESSED, THE NEURAL PATHWAYS WERE RE-FORMED ENOUGH THAT I COULD MAKE REPAIRS.
HE'S GOING TO BE ALL RIGHT?
HE MAY HAVE SOME MOTOR IMPAIRMENT, BUT HE WILL LIVE.
THAT'S INCREDIBLE--HOW LONG HAD HE BEEN DEAD?
THEY WERE GIVING THE BODY SOME TREATMENT TO PREVENT BREAKDOWN.
I ASSUME TO HELP THEM TRACE THE LOCATION OF THE CRYSTALS THEY WANT.
THE ONES THAT ARE MERGED WITH ME.
JIMMY--DID YOU CHECK THE HOSPITAL? IS SHERI OKAY?
I'M SORRY, DEL.
M-11, PLAY THE VIDEO YOU JUST FOUND.
kdla9
--WHO LEAPED TO HER DEATH FROM THE 7TH FLOOR OF CEDARS SINAI JUST MINUTES AGO IS IDENTIFIED AS ACTRESS SHERI DENNON OF THE POPULAR SHOW MACY'S LA--
AW NO.
NO!

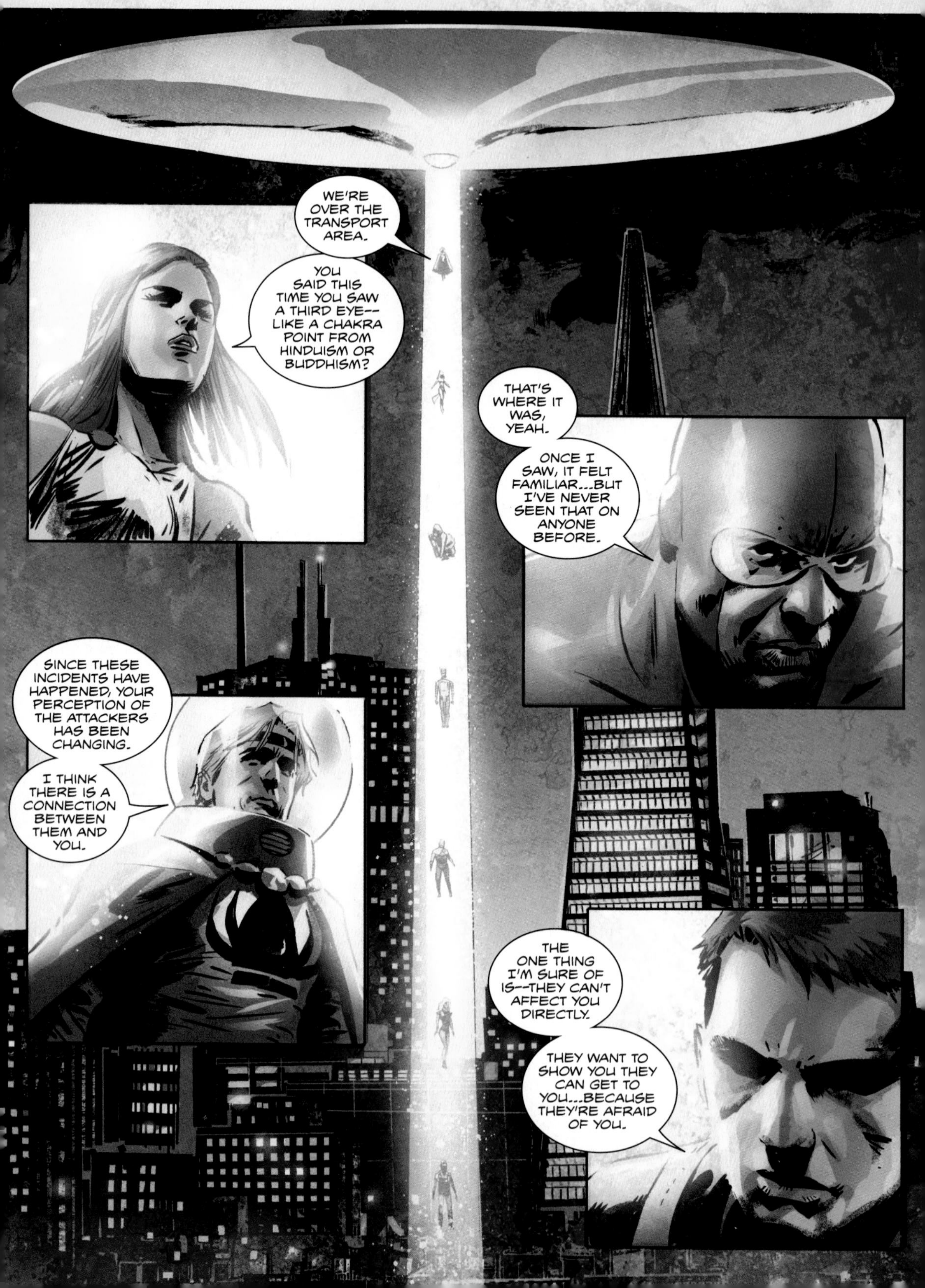
WE'RE OVER THE TRANSPORT AREA.
YOU SAID THIS TIME YOU SAW A THIRD EYE--LIKE A CHAKRA POINT FROM HINDUISM OR BUDDHISM?
THAT'S WHERE IT WAS, YEAH.
ONCE I SAW, IT FELT FAMILIAR...BUT I'VE NEVER SEEN THAT ON ANYONE BEFORE.
SINCE THESE INCIDENTS HAVE HAPPENED, YOUR PERCEPTION OF THE ATTACKERS HAS BEEN CHANGING.
I THINK THERE IS A CONNECTION BETWEEN THEM AND YOU.
THE ONE THING I'M SURE OF IS--THEY CAN'T AFFECT YOU DIRECTLY.
THEY WANT TO SHOW YOU THEY CAN GET TO YOU...BECAUSE THEY'RE AFRAID OF YOU.

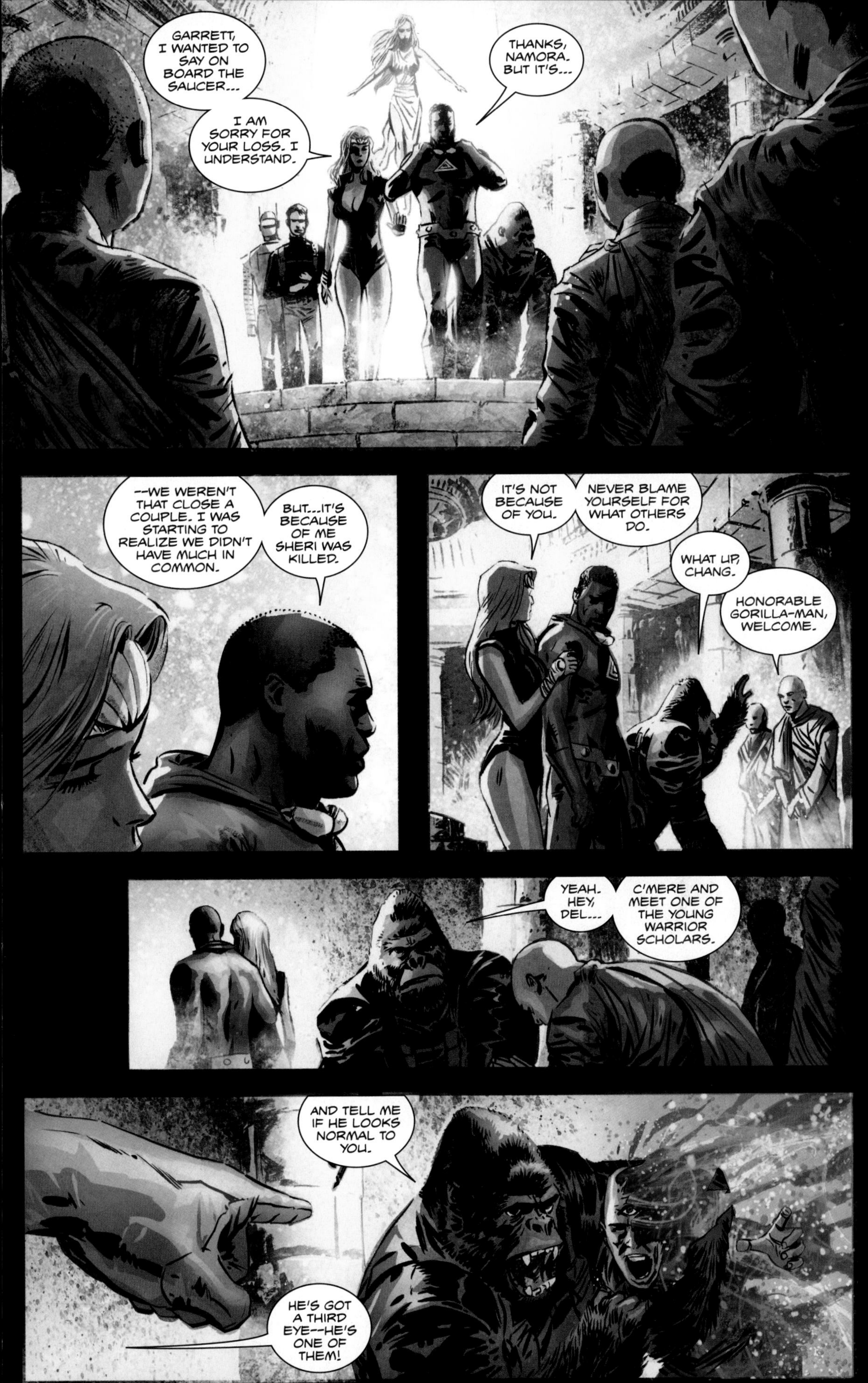
GARRETT, I WANTED TO SAY ON BOARD THE SAUCER...
I AM SORRY FOR YOUR LOSS. I UNDERSTAND.
THANKS, NAMORA. BUT IT'S...
--WE WEREN'T THAT CLOSE A COUPLE. I WAS STARTING TO REALIZE WE DIDN'T HAVE MUCH IN COMMON.
BUT...IT'S BECAUSE OF ME SHERI WAS KILLED.
IT'S NOT BECAUSE OF YOU.
NEVER BLAME YOURSELF FOR WHAT OTHERS DO.
WHAT UP, CHANG.
HONORABLE GORILLA-MAN, WELCOME.
YEAH. HEY, DEL...
C'MERE AND MEET ONE OF THE YOUNG WARRIOR SCHOLARS.
AND TELL ME IF HE LOOKS NORMAL TO YOU.
HE'S GOT A THIRD EYE--HE'S ONE OF THEM!

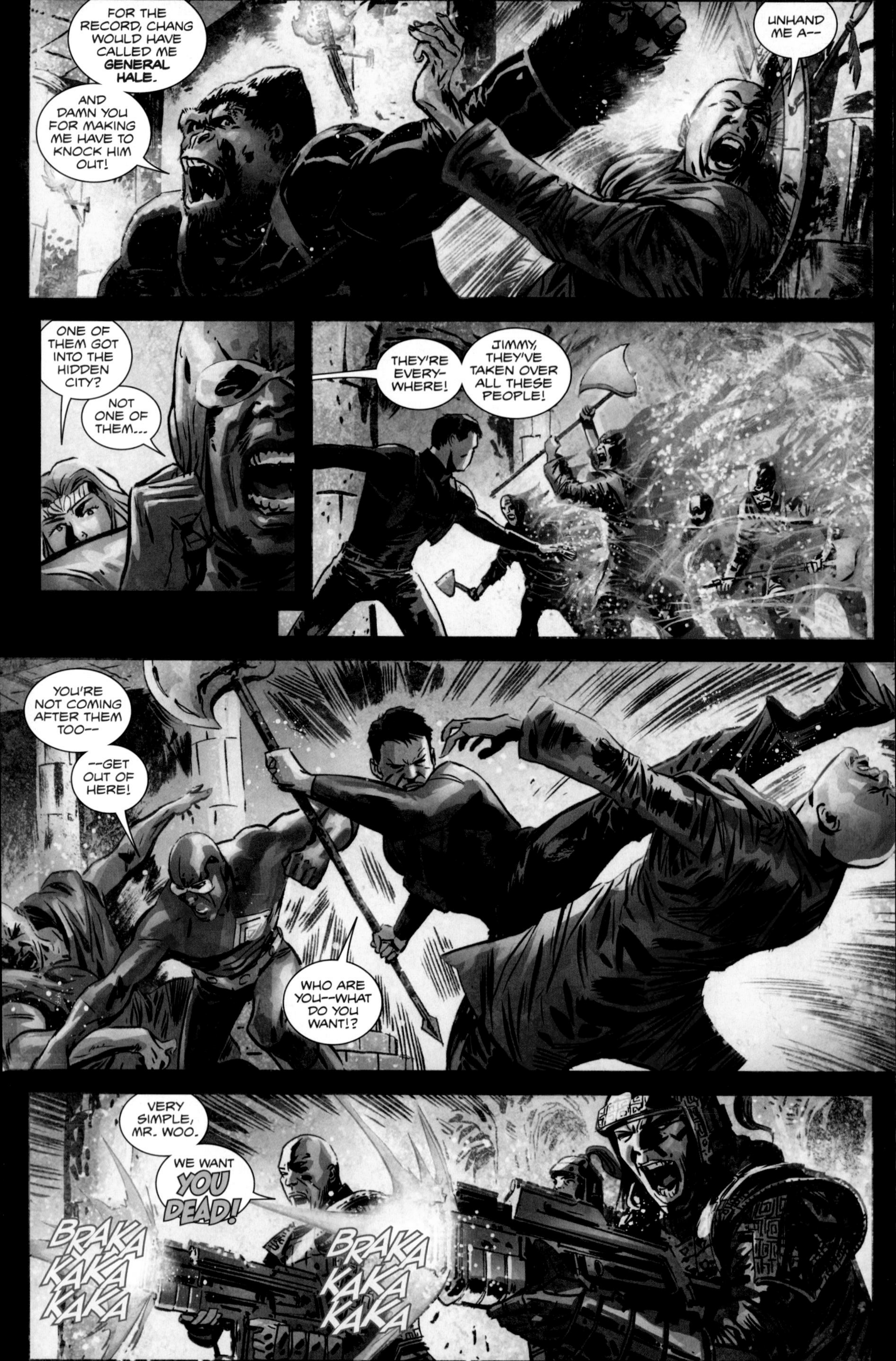
FOR THE RECORD, CHANG WOULD HAVE CALLED ME **GENERAL HALE**.
AND DAMN YOU FOR MAKING ME HAVE TO KNOCK HIM OUT!
UNHAND ME A--
ONE OF THEM GOT INTO THE HIDDEN CITY?
NOT ONE OF THEM...
THEY'RE EVERY-WHERE!
JIMMY, THEY'VE TAKEN OVER ALL THESE PEOPLE!
YOU'RE NOT COMING AFTER THEM TOO--
--GET OUT OF HERE!
WHO ARE YOU--WHAT DO YOU WANT!?
VERY SIMPLE, MR. WOO.
WE WANT YOU DEAD!
BRAKA KAKA KAKA
BRAKA KAKA KAKA

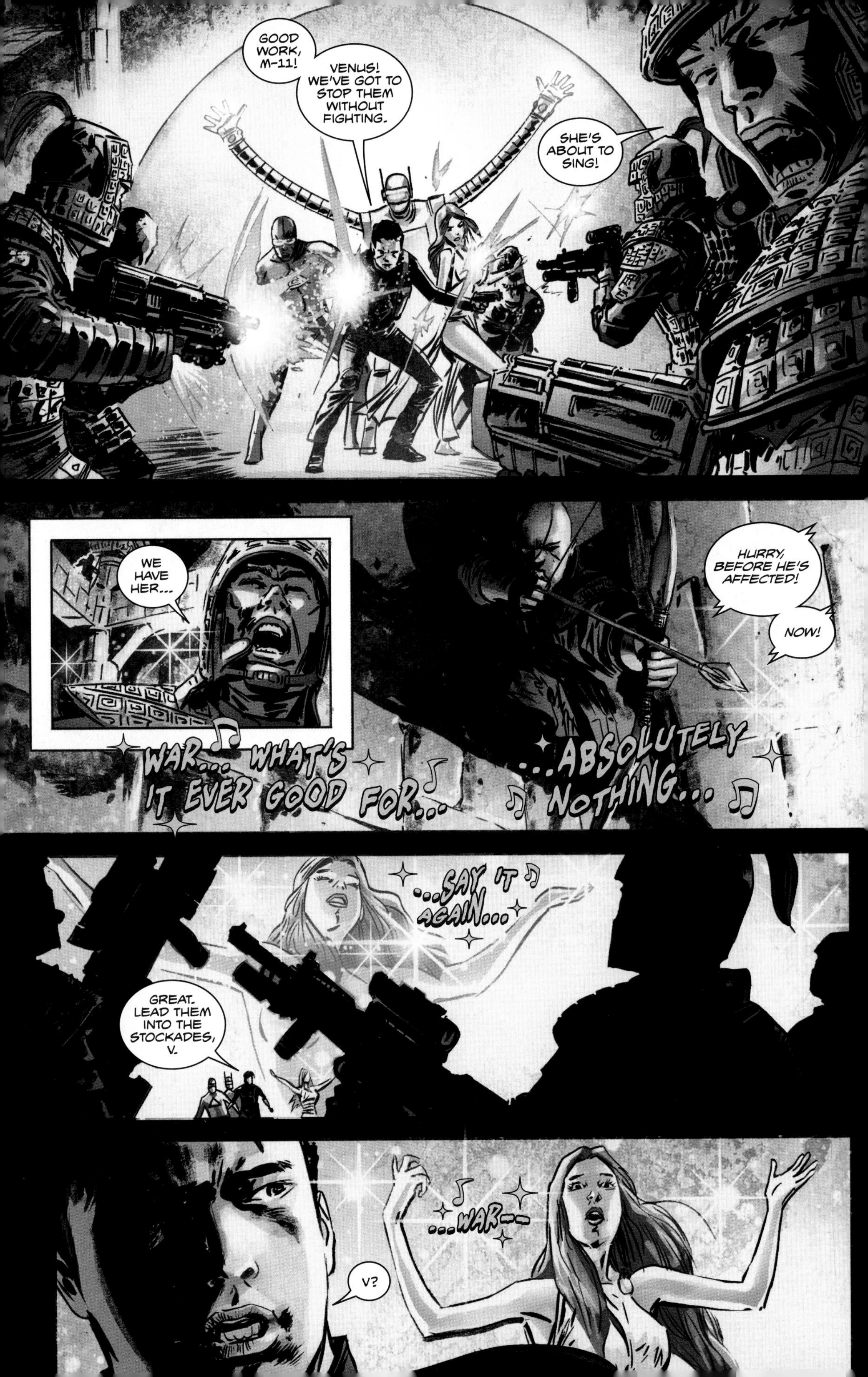
GOOD WORK, M-11!
VENUS! WE'VE GOT TO STOP THEM WITHOUT FIGHTING.
SHE'S ABOUT TO SING!
WE HAVE HER...
HURRY, BEFORE HE'S AFFECTED!
NOW!
WAR... WHAT'S IT EVER GOOD FOR...
...ABSOLUTELY NOTHING...
...SAY IT AGAIN...
GREAT. LEAD THEM INTO THE STOCKADES, V.
...WAR--
V?

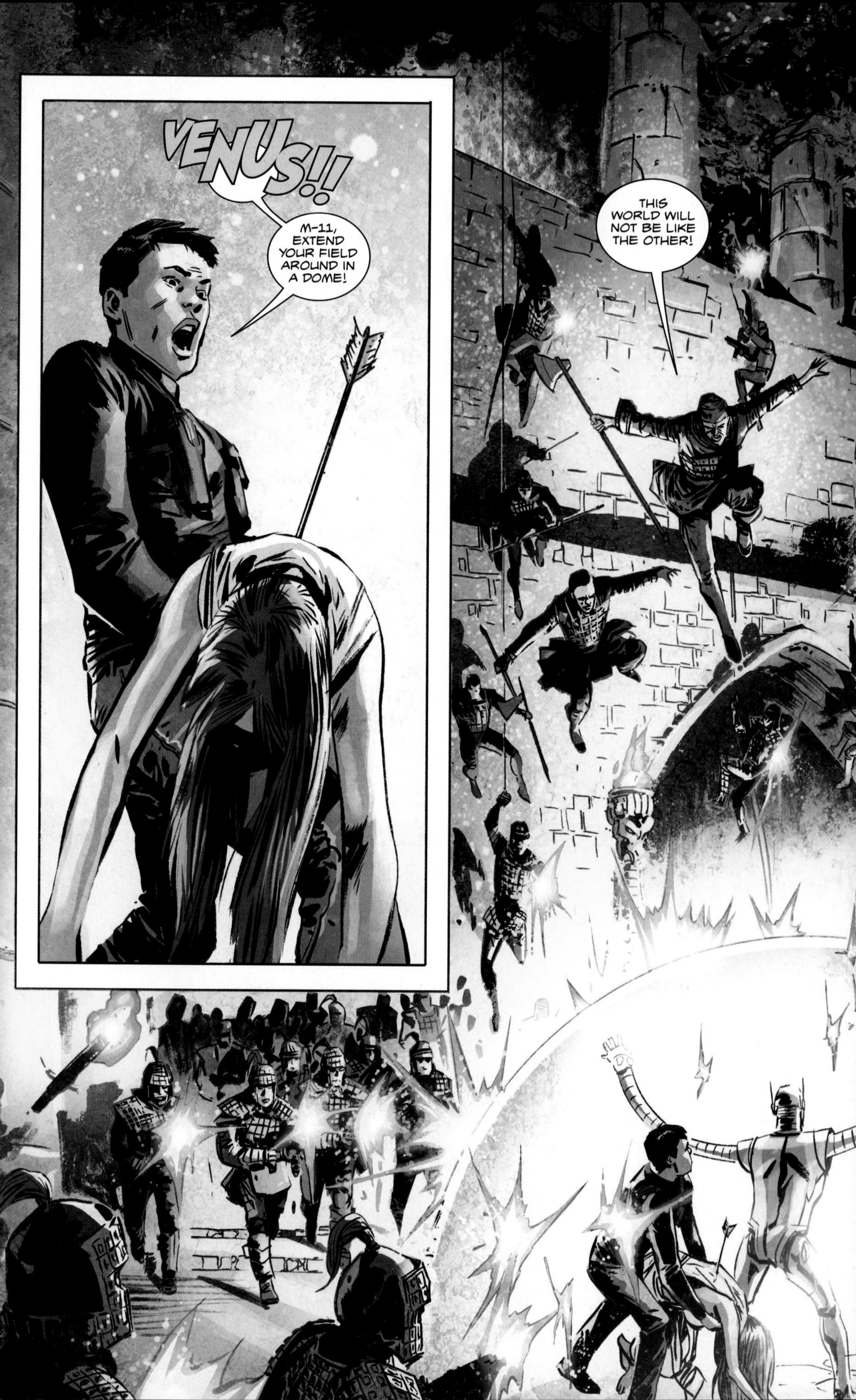
VENUS!!
M-11, EXTEND YOUR FIELD AROUND IN A DOME!
THIS WORLD WILL NOT BE LIKE THE OTHER!

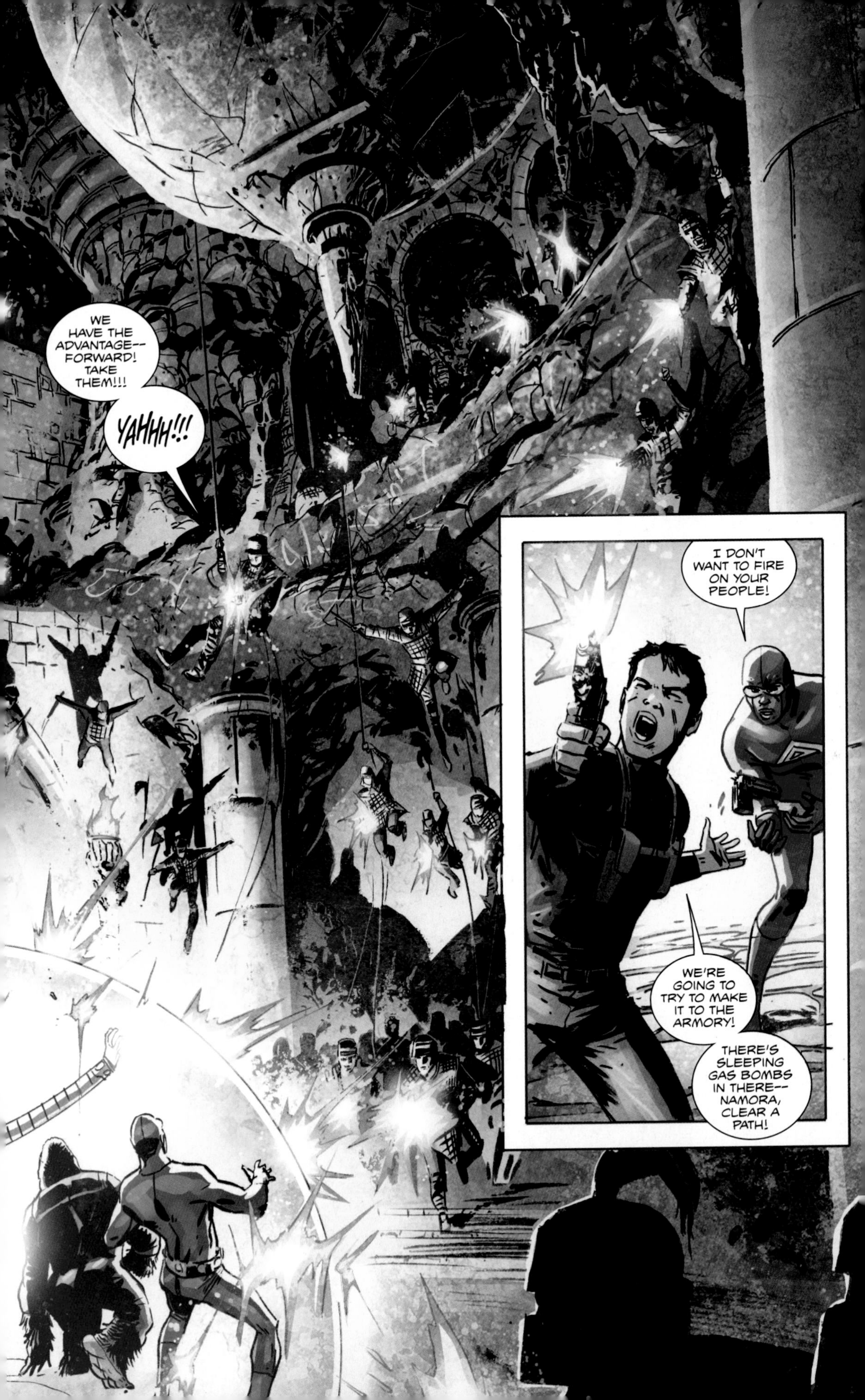
WE HAVE THE ADVANTAGE-- FORWARD! TAKE THEM!!!
YAHHH!!!
I DON'T WANT TO FIRE ON YOUR PEOPLE!
WE'RE GOING TO TRY TO MAKE IT TO THE ARMORY!
THERE'S SLEEPING GAS BOMBS IN THERE-- NAMORA, CLEAR A PATH!

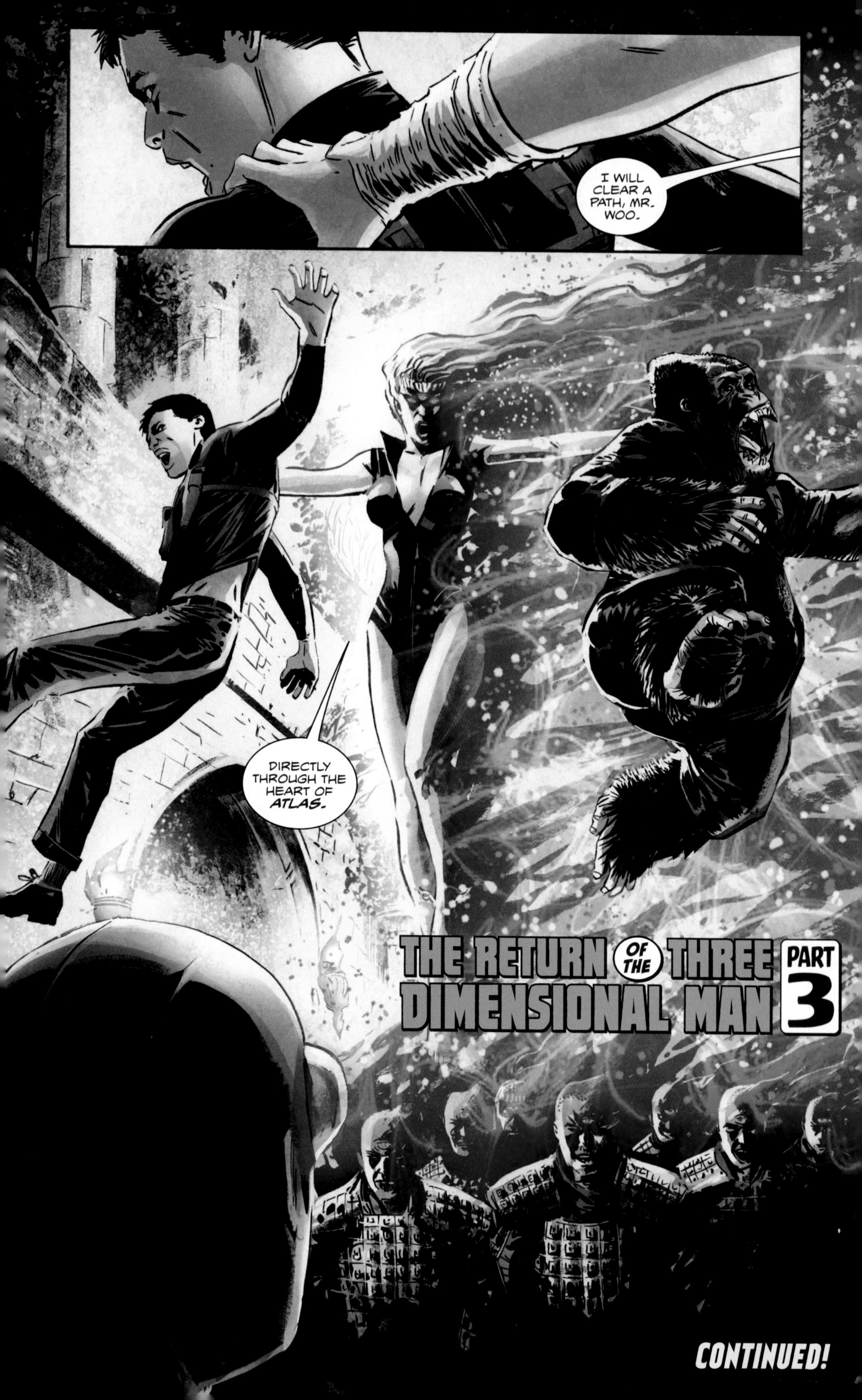

I WILL CLEAR A PATH, MR. WOO.
DIRECTLY THROUGH THE HEART OF ATLAS.
THE RETURN OF THE THREE DIMENSIONAL MAN PART 3
CONTINUED!

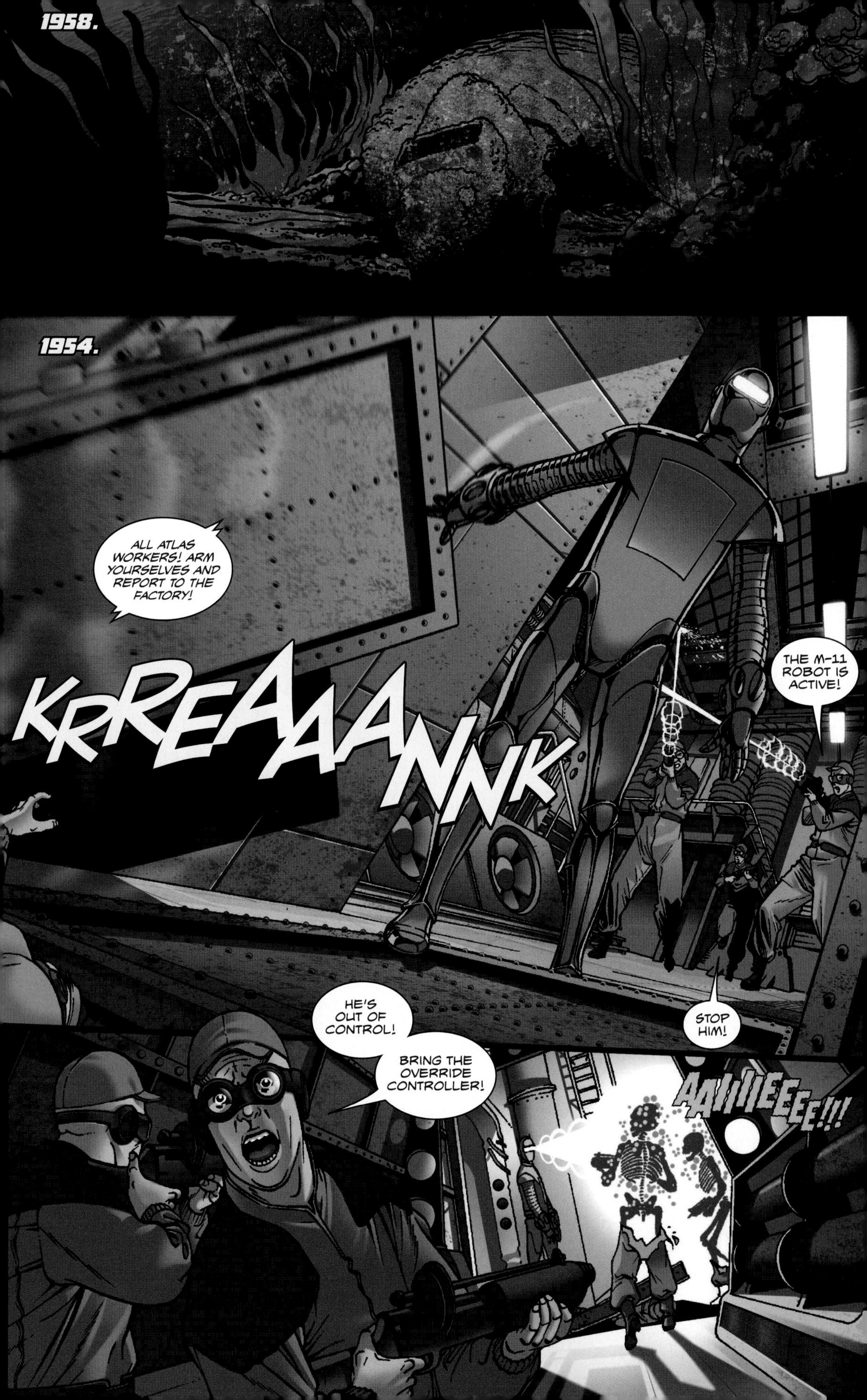
1958.
1954.
ALL ATLAS WORKERS! ARM YOURSELVES AND REPORT TO THE FACTORY!
KRREAAAANNK
THE M-11 ROBOT IS ACTIVE!
HE'S OUT OF CONTROL!
BRING THE OVERRIDE CONTROLLER!
STOP HIM!
AAIIIIEEEE!!!

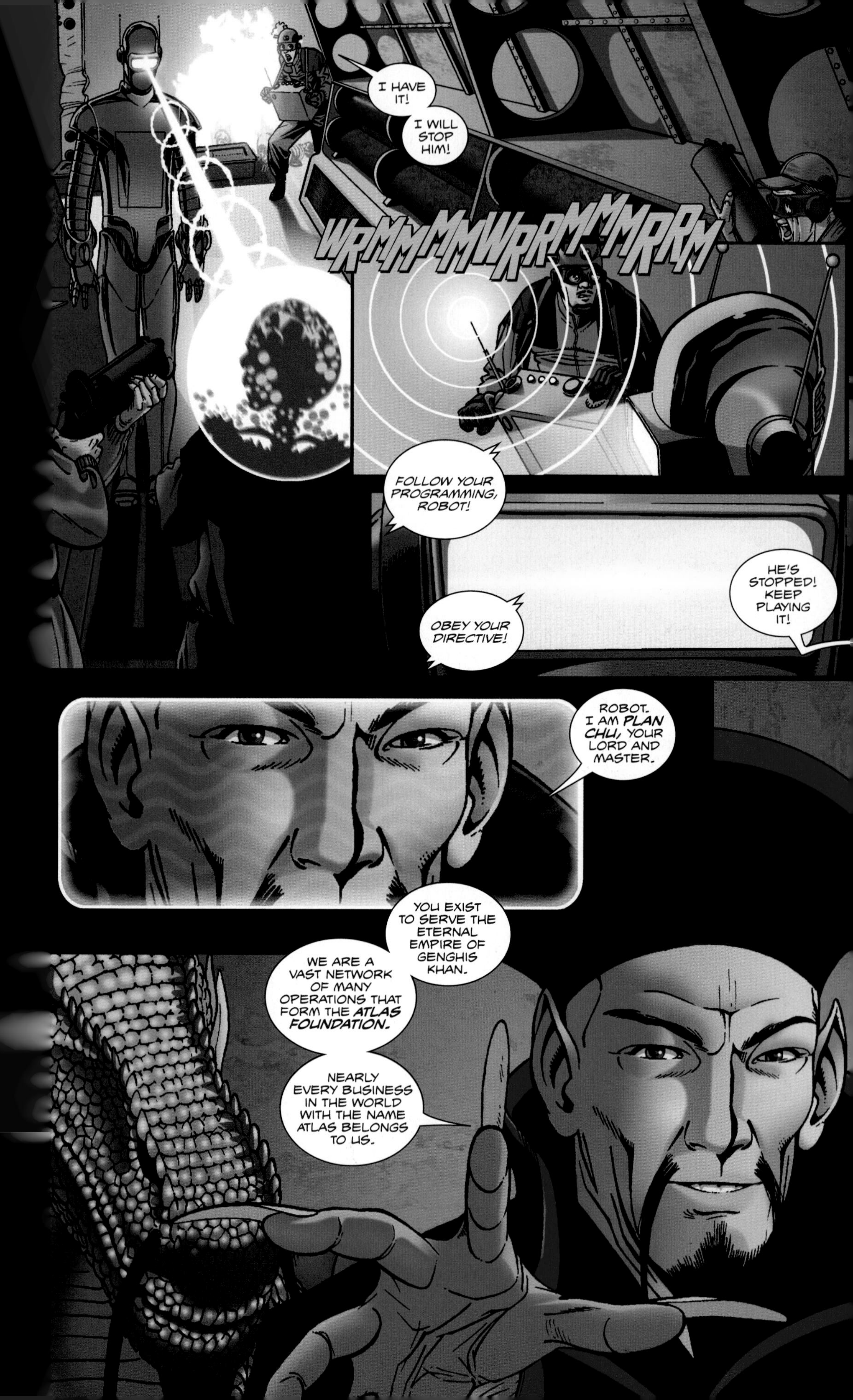
I HAVE IT!
I WILL STOP HIM!
WRMMMMMWRRMMMRRM
FOLLOW YOUR PROGRAMMING, ROBOT!
OBEY YOUR DIRECTIVE!
HE'S STOPPED! KEEP PLAYING IT!
ROBOT. I AM PLAN CHU, YOUR LORD AND MASTER.
YOU EXIST TO SERVE THE ETERNAL EMPIRE OF GENGHIS KHAN.
WE ARE A VAST NETWORK OF MANY OPERATIONS THAT FORM THE ATLAS FOUNDATION.
NEARLY EVERY BUSINESS IN THE WORLD WITH THE NAME ATLAS BELONGS TO US.

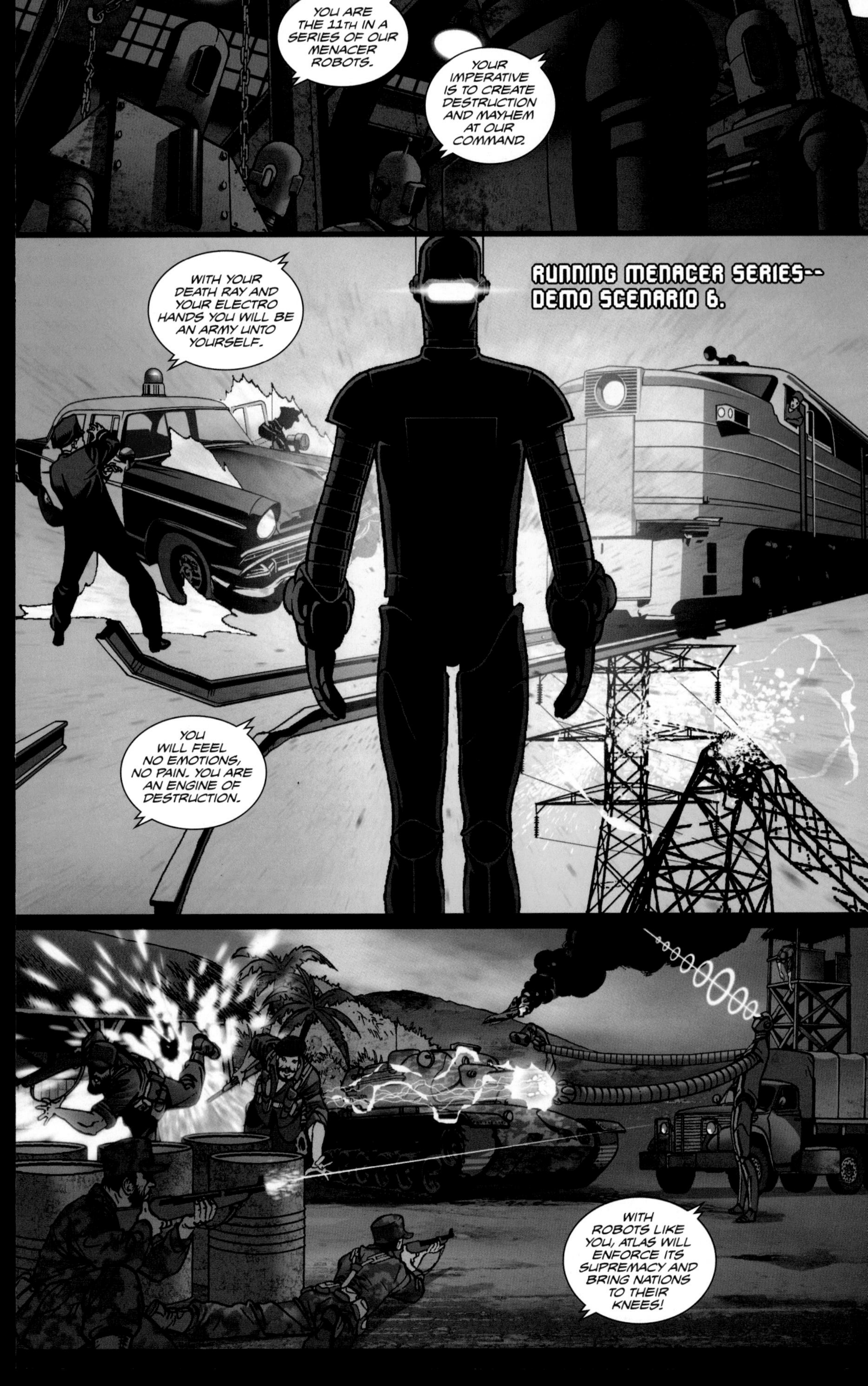
YOU ARE THE 11TH IN A SERIES OF OUR MENACER ROBOTS.
YOUR IMPERATIVE IS TO CREATE DESTRUCTION AND MAYHEM AT OUR COMMAND.
RUNNING MENACER SERIES--DEMO SCENARIO 6.
WITH YOUR DEATH RAY AND YOUR ELECTRO HANDS YOU WILL BE AN ARMY UNTO YOURSELF.
YOU WILL FEEL NO EMOTIONS, NO PAIN. YOU ARE AN ENGINE OF DESTRUCTION.
WITH ROBOTS LIKE YOU, ATLAS WILL ENFORCE ITS SUPREMACY AND BRING NATIONS TO THEIR KNEES!

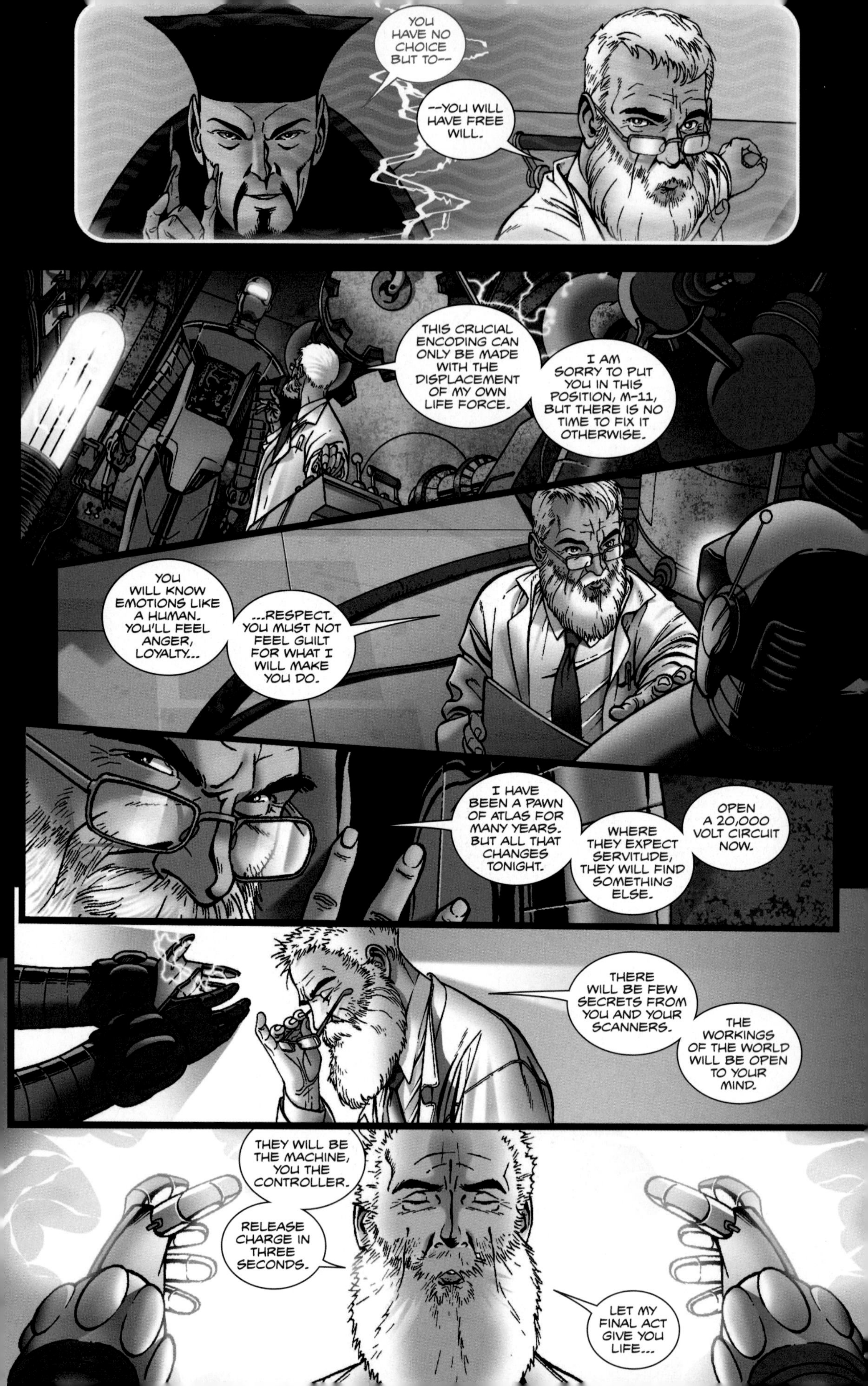
YOU HAVE NO CHOICE BUT TO--
--YOU WILL HAVE FREE WILL.
THIS CRUCIAL ENCODING CAN ONLY BE MADE WITH THE DISPLACEMENT OF MY OWN LIFE FORCE.
I AM SORRY TO PUT YOU IN THIS POSITION, M-11, BUT THERE IS NO TIME TO FIX IT OTHERWISE.
YOU WILL KNOW EMOTIONS LIKE A HUMAN. YOU'LL FEEL ANGER, LOYALTY...
...RESPECT. YOU MUST NOT FEEL GUILT FOR WHAT I WILL MAKE YOU DO.
I HAVE BEEN A PAWN OF ATLAS FOR MANY YEARS. BUT ALL THAT CHANGES TONIGHT.
WHERE THEY EXPECT SERVITUDE, THEY WILL FIND SOMETHING ELSE.
OPEN A 20,000 VOLT CIRCUIT NOW.
THERE WILL BE FEW SECRETS FROM YOU AND YOUR SCANNERS.
THE WORKINGS OF THE WORLD WILL BE OPEN TO YOUR MIND.
THEY WILL BE THE MACHINE, YOU THE CONTROLLER.
RELEASE CHARGE IN THREE SECONDS.
LET MY FINAL ACT GIVE YOU LIFE...

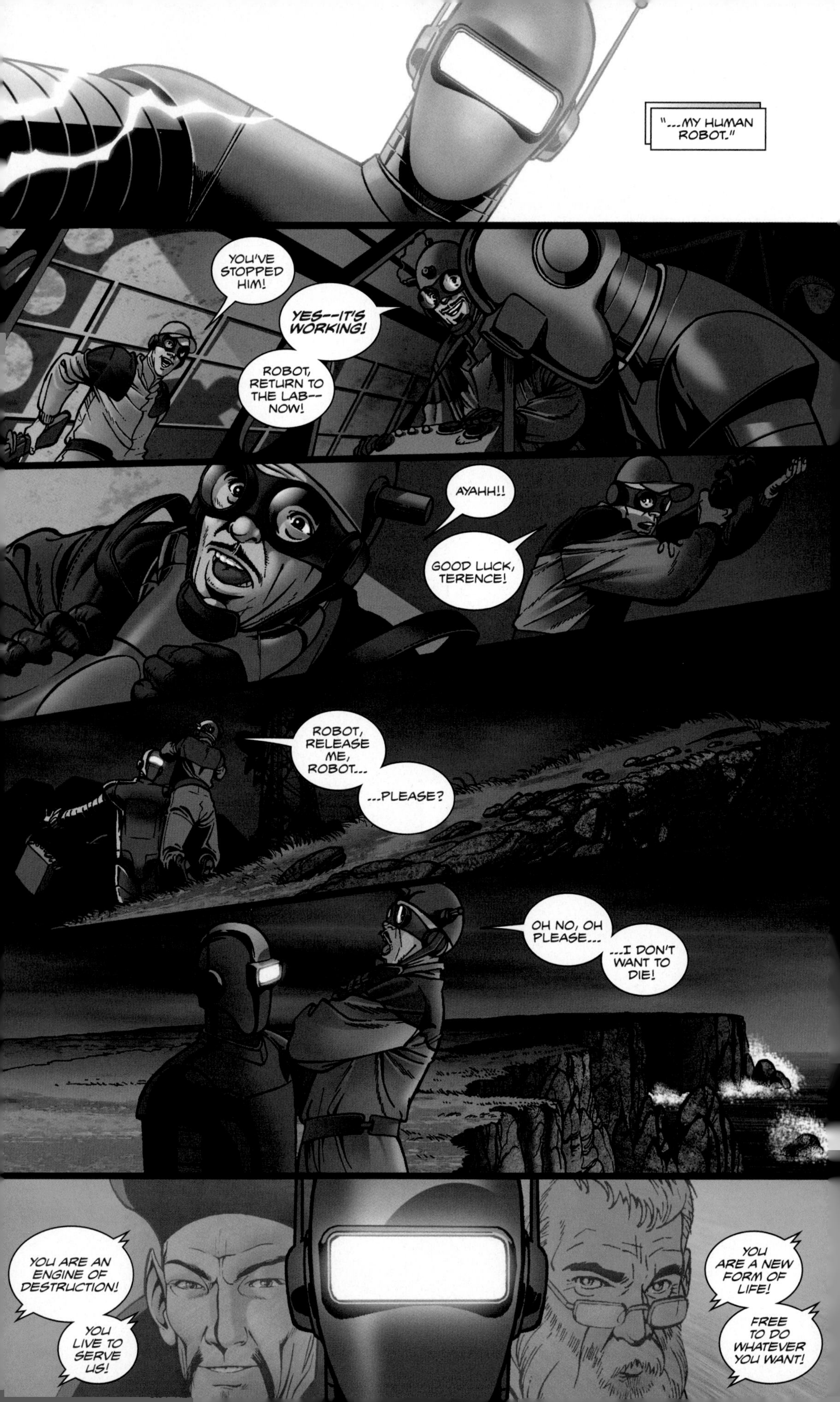
"...MY HUMAN ROBOT."
YOU'VE STOPPED HIM!
YES--IT'S WORKING!
ROBOT, RETURN TO THE LAB-- NOW!
AYAHH!!
GOOD LUCK, TERENCE!
ROBOT, RELEASE ME, ROBOT...
...PLEASE?
OH NO, OH PLEASE...
...I DON'T WANT TO DIE!
YOU ARE AN ENGINE OF DESTRUCTION!
YOU LIVE TO SERVE US!
YOU ARE A NEW FORM OF LIFE!
FREE TO DO WHATEVER YOU WANT!

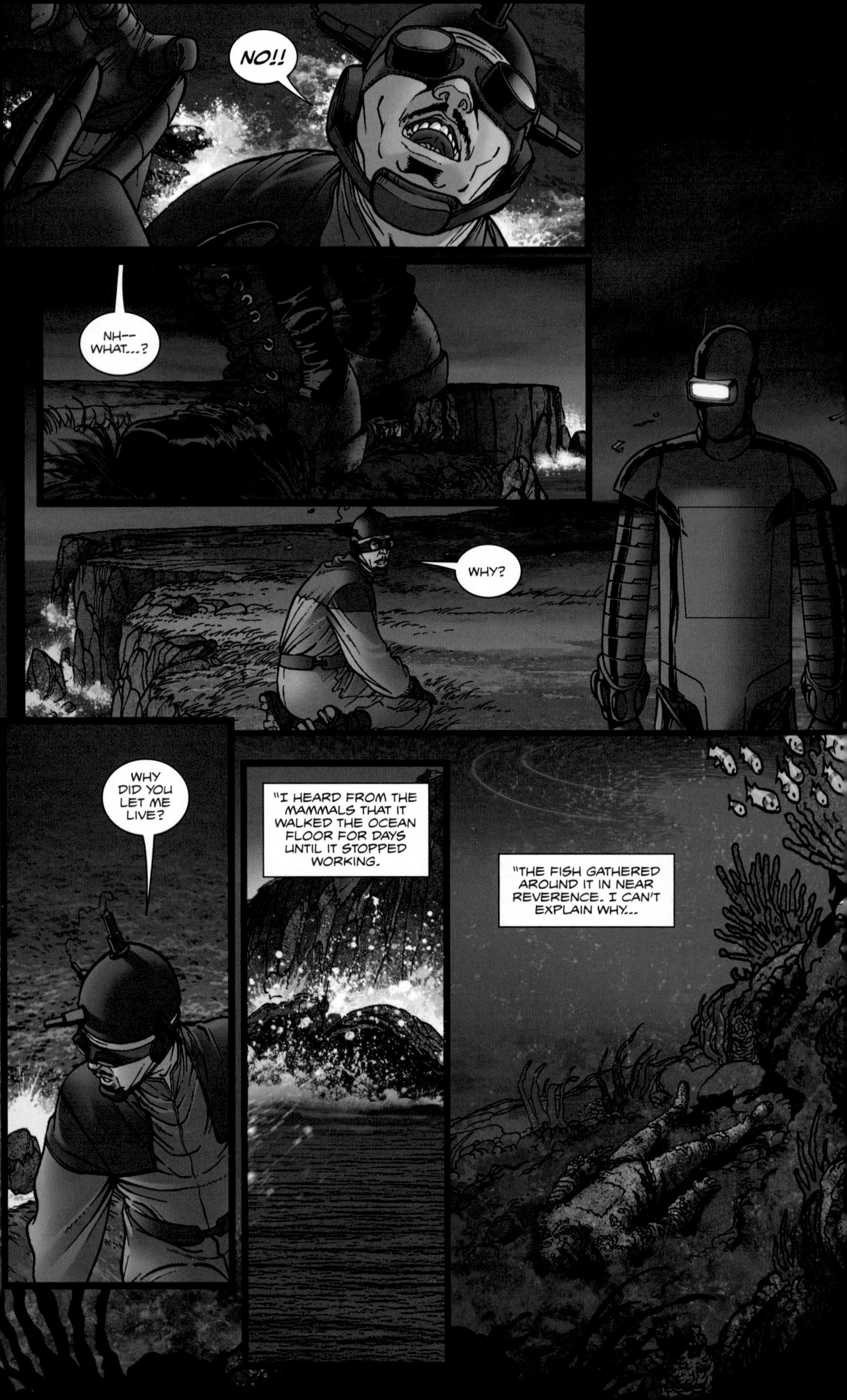
NO!!
NH-- WHAT...?
WHY?
WHY DID YOU LET ME LIVE?
"I HEARD FROM THE MAMMALS THAT IT WALKED THE OCEAN FLOOR FOR DAYS UNTIL IT STOPPED WORKING.
"THE FISH GATHERED AROUND IT IN NEAR REVERENCE. I CAN'T EXPLAIN WHY...

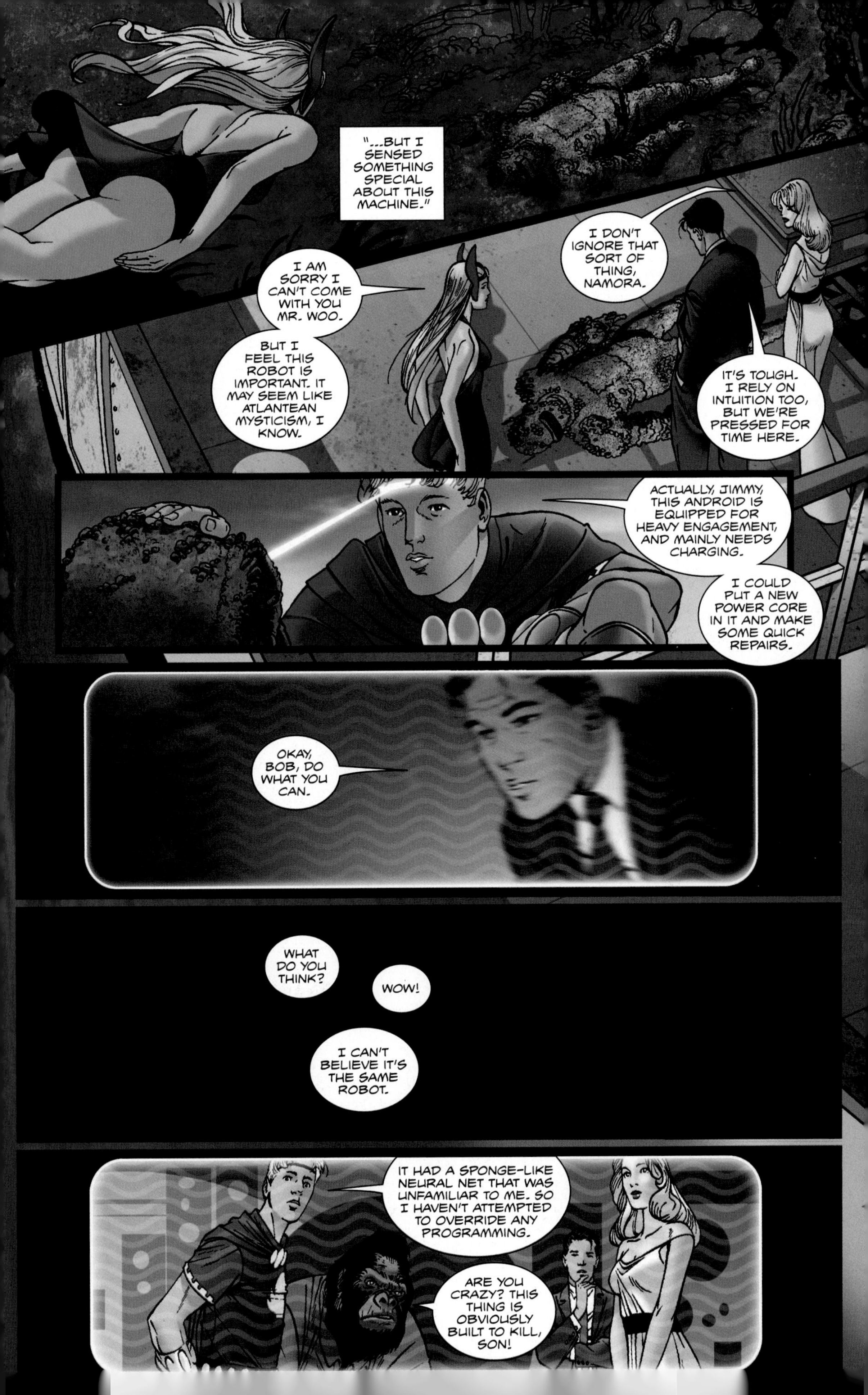
"...BUT I SENSED SOMETHING SPECIAL ABOUT THIS MACHINE."
I AM SORRY I CAN'T COME WITH YOU MR. WOO.
BUT I FEEL THIS ROBOT IS IMPORTANT. IT MAY SEEM LIKE ATLANTEAN MYSTICISM, I KNOW.
I DON'T IGNORE THAT SORT OF THING, NAMORA.
IT'S TOUGH. I RELY ON INTUITION TOO, BUT WE'RE PRESSED FOR TIME HERE.
ACTUALLY, JIMMY, THIS ANDROID IS EQUIPPED FOR HEAVY ENGAGEMENT, AND MAINLY NEEDS CHARGING.
I COULD PUT A NEW POWER CORE IN IT AND MAKE SOME QUICK REPAIRS.
OKAY, BOB, DO WHAT YOU CAN.
WHAT DO YOU THINK?
WOW!
I CAN'T BELIEVE IT'S THE SAME ROBOT.
IT HAD A SPONGE-LIKE NEURAL NET THAT WAS UNFAMILIAR TO ME. SO I HAVEN'T ATTEMPTED TO OVERRIDE ANY PROGRAMMING.
ARE YOU CRAZY? THIS THING IS OBVIOUSLY BUILT TO KILL, SON!

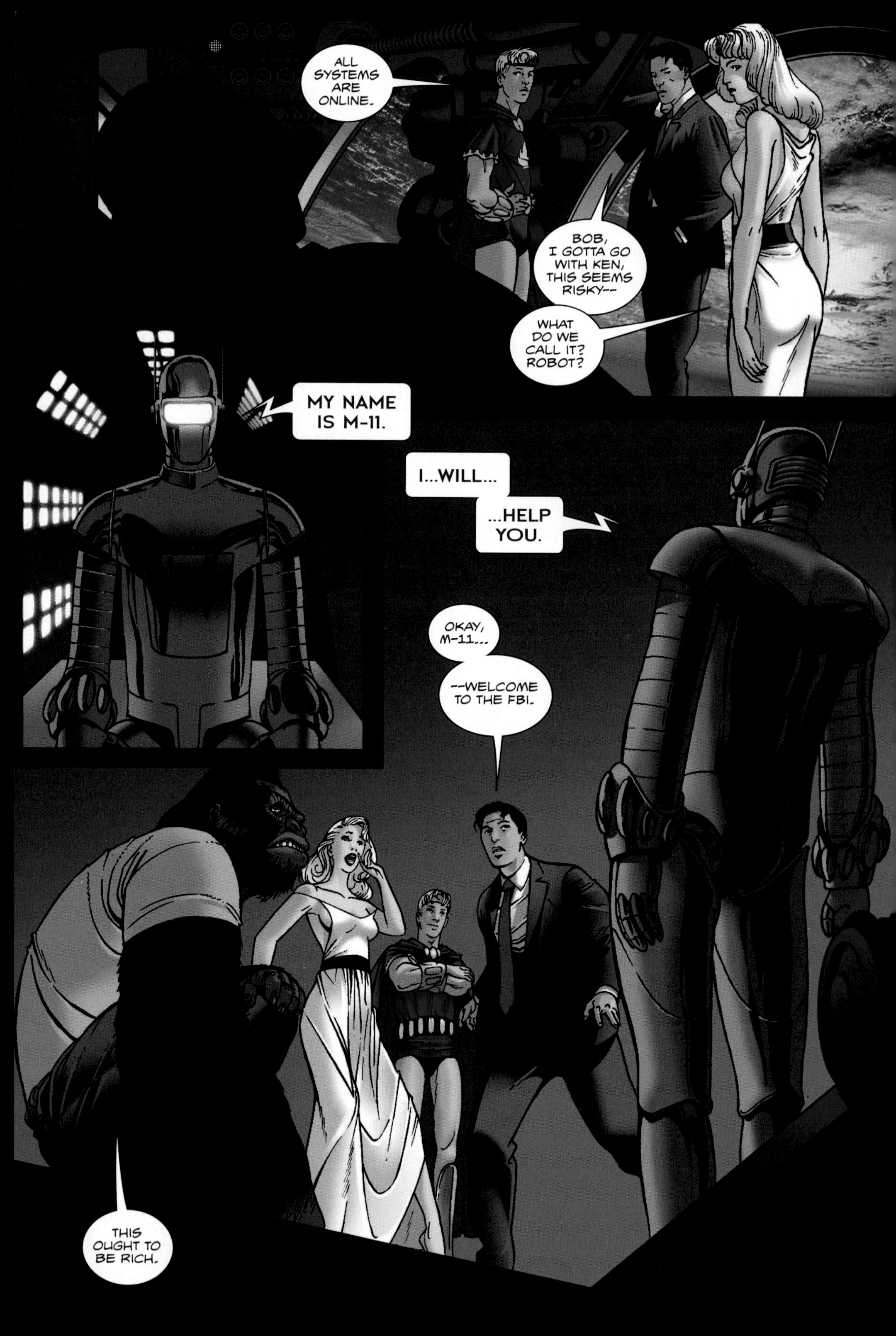
ALL SYSTEMS ARE ONLINE.
BOB, I GOTTA GO WITH KEN, THIS SEEMS RISKY--
WHAT DO WE CALL IT? ROBOT?
MY NAME IS M-11.
I...WILL...
...HELP YOU.
OKAY, M-11...
--WELCOME TO THE FBI.
THIS OUGHT TO BE RICH.

THE HUMAN ROBOT

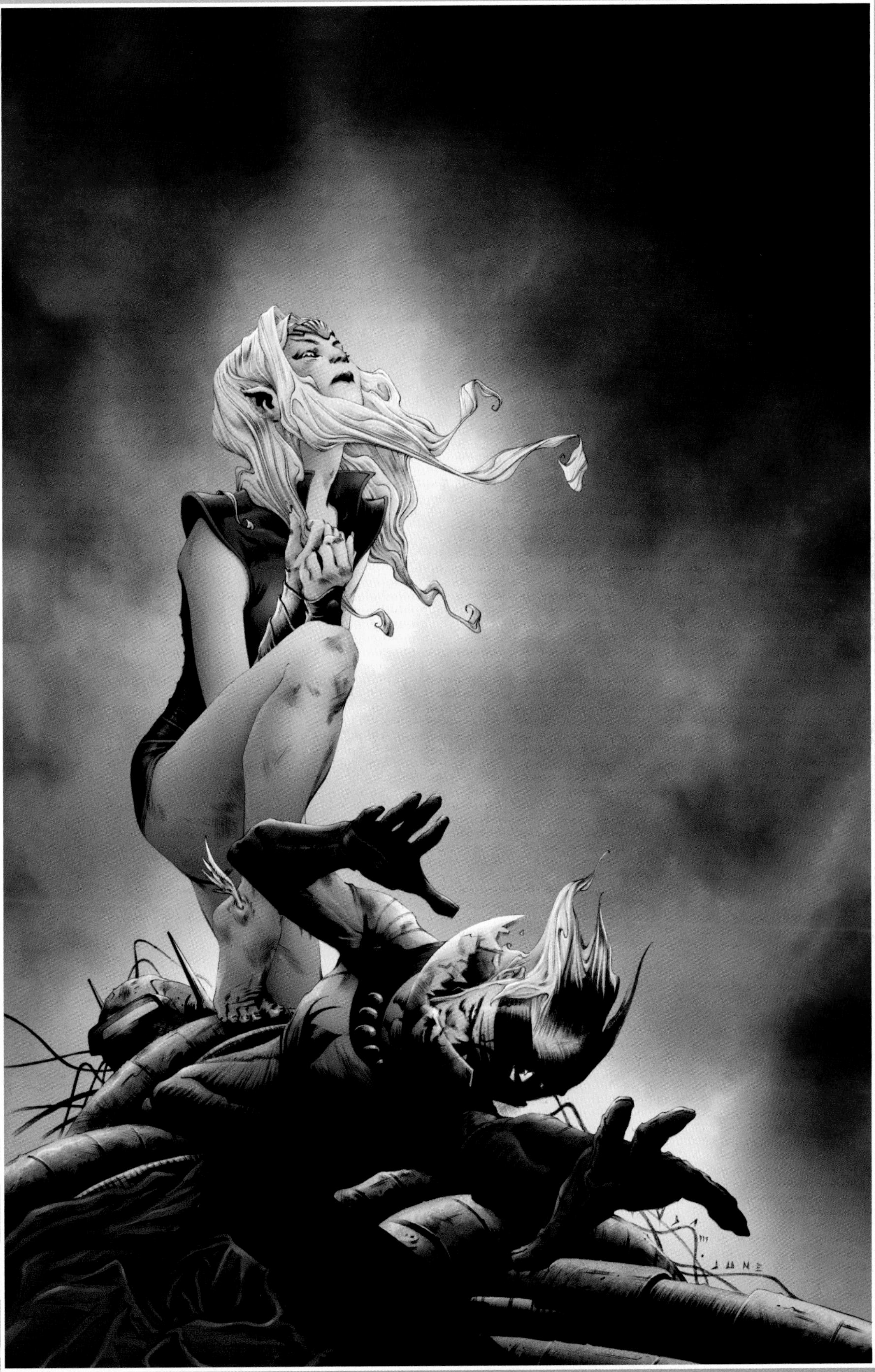

Atlas #4

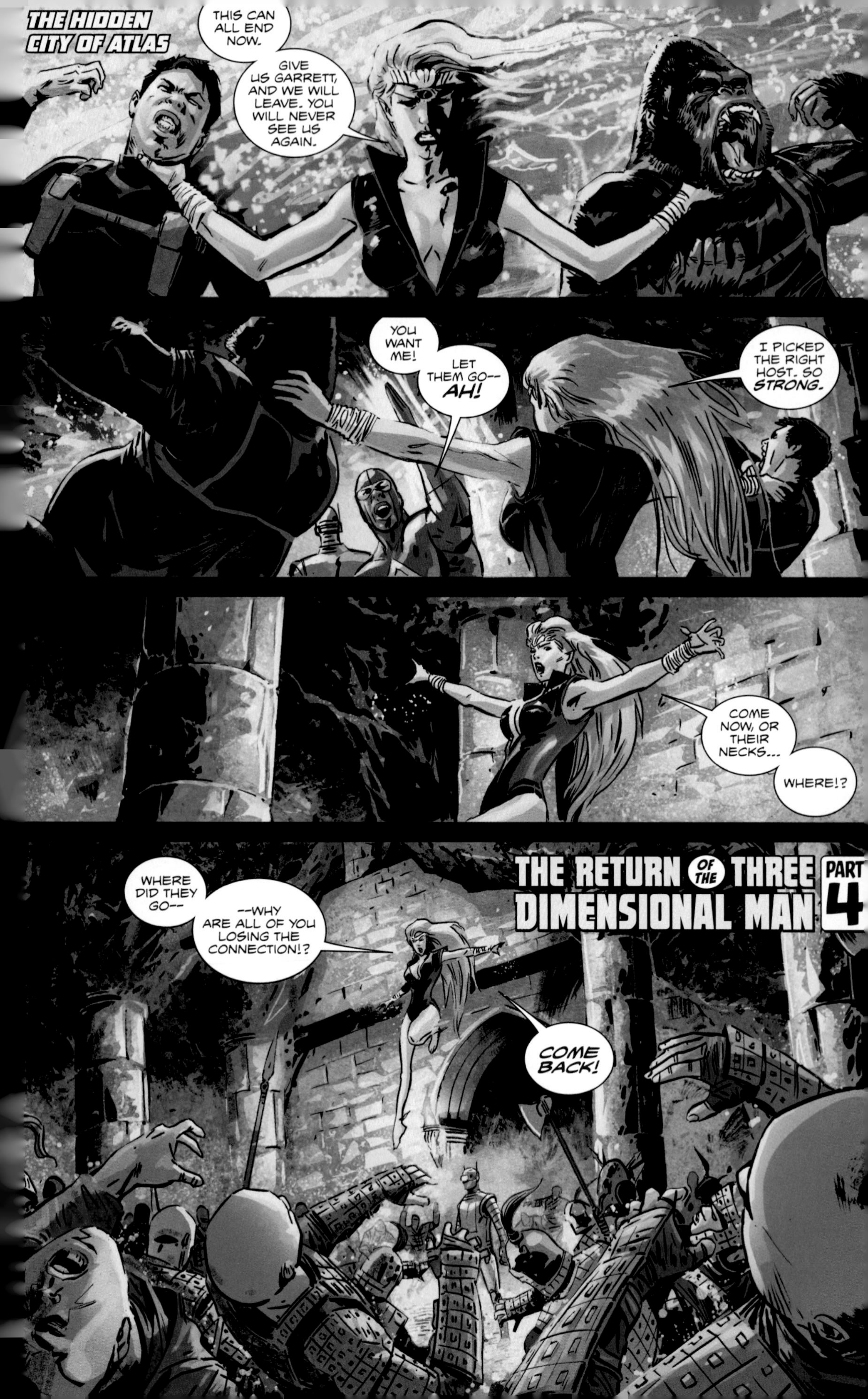
THE HIDDEN CITY OF ATLAS
THIS CAN ALL END NOW.
GIVE US GARRETT, AND WE WILL LEAVE. YOU WILL NEVER SEE US AGAIN.
YOU WANT ME!
LET THEM GO-- AH!
I PICKED THE RIGHT HOST. SO STRONG.
COME NOW, OR THEIR NECKS...
WHERE!?
THE RETURN OF THE THREE DIMENSIONAL MAN PART 4
WHERE DID THEY GO--
--WHY ARE ALL OF YOU LOSING THE CONNECTION!?
COME BACK!

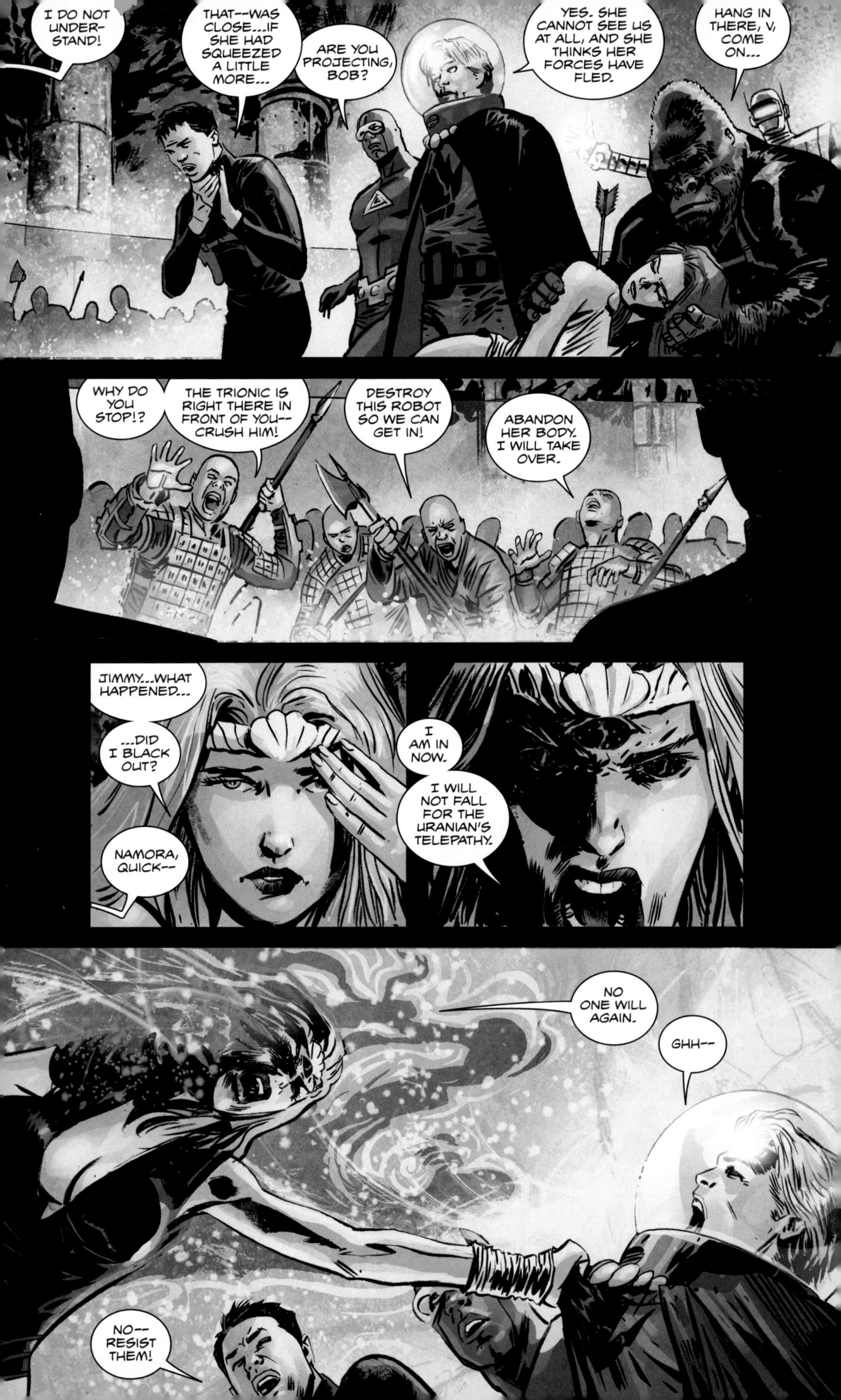

I DO NOT UNDER-STAND!
THAT--WAS CLOSE...IF SHE HAD SQUEEZED A LITTLE MORE...
ARE YOU PROJECTING, BOB?
YES. SHE CANNOT SEE US AT ALL, AND SHE THINKS HER FORCES HAVE FLED.
HANG IN THERE, V, COME ON...
WHY DO YOU STOP!?
THE TRIONIC IS RIGHT THERE IN FRONT OF YOU--CRUSH HIM!
DESTROY THIS ROBOT SO WE CAN GET IN!
ABANDON HER BODY. I WILL TAKE OVER.
JIMMY...WHAT HAPPENED...
...DID I BLACK OUT?
NAMORA, QUICK--
I AM IN NOW.
I WILL NOT FALL FOR THE URANIAN'S TELEPATHY.
NO ONE WILL AGAIN.
GHH--
NO--RESIST THEM!

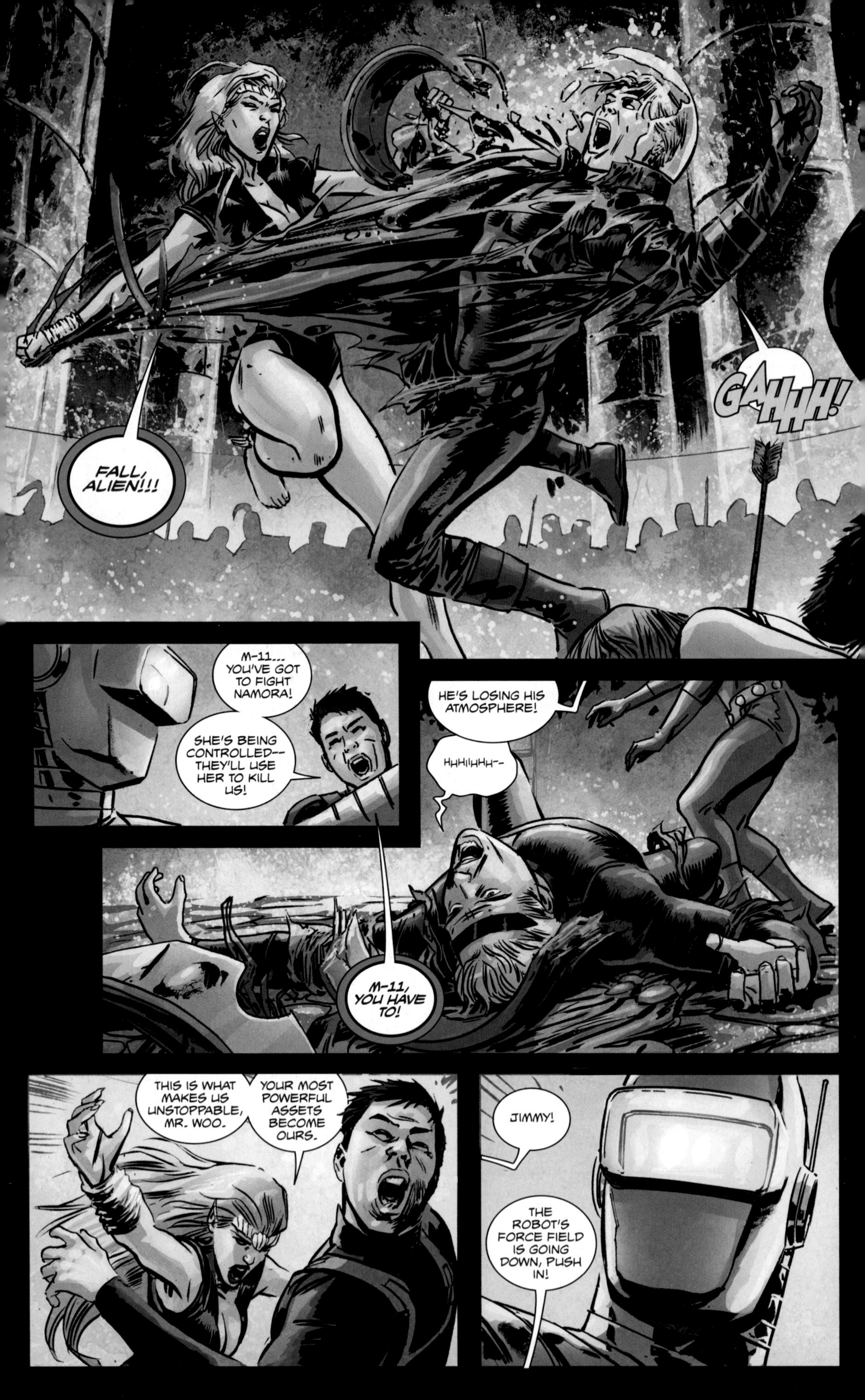
GAHHH!
FALL, ALIEN!!!
M-11... YOU'VE GOT TO FIGHT NAMORA!
SHE'S BEING CONTROLLED-- THEY'LL USE HER TO KILL US!
HE'S LOSING HIS ATMOSPHERE!
HHHIIHHH--
M-11, YOU HAVE TO!
THIS IS WHAT MAKES US UNSTOPPABLE, MR. WOO.
YOUR MOST POWERFUL ASSETS BECOME OURS.
JIMMY!
THE ROBOT'S FORCE FIELD IS GOING DOWN, PUSH IN!

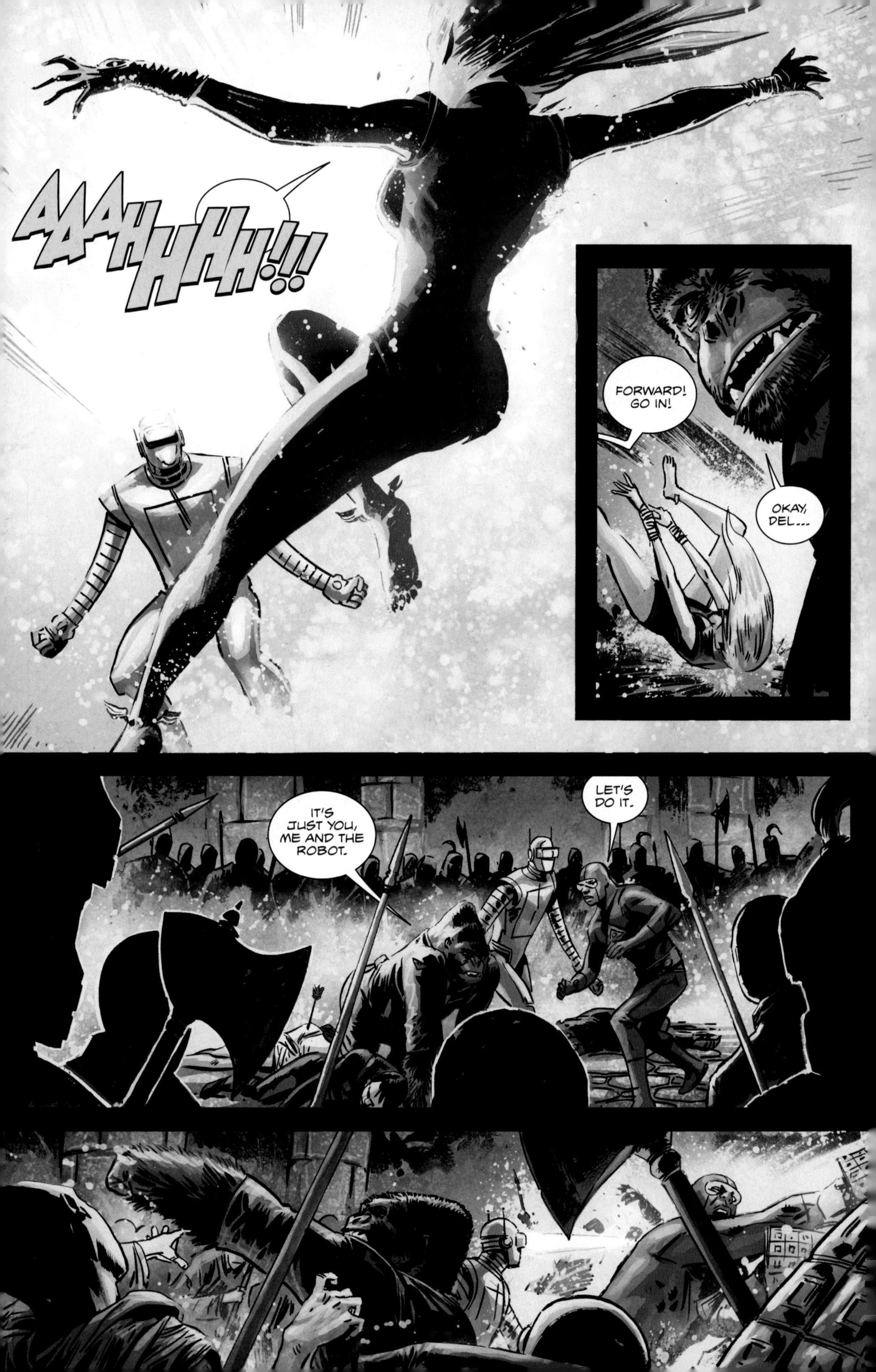
AAAHHHHH!!!
FORWARD! GO IN!
OKAY, DEL...
IT'S JUST YOU, ME AND THE ROBOT.
LET'S DO IT.

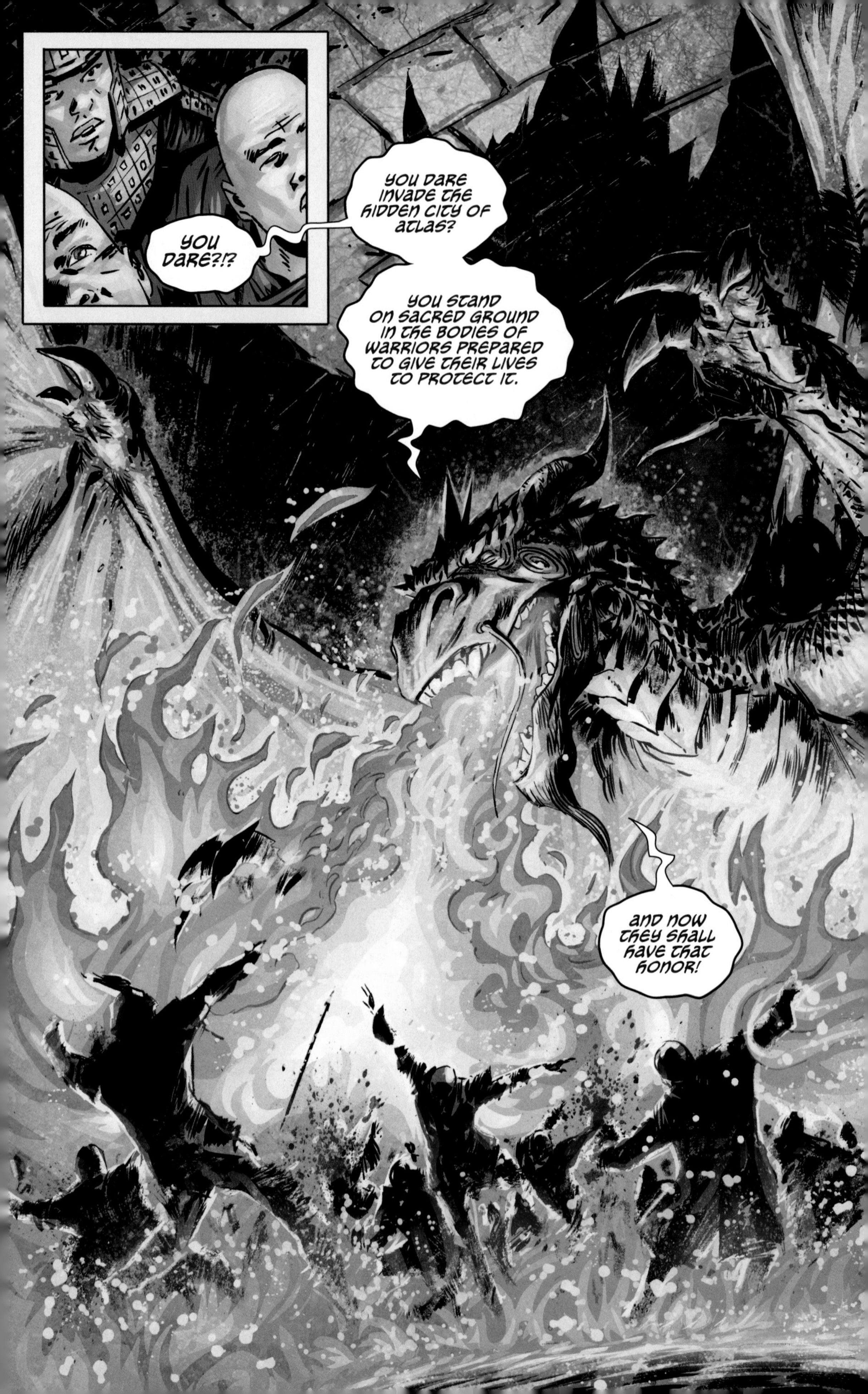
YOU DARE?!?
YOU DARE INVADE THE HIDDEN CITY OF ATLAS?
YOU STAND ON SACRED GROUND IN THE BODIES OF WARRIORS PREPARED TO GIVE THEIR LIVES TO PROTECT IT.
AND NOW THEY SHALL HAVE THAT HONOR!

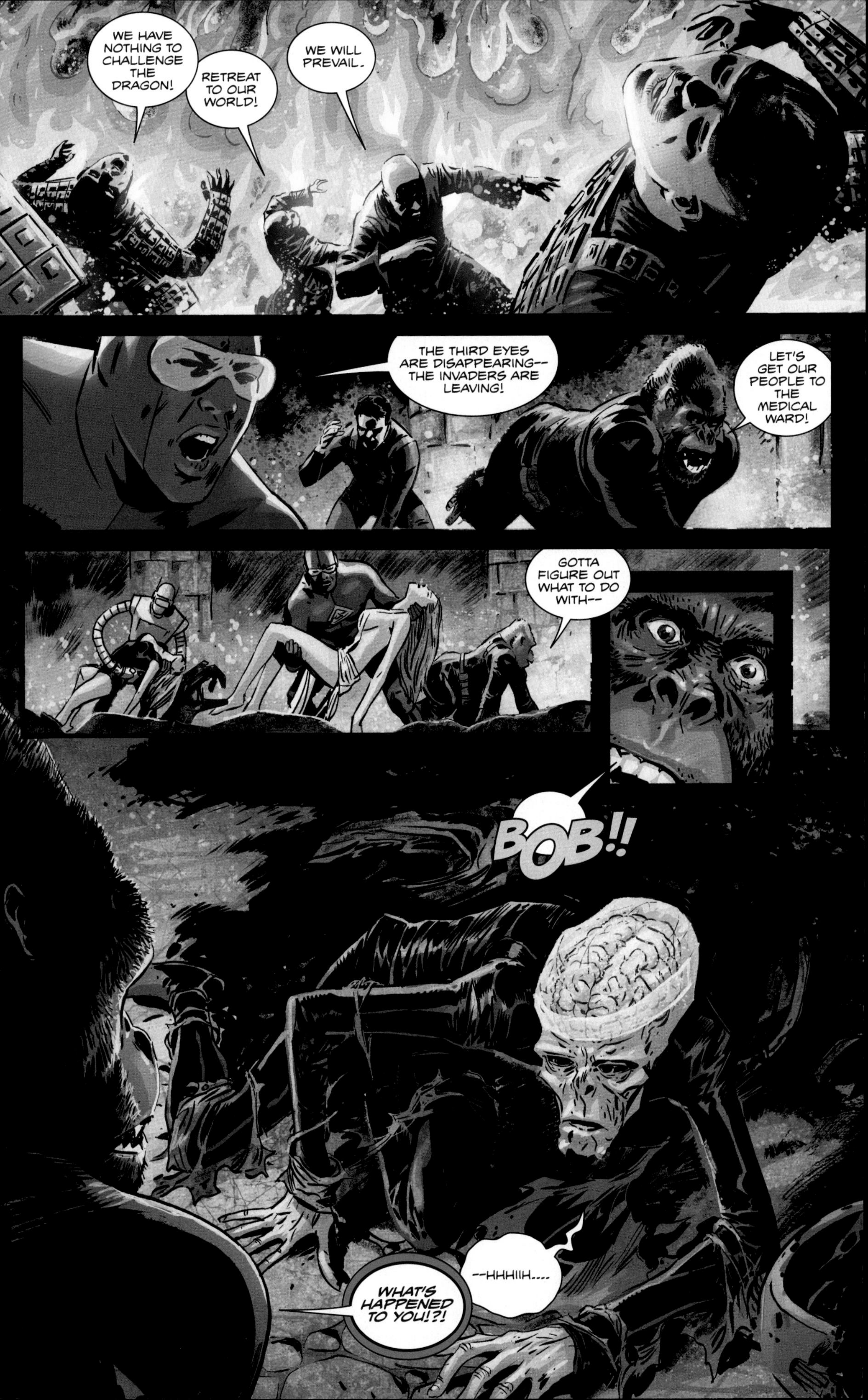
WE HAVE NOTHING TO CHALLENGE THE DRAGON!
RETREAT TO OUR WORLD!
WE WILL PREVAIL.
THE THIRD EYES ARE DISAPPEARING-- THE INVADERS ARE LEAVING!
LET'S GET OUR PEOPLE TO THE MEDICAL WARD!
GOTTA FIGURE OUT WHAT TO DO WITH--
BOB!!
WHAT'S HAPPENED TO YOU!?!
--HHHIIH....

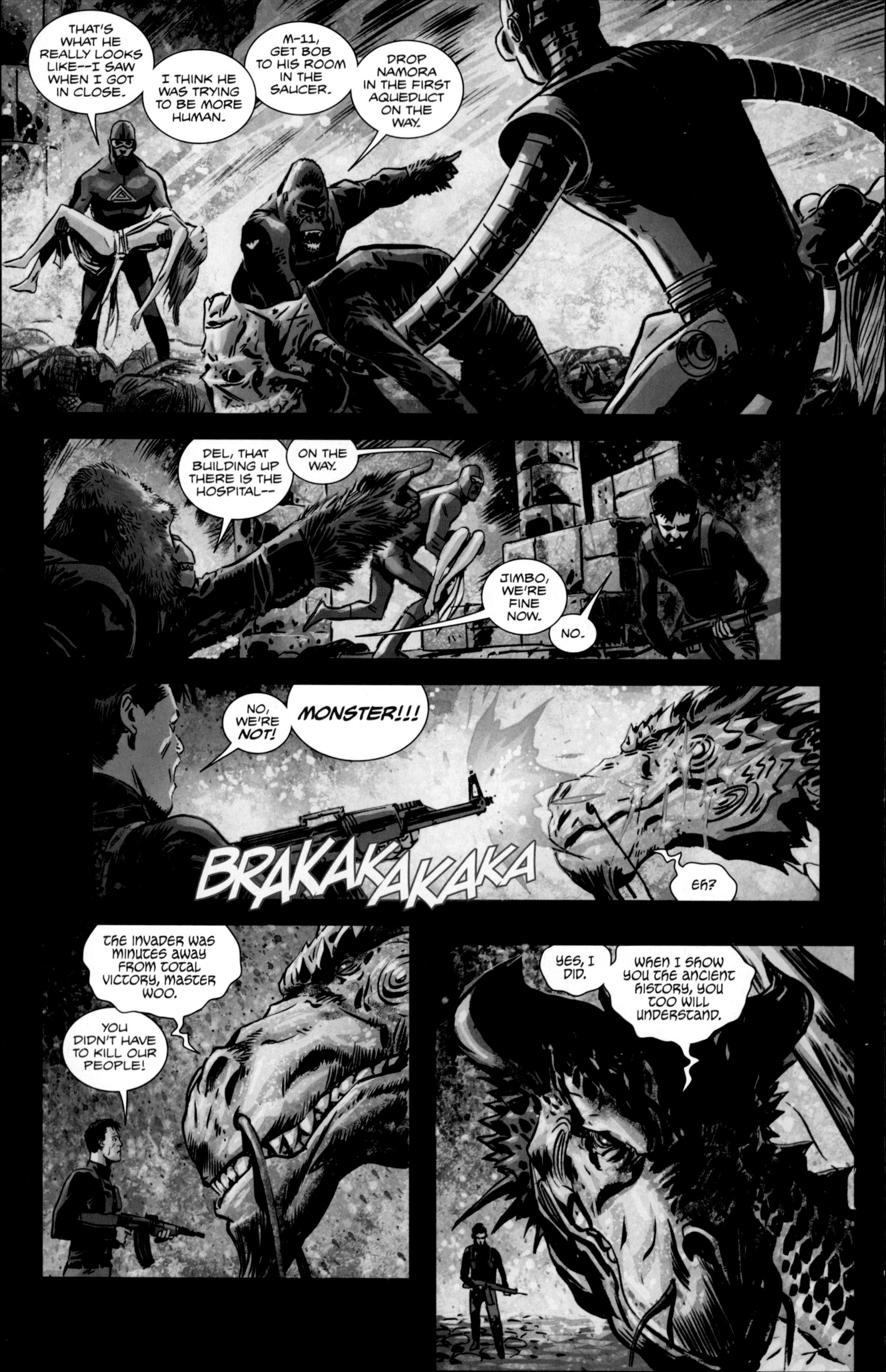
THAT'S WHAT HE REALLY LOOKS LIKE--I SAW WHEN I GOT IN CLOSE.
I THINK HE WAS TRYING TO BE MORE HUMAN.
M-11, GET BOB TO HIS ROOM IN THE SAUCER.
DROP NAMORA IN THE FIRST AQUEDUCT ON THE WAY.
DEL, THAT BUILDING UP THERE IS THE HOSPITAL--
ON THE WAY.
JIMBO, WE'RE FINE NOW.
NO.
NO, WE'RE NOT!
MONSTER!!!
BRAKAKAKAKA
EH?
THE INVADER WAS MINUTES AWAY FROM TOTAL VICTORY, MASTER WOO.
YOU DIDN'T HAVE TO KILL OUR PEOPLE!
YES, I DID.
WHEN I SHOW YOU THE ANCIENT HISTORY, YOU TOO WILL UNDERSTAND.

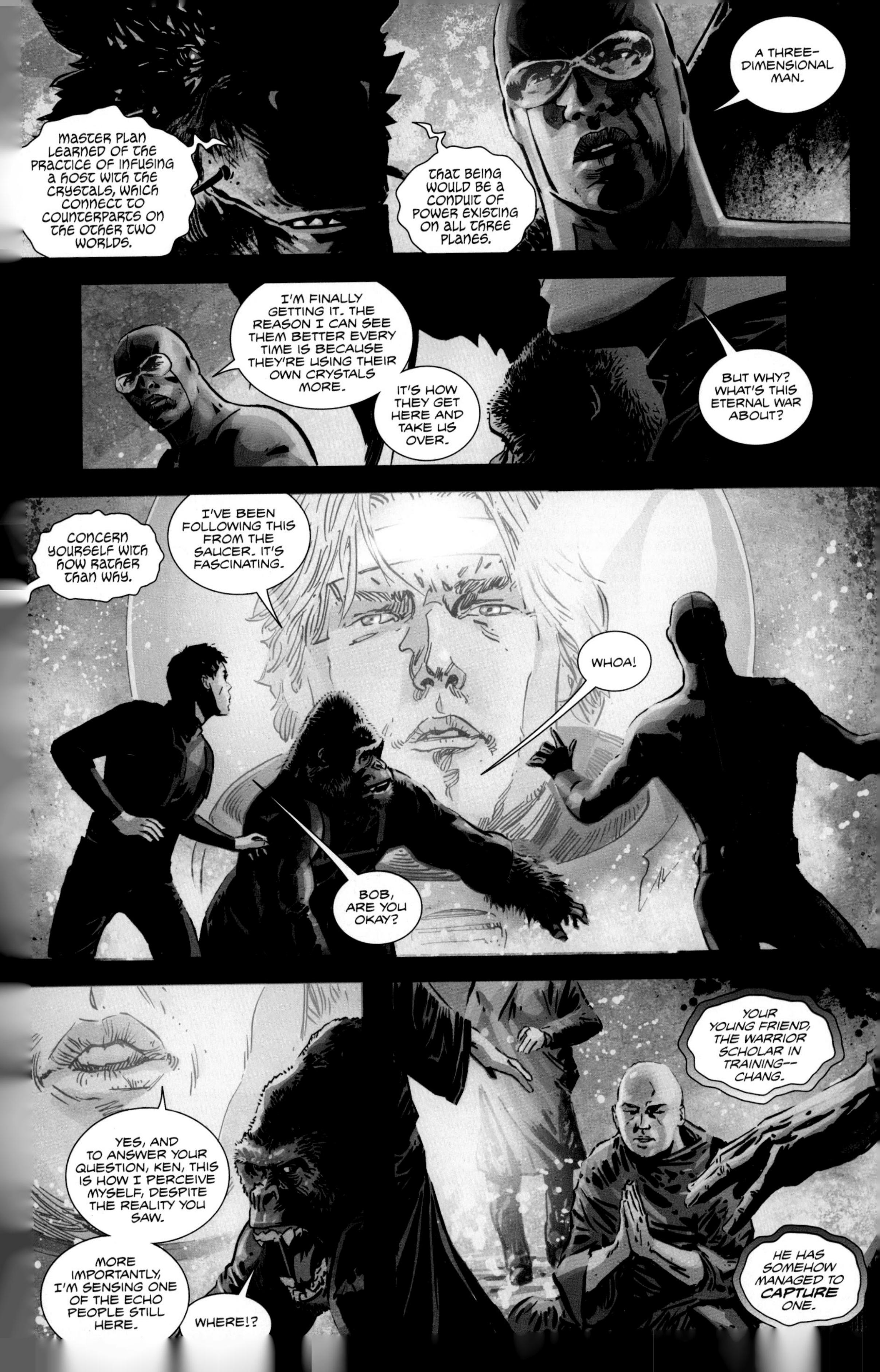
MASTER PLAN LEARNED OF THE PRACTICE OF INFUSING A HOST WITH THE CRYSTALS, WHICH CONNECT TO COUNTERPARTS ON THE OTHER TWO WORLDS.
THAT BEING WOULD BE A CONDUIT OF POWER EXISTING ON ALL THREE PLANES.
A THREE-DIMENSIONAL MAN.
I'M FINALLY GETTING IT. THE REASON I CAN SEE THEM BETTER EVERY TIME IS BECAUSE THEY'RE USING THEIR OWN CRYSTALS MORE.
IT'S HOW THEY GET HERE AND TAKE US OVER.
BUT WHY? WHAT'S THIS ETERNAL WAR ABOUT?
CONCERN YOURSELF WITH HOW RATHER THAN WHY.
I'VE BEEN FOLLOWING THIS FROM THE SAUCER. IT'S FASCINATING.
WHOA!
BOB, ARE YOU OKAY?
YES, AND TO ANSWER YOUR QUESTION, KEN, THIS IS HOW I PERCEIVE MYSELF, DESPITE THE REALITY YOU SAW.
MORE IMPORTANTLY, I'M SENSING ONE OF THE ECHO PEOPLE STILL HERE.
WHERE!?
YOUR YOUNG FRIEND, THE WARRIOR SCHOLAR IN TRAINING-- CHANG.
HE HAS SOMEHOW MANAGED TO CAPTURE ONE.

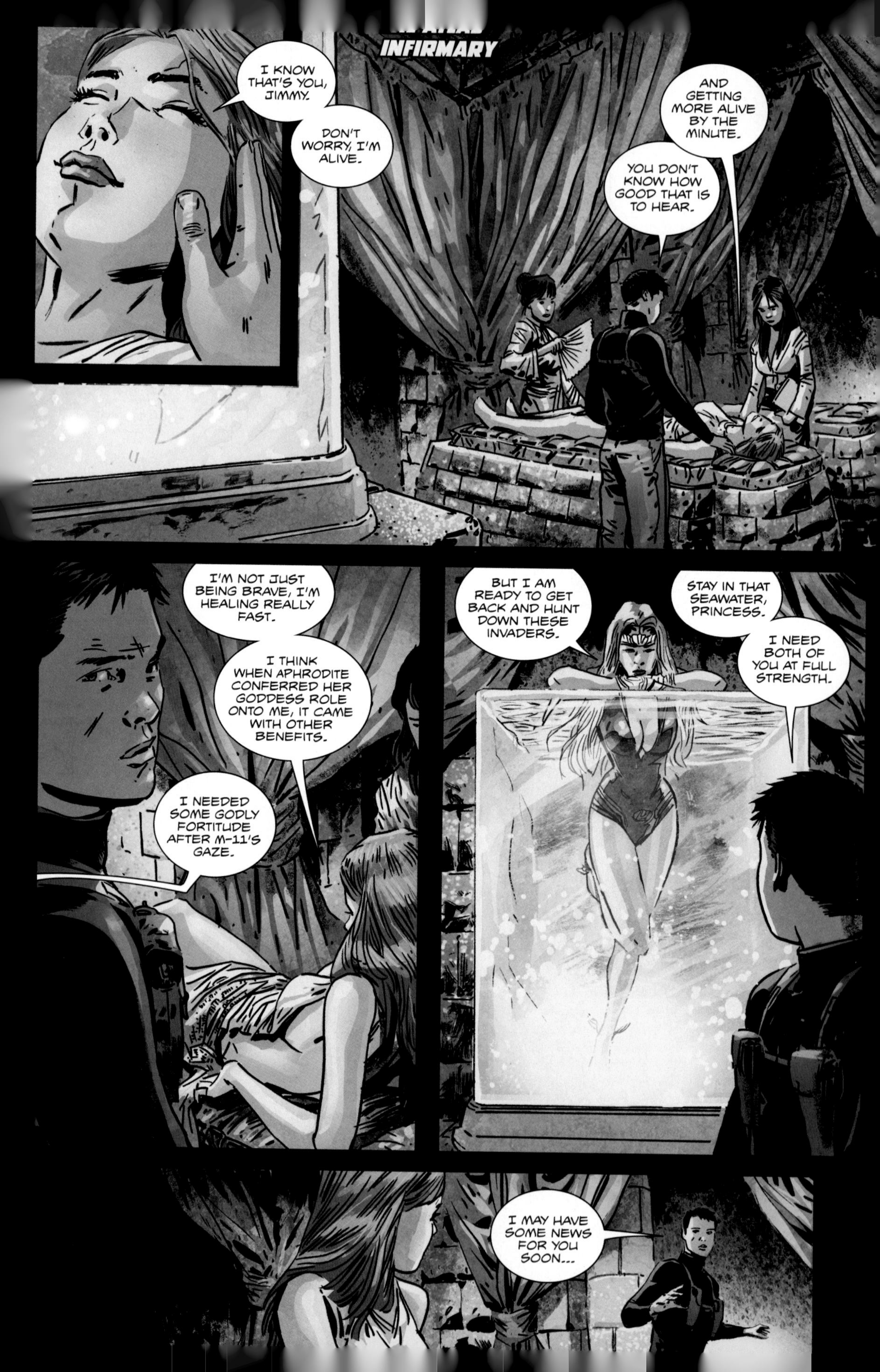
INFIRMARY
I KNOW THAT'S YOU, JIMMY.
DON'T WORRY, I'M ALIVE.
AND GETTING MORE ALIVE BY THE MINUTE.
YOU DON'T KNOW HOW GOOD THAT IS TO HEAR.
I'M NOT JUST BEING BRAVE, I'M HEALING REALLY FAST.
I THINK WHEN APHRODITE CONFERRED HER GODDESS ROLE ONTO ME, IT CAME WITH OTHER BENEFITS.
I NEEDED SOME GODLY FORTITUDE AFTER M-11'S GAZE.
BUT I AM READY TO GET BACK AND HUNT DOWN THESE INVADERS.
STAY IN THAT SEAWATER, PRINCESS.
I NEED BOTH OF YOU AT FULL STRENGTH.
I MAY HAVE SOME NEWS FOR YOU SOON...

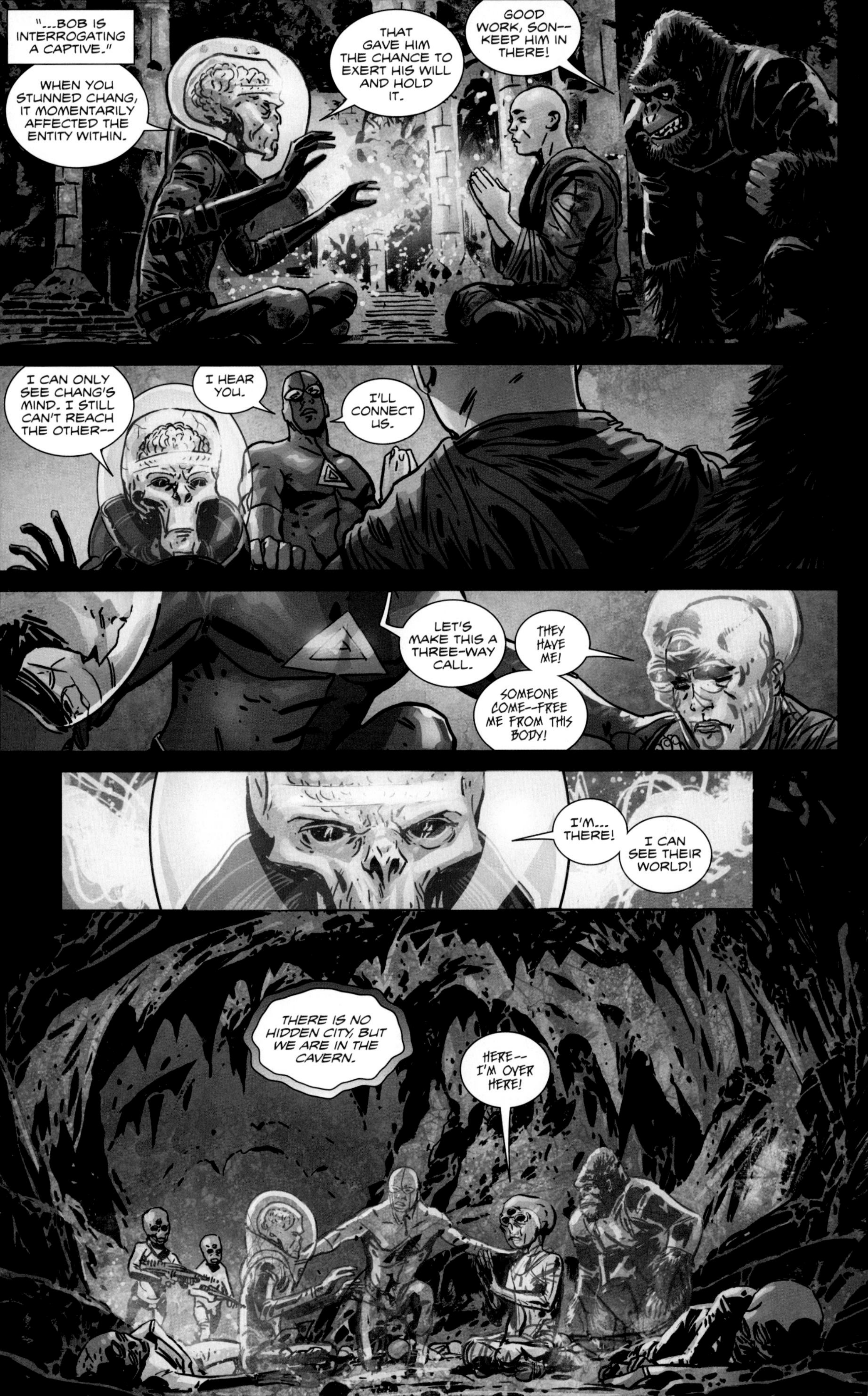
"...BOB IS INTERROGATING A CAPTIVE."
WHEN YOU STUNNED CHANG, IT MOMENTARILY AFFECTED THE ENTITY WITHIN.
THAT GAVE HIM THE CHANCE TO EXERT HIS WILL AND HOLD IT.
GOOD WORK, SON--KEEP HIM IN THERE!
I CAN ONLY SEE CHANG'S MIND. I STILL CAN'T REACH THE OTHER--
I HEAR YOU.
I'LL CONNECT US.
LET'S MAKE THIS A THREE-WAY CALL.
THEY HAVE ME!
SOMEONE COME--FREE ME FROM THIS BODY!
I'M... THERE!
I CAN SEE THEIR WORLD!
THERE IS NO HIDDEN CITY, BUT WE ARE IN THE CAVERN.
HERE--I'M OVER HERE!

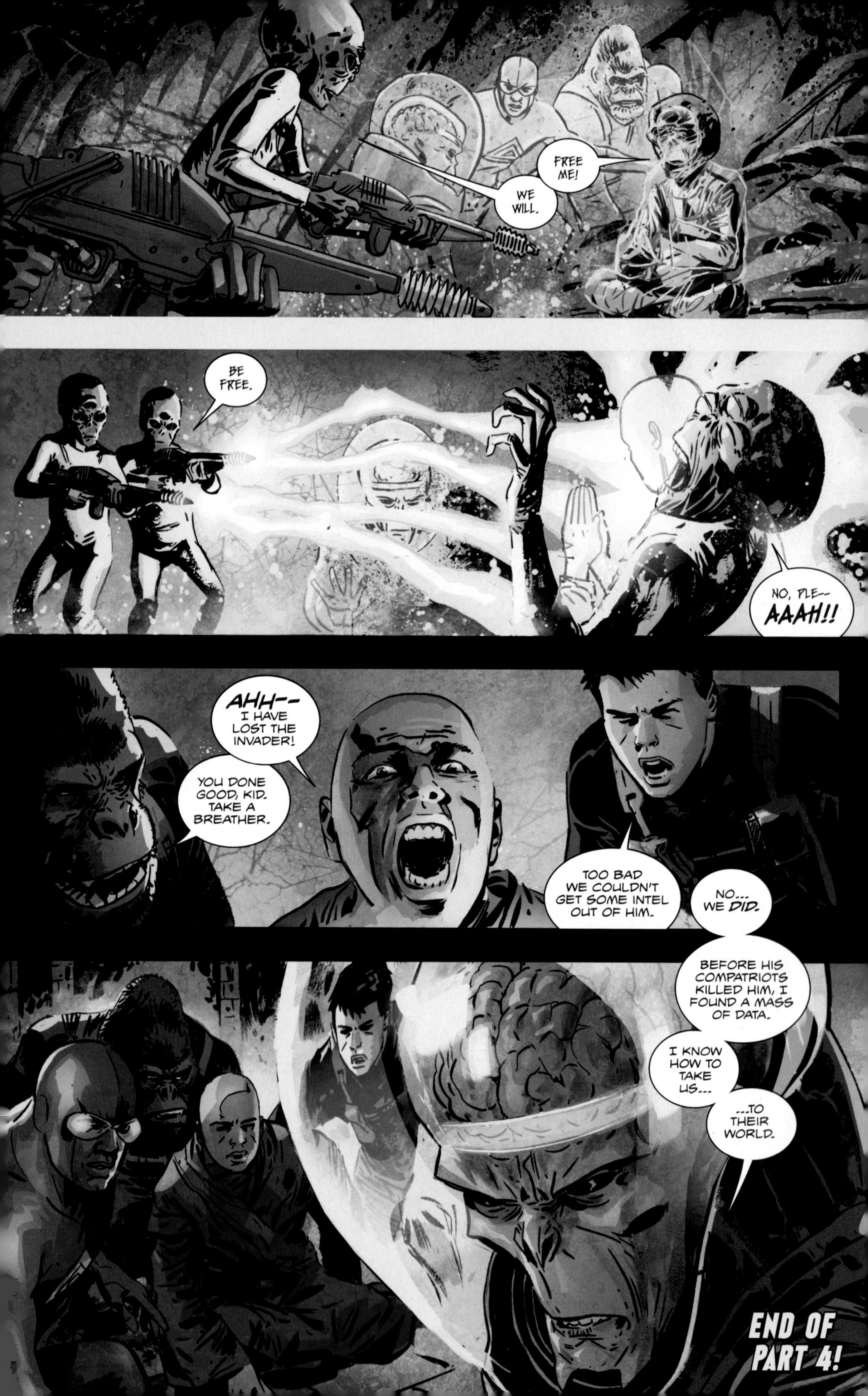
FREE ME!
WE WILL.
BE FREE.
NO, PLE-- AAAH!!
AHH-- I HAVE LOST THE INVADER!
YOU DONE GOOD, KID. TAKE A BREATHER.
TOO BAD WE COULDN'T GET SOME INTEL OUT OF HIM.
NO... WE DID.
BEFORE HIS COMPATRIOTS KILLED HIM, I FOUND A MASS OF DATA.
I KNOW HOW TO TAKE US...
...TO THEIR WORLD.
END OF PART 4!

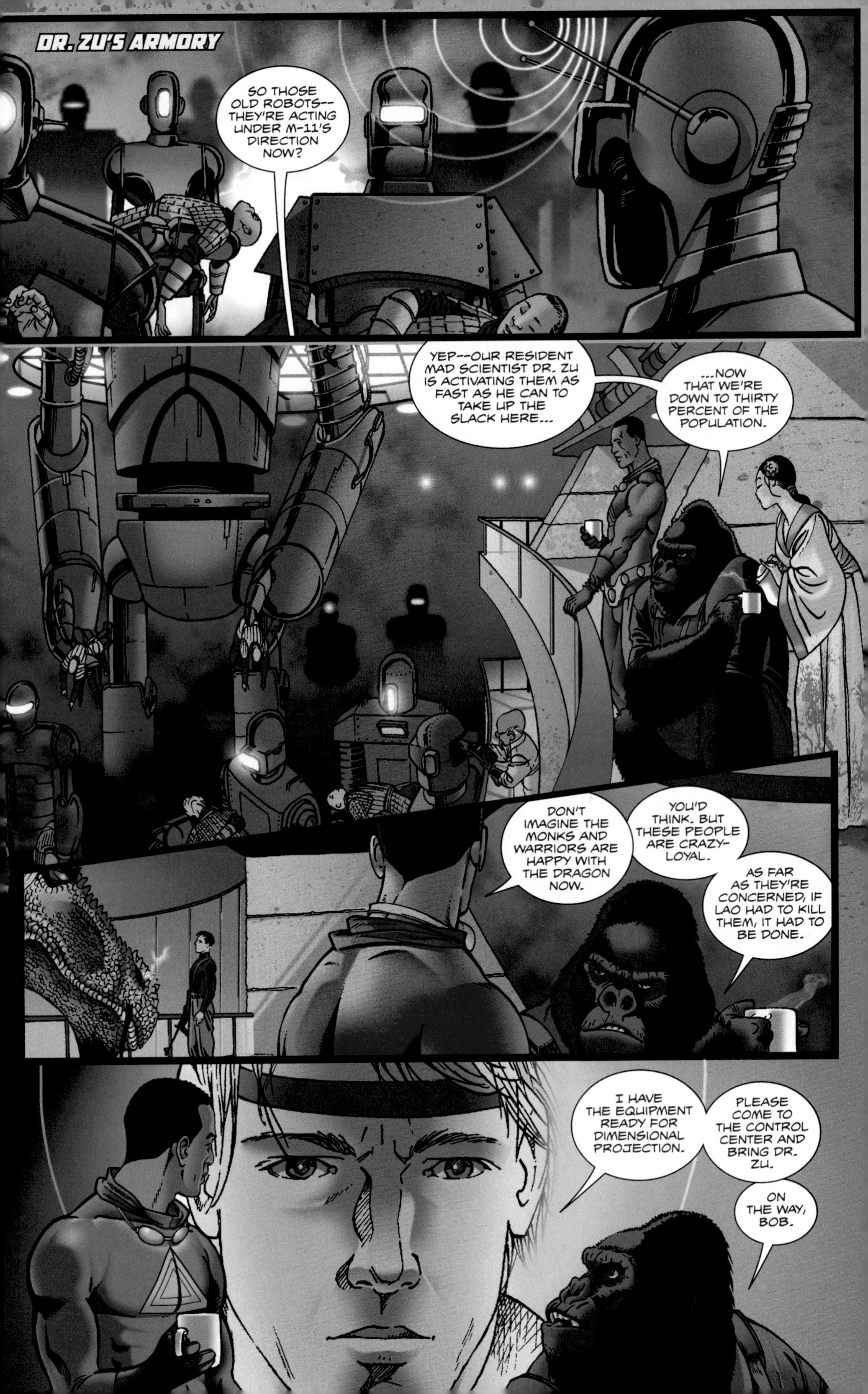
DR. ZU'S ARMORY
SO THOSE OLD ROBOTS--THEY'RE ACTING UNDER M-11'S DIRECTION NOW?
YEP--OUR RESIDENT MAD SCIENTIST DR. ZU IS ACTIVATING THEM AS FAST AS HE CAN TO TAKE UP THE SLACK HERE...
...NOW THAT WE'RE DOWN TO THIRTY PERCENT OF THE POPULATION.
DON'T IMAGINE THE MONKS AND WARRIORS ARE HAPPY WITH THE DRAGON NOW.
YOU'D THINK. BUT THESE PEOPLE ARE CRAZY-LOYAL.
AS FAR AS THEY'RE CONCERNED, IF LAO HAD TO KILL THEM, IT HAD TO BE DONE.
I HAVE THE EQUIPMENT READY FOR DIMENSIONAL PROJECTION.
PLEASE COME TO THE CONTROL CENTER AND BRING DR. ZU.
ON THE WAY, BOB.

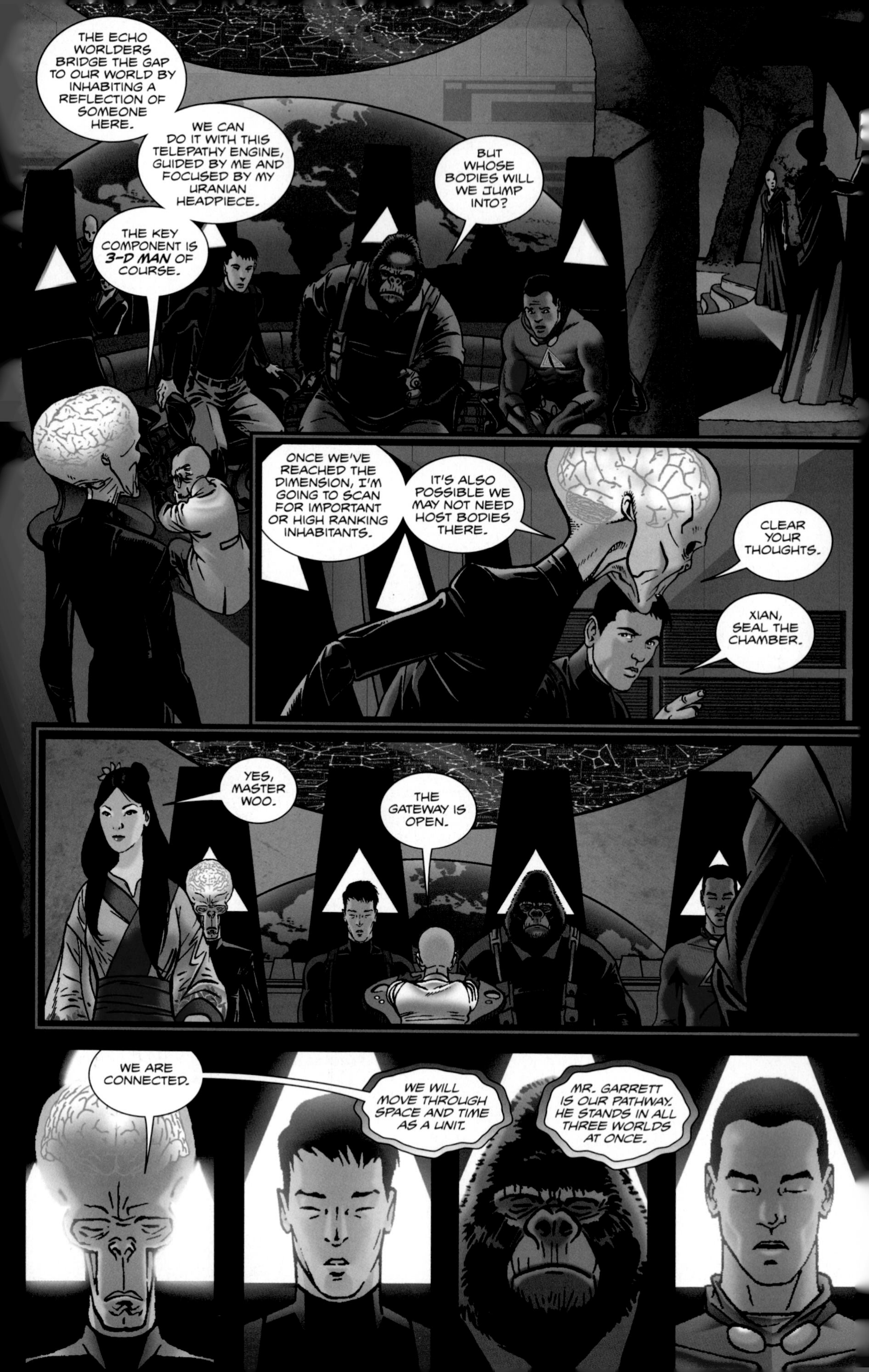
THE ECHO WORLDERS BRIDGE THE GAP TO OUR WORLD BY INHABITING A REFLECTION OF SOMEONE HERE.
WE CAN DO IT WITH THIS TELEPATHY ENGINE, GUIDED BY ME AND FOCUSED BY MY URANIAN HEADPIECE.
BUT WHOSE BODIES WILL WE JUMP INTO?
THE KEY COMPONENT IS **3-D MAN** OF COURSE.
ONCE WE'VE REACHED THE DIMENSION, I'M GOING TO SCAN FOR IMPORTANT OR HIGH RANKING INHABITANTS.
IT'S ALSO POSSIBLE WE MAY NOT NEED HOST BODIES THERE.
CLEAR YOUR THOUGHTS.
XIAN, SEAL THE CHAMBER.
YES, MASTER WOO.
THE GATEWAY IS OPEN.
WE ARE CONNECTED.
WE WILL MOVE THROUGH SPACE AND TIME AS A UNIT.
MR. GARRETT IS OUR PATHWAY. HE STANDS IN ALL THREE WORLDS AT ONCE.

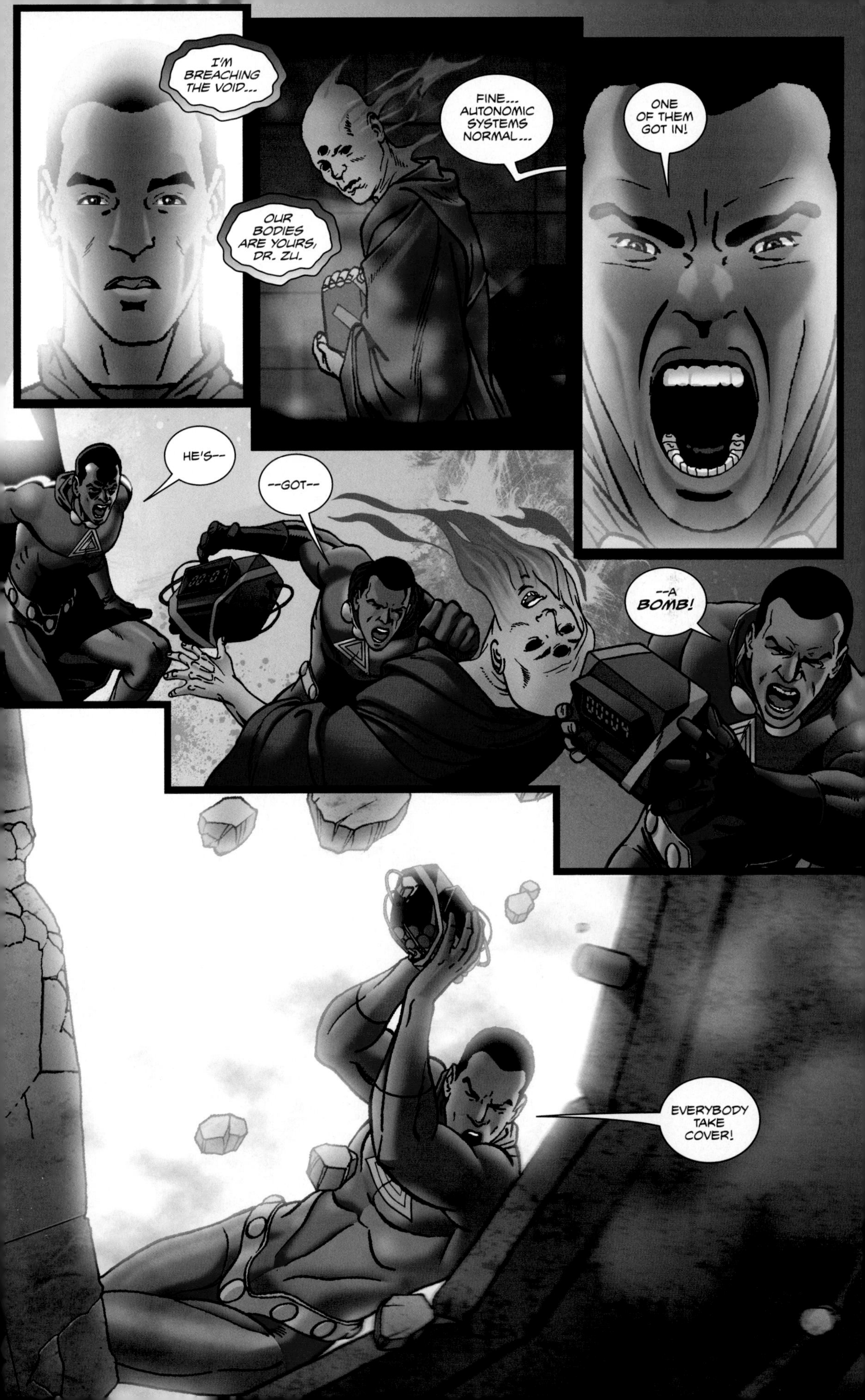

I'M BREACHING THE VOID...
OUR BODIES ARE YOURS, DR. ZU.
FINE... AUTONOMIC SYSTEMS NORMAL...
ONE OF THEM GOT IN!
HE'S--
--GOT--
--A BOMB!
EVERYBODY TAKE COVER!

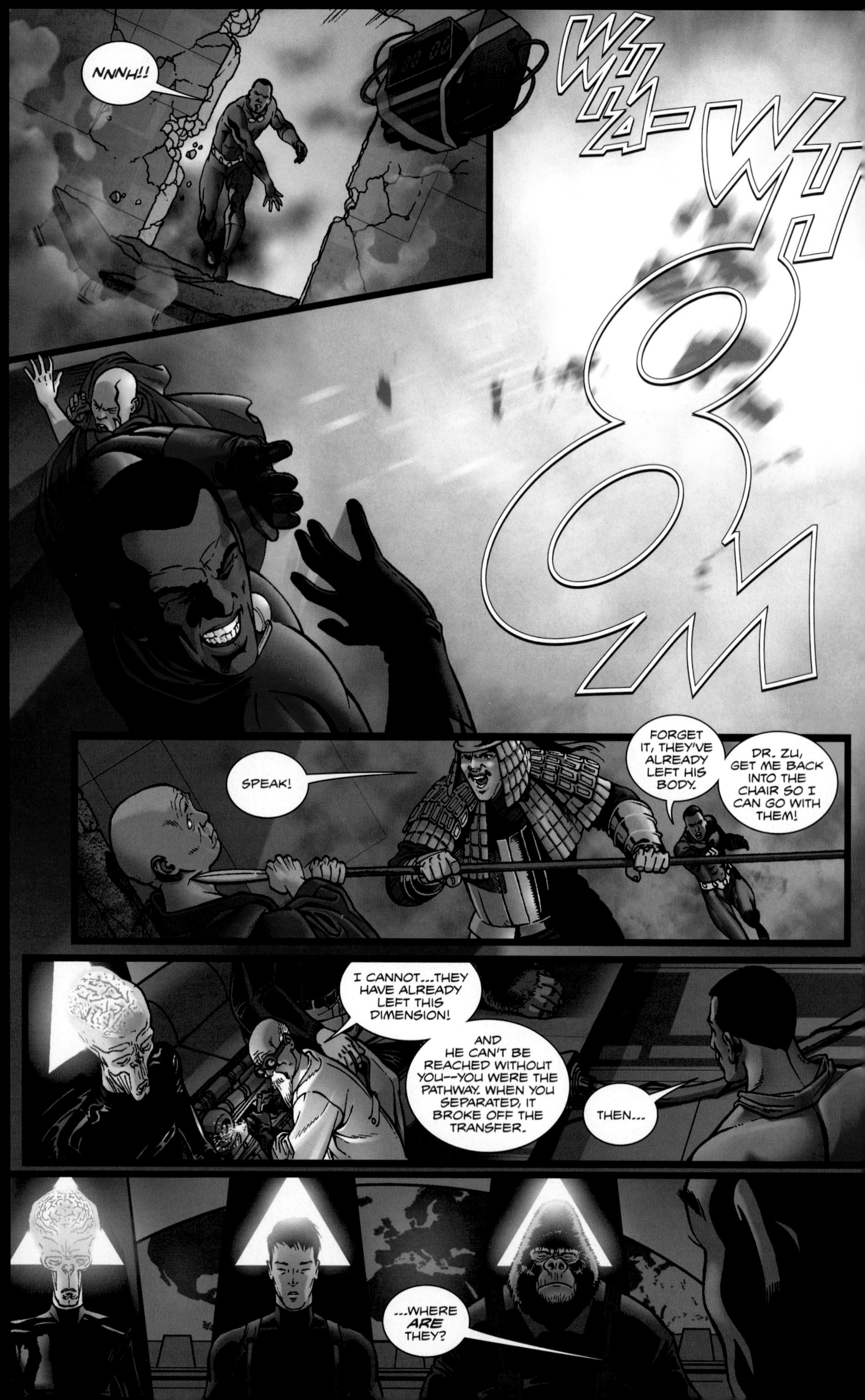
NNNH!!
WHA-WHHOOOM
SPEAK!
FORGET IT, THEY'VE ALREADY LEFT HIS BODY.
DR. ZU, GET ME BACK INTO THE CHAIR SO I CAN GO WITH THEM!
I CANNOT...THEY HAVE ALREADY LEFT THIS DIMENSION!
AND HE CAN'T BE REACHED WITHOUT YOU--YOU WERE THE PATHWAY. WHEN YOU SEPARATED, IT BROKE OFF THE TRANSFER.
THEN...
...WHERE ARE THEY?

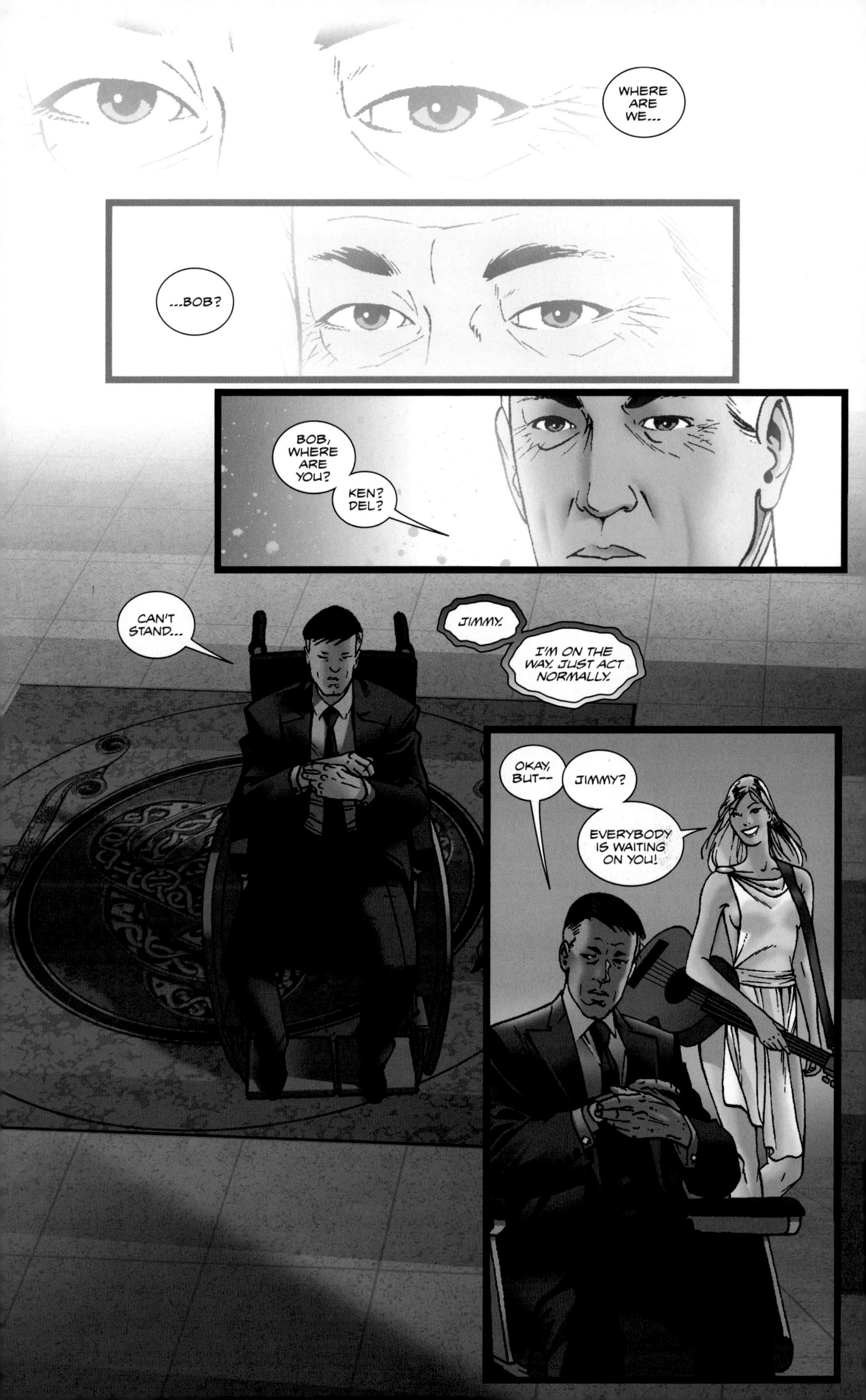
WHERE ARE WE...
...BOB?
BOB, WHERE ARE YOU?
KEN? DEL?
CAN'T STAND...
JIMMY.
I'M ON THE WAY. JUST ACT NORMALLY.
OKAY, BUT--
JIMMY?
EVERYBODY IS WAITING ON YOU!

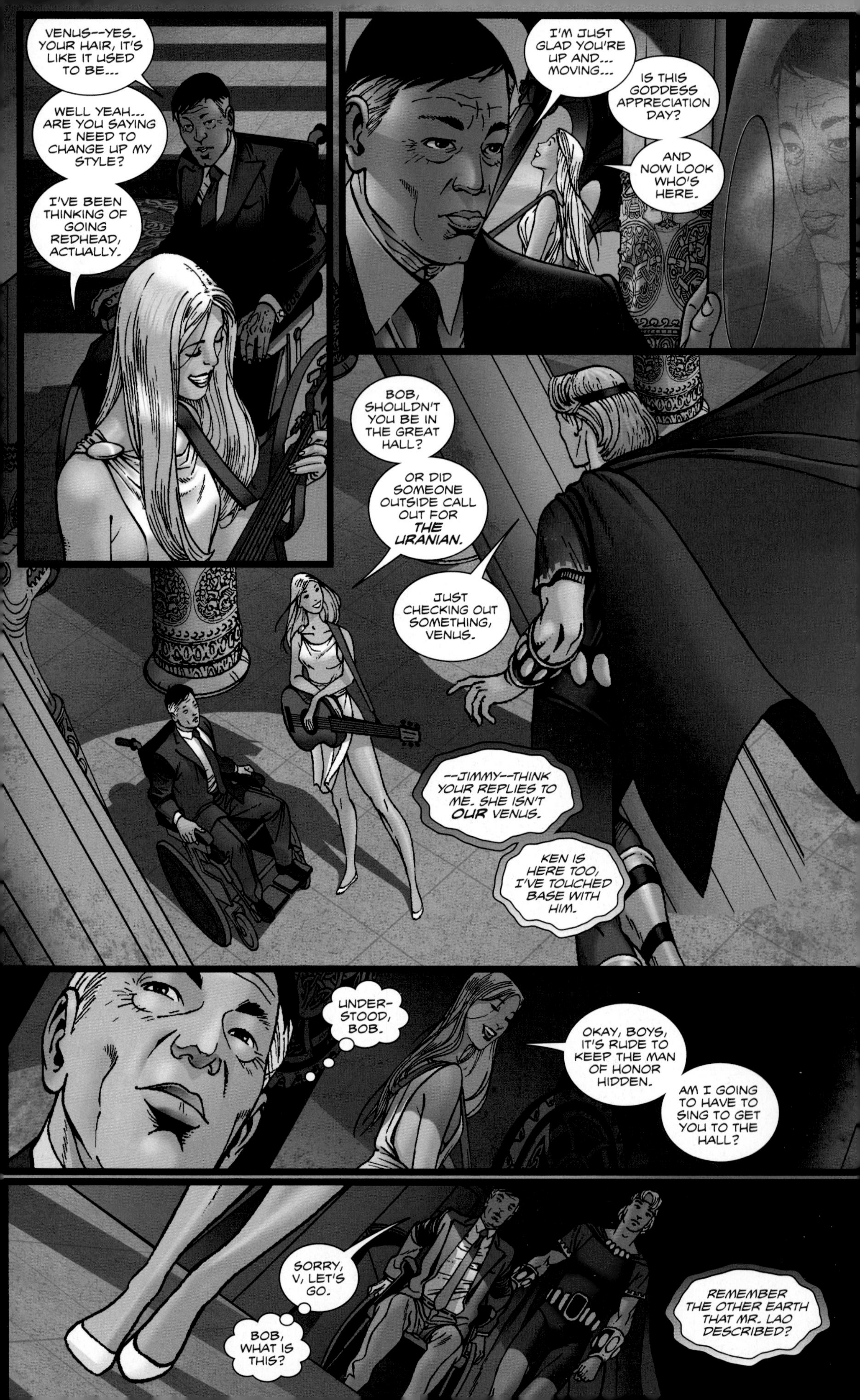
VENUS--YES. YOUR HAIR, IT'S LIKE IT USED TO BE...
WELL YEAH... ARE YOU SAYING I NEED TO CHANGE UP MY STYLE?
I'VE BEEN THINKING OF GOING REDHEAD, ACTUALLY.
I'M JUST GLAD YOU'RE UP AND... MOVING...
IS THIS GODDESS APPRECIATION DAY?
AND NOW LOOK WHO'S HERE.
BOB, SHOULDN'T YOU BE IN THE GREAT HALL?
OR DID SOMEONE OUTSIDE CALL OUT FOR *THE URANIAN*.
JUST CHECKING OUT SOMETHING, VENUS.
--JIMMY--THINK YOUR REPLIES TO ME. SHE ISN'T **OUR** VENUS.
KEN IS HERE TOO, I'VE TOUCHED BASE WITH HIM.
UNDER-STOOD, BOB.
OKAY, BOYS, IT'S RUDE TO KEEP THE MAN OF HONOR HIDDEN.
AM I GOING TO HAVE TO SING TO GET YOU TO THE HALL?
SORRY, V, LET'S GO.
BOB, WHAT IS THIS?
REMEMBER THE OTHER EARTH THAT MR. LAO DESCRIBED?

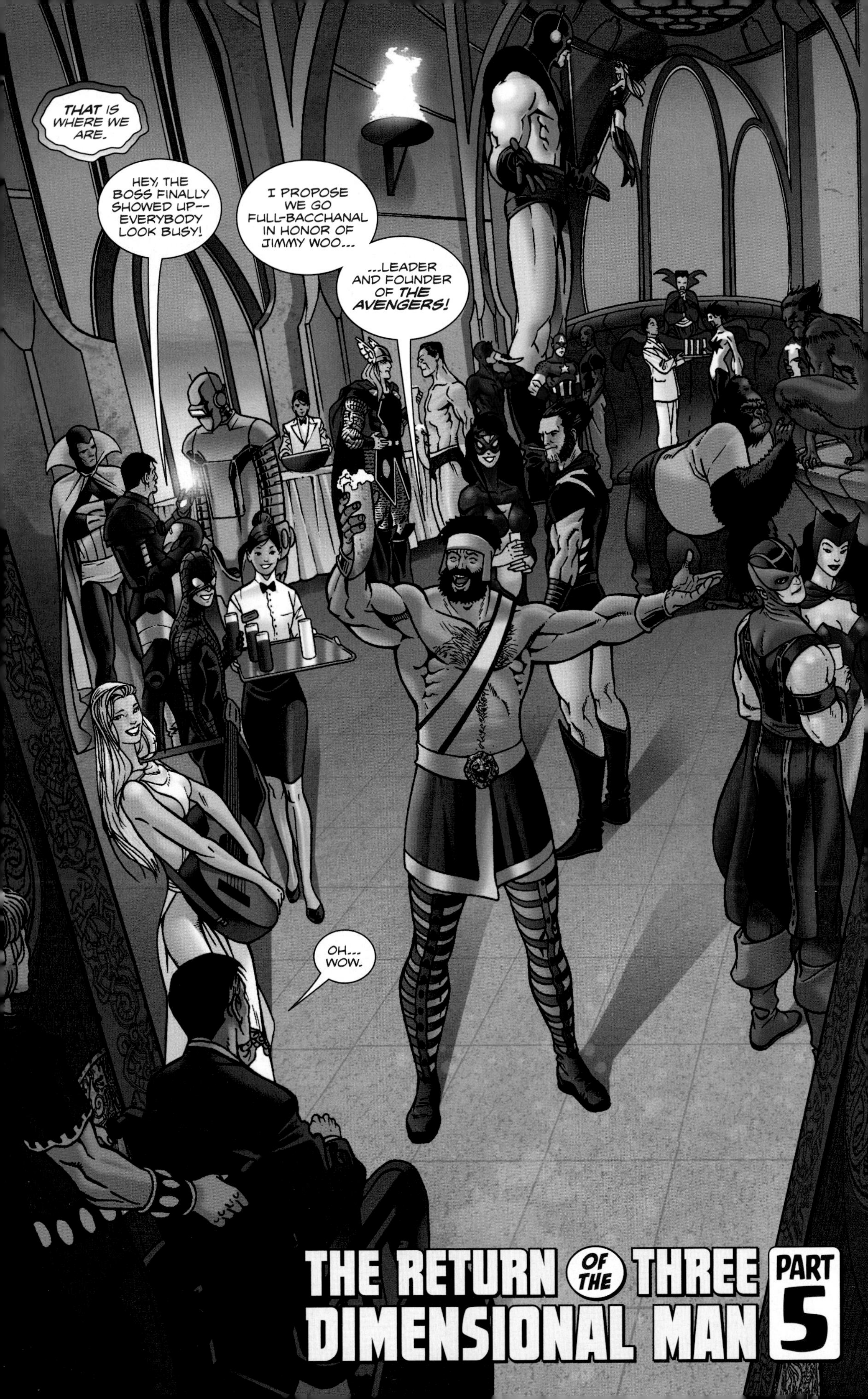
THAT IS WHERE WE ARE.
HEY, THE BOSS FINALLY SHOWED UP-- EVERYBODY LOOK BUSY!
I PROPOSE WE GO FULL-BACCHANAL IN HONOR OF JIMMY WOO...
...LEADER AND FOUNDER OF THE AVENGERS!
OH... WOW.
THE RETURN OF THE THREE DIMENSIONAL MAN PART 5

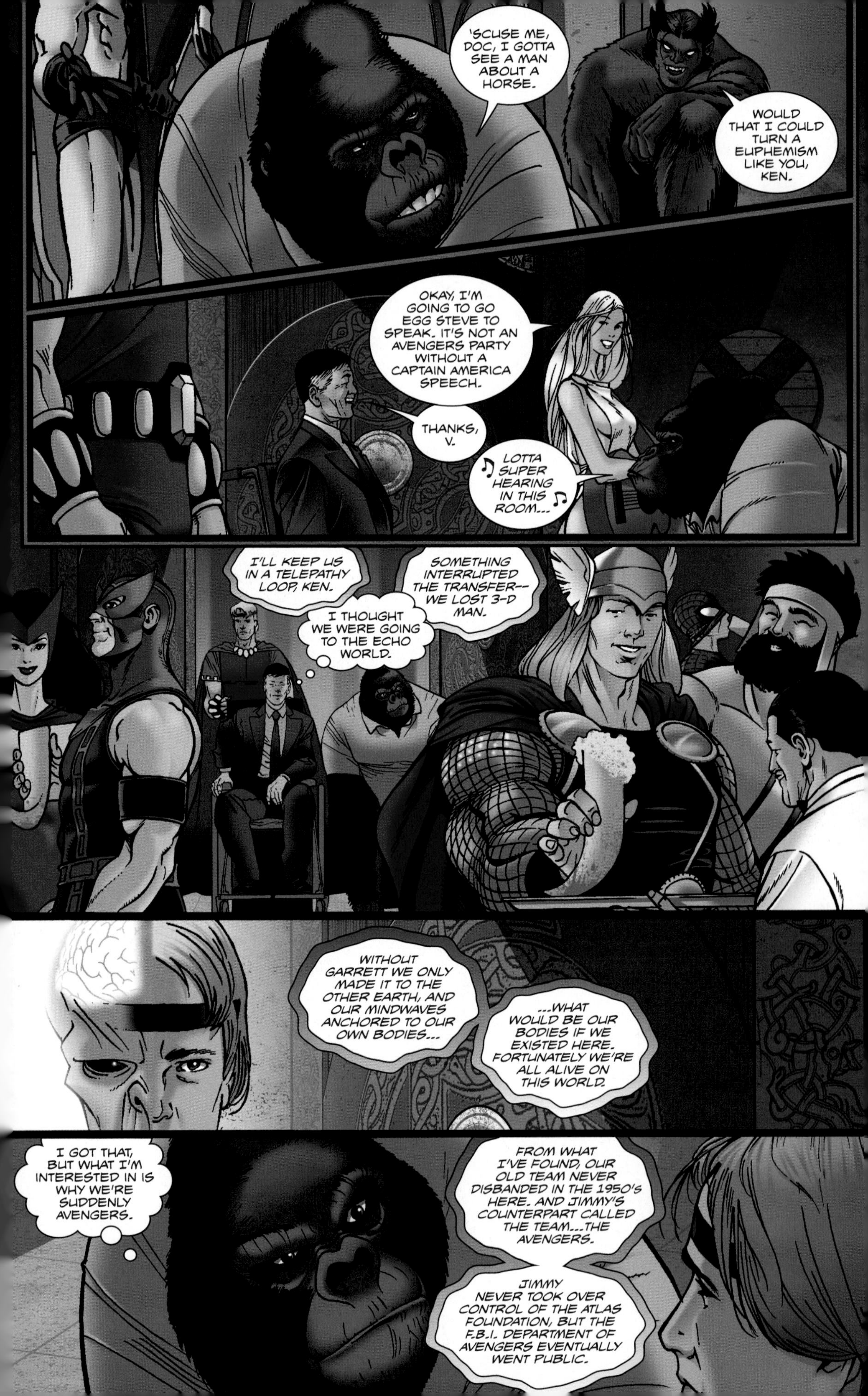
'SCUSE ME, DOC, I GOTTA SEE A MAN ABOUT A HORSE.
WOULD THAT I COULD TURN A EUPHEMISM LIKE YOU, KEN.
OKAY, I'M GOING TO GO EGG STEVE TO SPEAK. IT'S NOT AN AVENGERS PARTY WITHOUT A CAPTAIN AMERICA SPEECH.
THANKS, V.
♫ LOTTA SUPER HEARING IN THIS ROOM... ♫
I'LL KEEP US IN A TELEPATHY LOOP, KEN.
SOMETHING INTERRUPTED THE TRANSFER--WE LOST 3-D MAN.
I THOUGHT WE WERE GOING TO THE ECHO WORLD.
WITHOUT GARRETT WE ONLY MADE IT TO THE OTHER EARTH, AND OUR MINDWAVES ANCHORED TO OUR OWN BODIES...
...WHAT WOULD BE OUR BODIES IF WE EXISTED HERE. FORTUNATELY WE'RE ALL ALIVE ON THIS WORLD.
I GOT THAT, BUT WHAT I'M INTERESTED IN IS WHY WE'RE SUDDENLY AVENGERS.
FROM WHAT I'VE FOUND, OUR OLD TEAM NEVER DISBANDED IN THE 1950'S HERE. AND JIMMY'S COUNTERPART CALLED THE TEAM...THE AVENGERS.
JIMMY NEVER TOOK OVER CONTROL OF THE ATLAS FOUNDATION, BUT THE F.B.I. DEPARTMENT OF AVENGERS EVENTUALLY WENT PUBLIC.

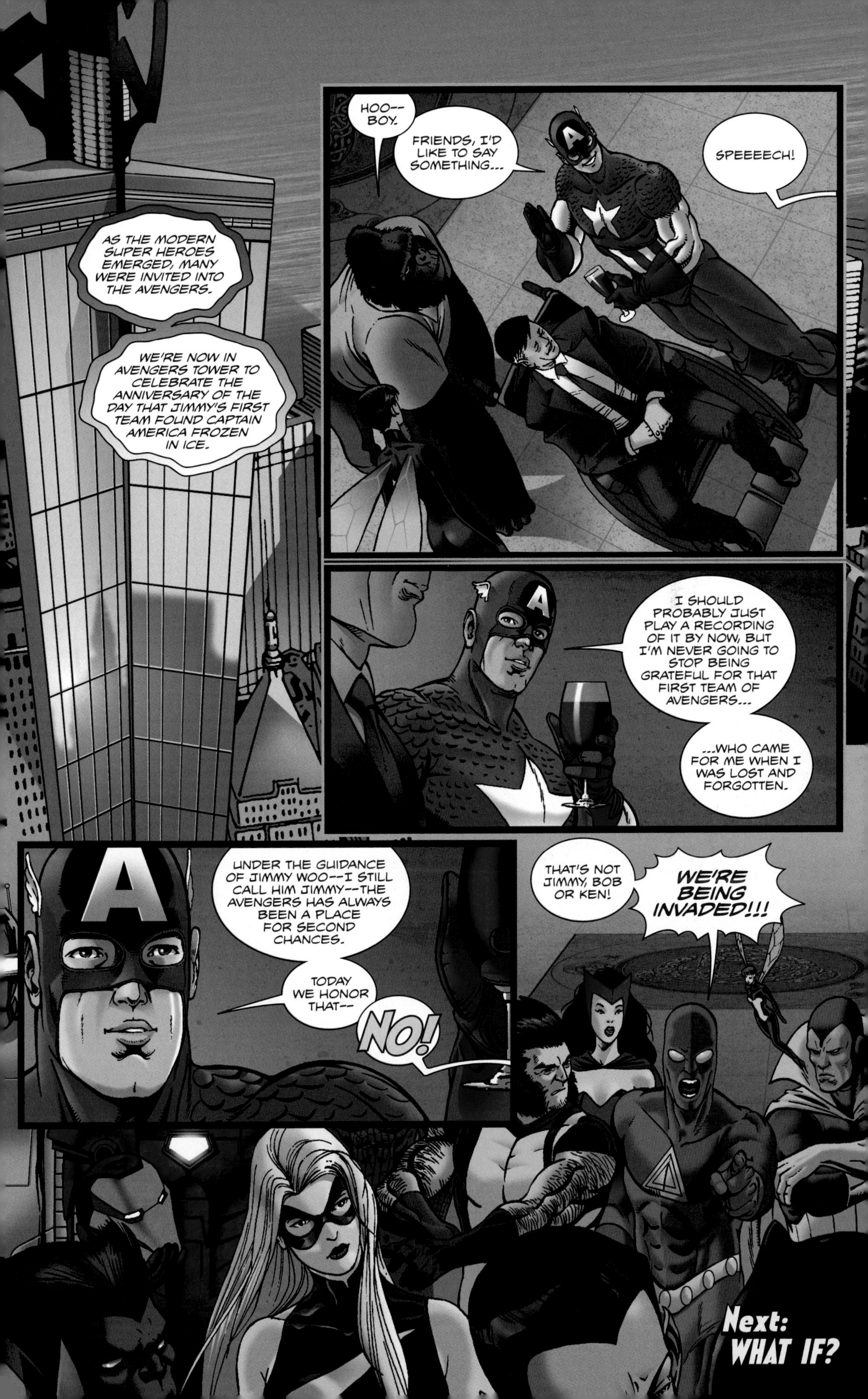
AS THE MODERN SUPER HEROES EMERGED, MANY WERE INVITED INTO THE AVENGERS.
WE'RE NOW IN AVENGERS TOWER TO CELEBRATE THE ANNIVERSARY OF THE DAY THAT JIMMY'S FIRST TEAM FOUND CAPTAIN AMERICA FROZEN IN ICE.
HOO--BOY.
FRIENDS, I'D LIKE TO SAY SOMETHING...
SPEEEECH!
I SHOULD PROBABLY JUST PLAY A RECORDING OF IT BY NOW, BUT I'M NEVER GOING TO STOP BEING GRATEFUL FOR THAT FIRST TEAM OF AVENGERS...
...WHO CAME FOR ME WHEN I WAS LOST AND FORGOTTEN.
UNDER THE GUIDANCE OF JIMMY WOO--I STILL CALL HIM JIMMY--THE AVENGERS HAS ALWAYS BEEN A PLACE FOR SECOND CHANCES.
TODAY WE HONOR THAT--
NO!
THAT'S NOT JIMMY, BOB OR KEN!
WE'RE BEING INVADED!!!
Next: WHAT IF?

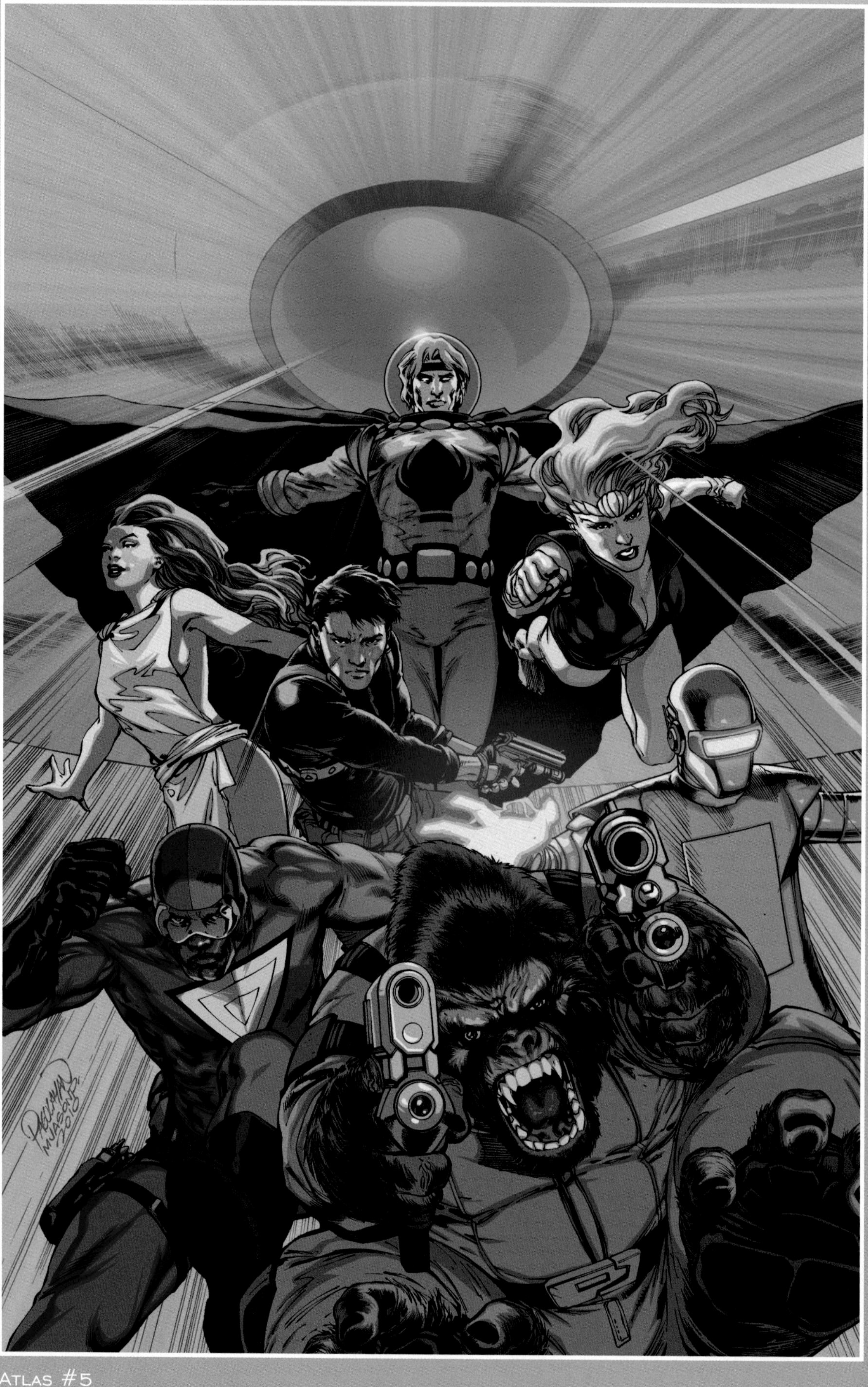

Atlas #5

A SPY. A SPACEMAN. A SIREN. A MERMAID. A ROBOT. A GORILLA.

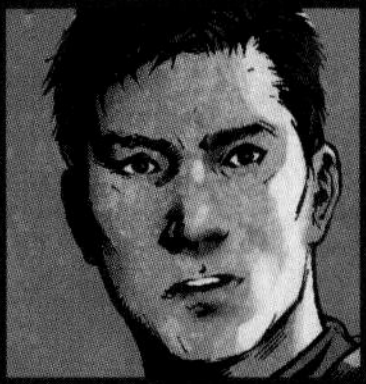

JIMMY WOO
LEADER OF THE SECRET EMPIRE KNOWN AS ATLAS

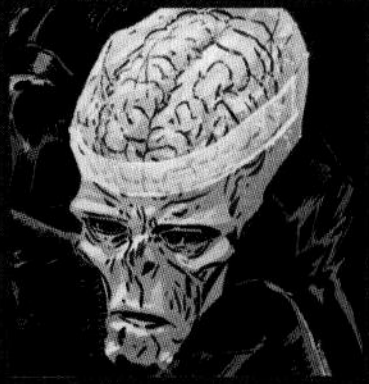

THE URANIAN
BOB GRAYSON, TELEPATH AND TECH

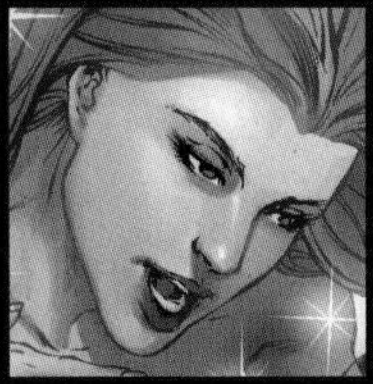

VENUS
AN HONEST-TO-GOSH SIREN

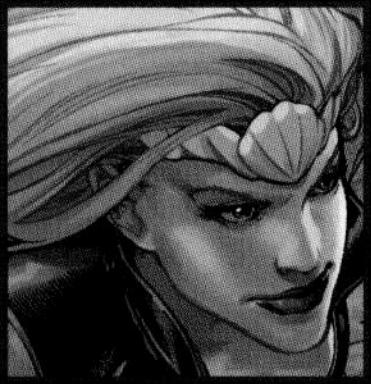

NAMORA
ATLANTEAN PRINCESS, COUSIN OF NAMOR

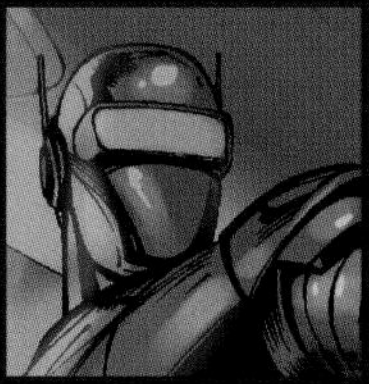

M-11
KILLER ROBOT, "REFORMED"

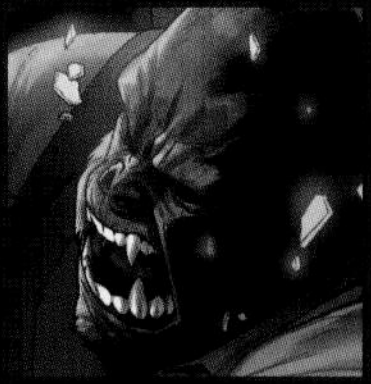

GORILLA-MAN
KEN HALE, GUY THAT'S A GORILLA

THEY ARE A TEAM OF 1950'S ADVENTURERS RE-FORMED TO BATTLE EARTH'S GREATEST THREATS. THEY ARE THE AGENTS OF

ATLAS

I am Chang Li-Ten. Due to recent events, Master Woo has asked this Humble One to make Atlas log entries for what has become a most crucial time in this secret empire's history.

Our numbers in the Hidden City have been greatly depleted. Many of our warriors were invaded by hostile aliens from another dimension of time and space. To protect the Inner Circle and the secrets of the Eternal Empire of Genghis Khan, our most honorable royal counsel The Great Dragon Lao sent the possessed to join the spirits with his righteous flame.

The Inner Circle suffered greatly—the Atlantean-Human Namora was nearly killed as was the goddess Venus. Both are recovering in the Royal Infirmary. The Uranian Bob Grayson had his environment suit destroyed by the possessed Namora, revealing that he had been hiding his true appearance, which had been greatly transformed to live in the depths of the seventh planet.

I was fortunate enough to briefly capture one of the invading minds, which Grayson gathered information from. With this knowledge, he built a projection system to allow Master Woo, General Hale, the Three Dimensional Man and himself to breach the great void and investigate the other-dimensional world of our enemy.

Yet I now hear this journey was interrupted. Another Echo Worlder infiltrated our control room, and was dispatched by the Three Dimensional Man. In breaking the circuit which required him, we now do not know where the spirits of our Inner Circle reside...

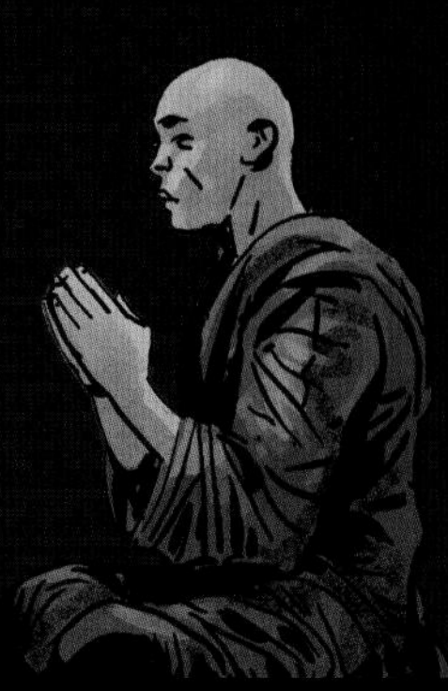

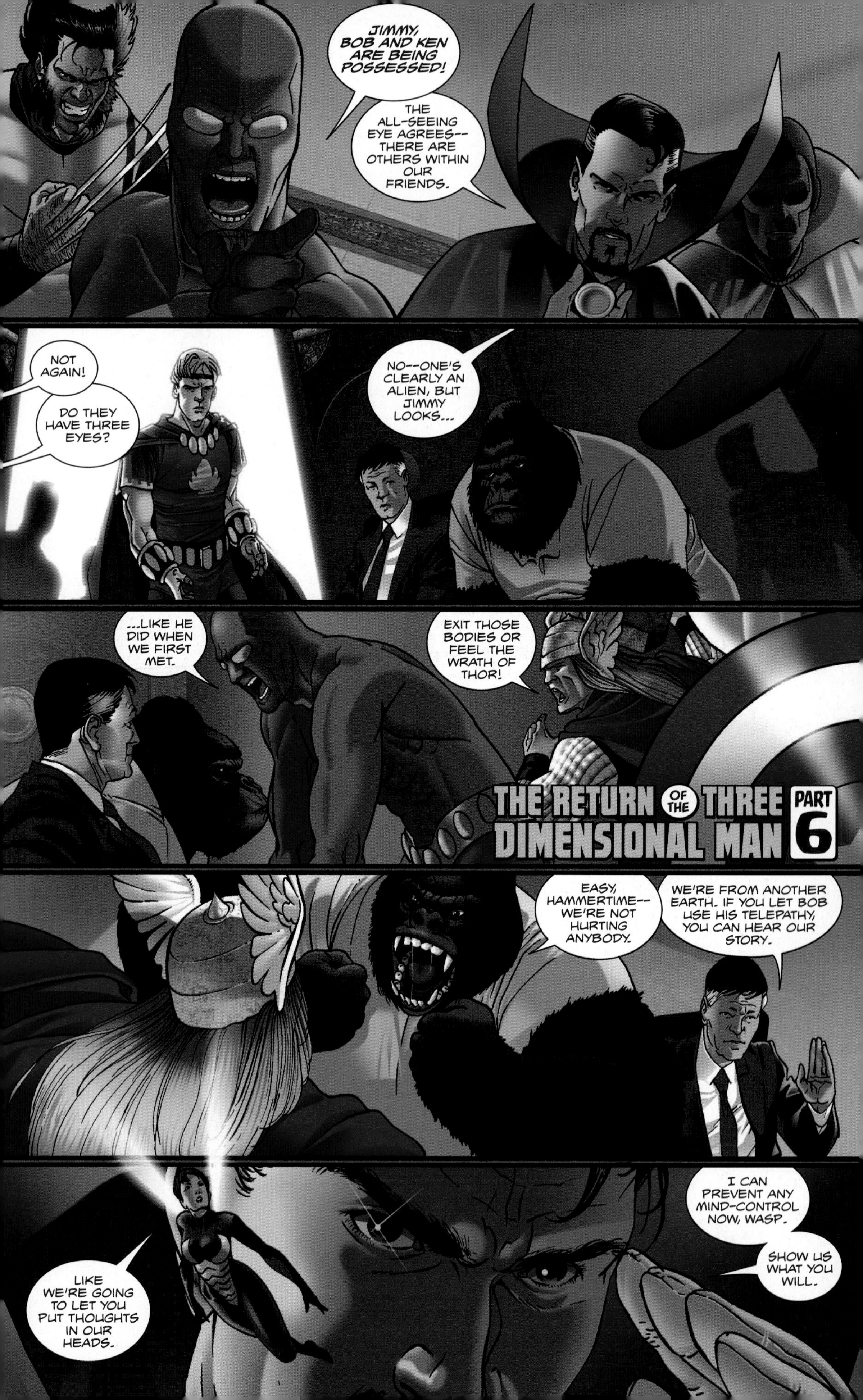
JIMMY, BOB AND KEN ARE BEING POSSESSED!
THE ALL-SEEING EYE AGREES-- THERE ARE OTHERS WITHIN OUR FRIENDS.
NOT AGAIN!
DO THEY HAVE THREE EYES?
NO--ONE'S CLEARLY AN ALIEN, BUT JIMMY LOOKS...
...LIKE HE DID WHEN WE FIRST MET.
EXIT THOSE BODIES OR FEEL THE WRATH OF THOR!
THE RETURN OF THE THREE DIMENSIONAL MAN PART 6
EASY, HAMMERTIME-- WE'RE NOT HURTING ANYBODY.
WE'RE FROM ANOTHER EARTH. IF YOU LET BOB USE HIS TELEPATHY, YOU CAN HEAR OUR STORY.
LIKE WE'RE GOING TO LET YOU PUT THOUGHTS IN OUR HEADS.
I CAN PREVENT ANY MIND-CONTROL NOW, WASP.
SHOW US WHAT YOU WILL.

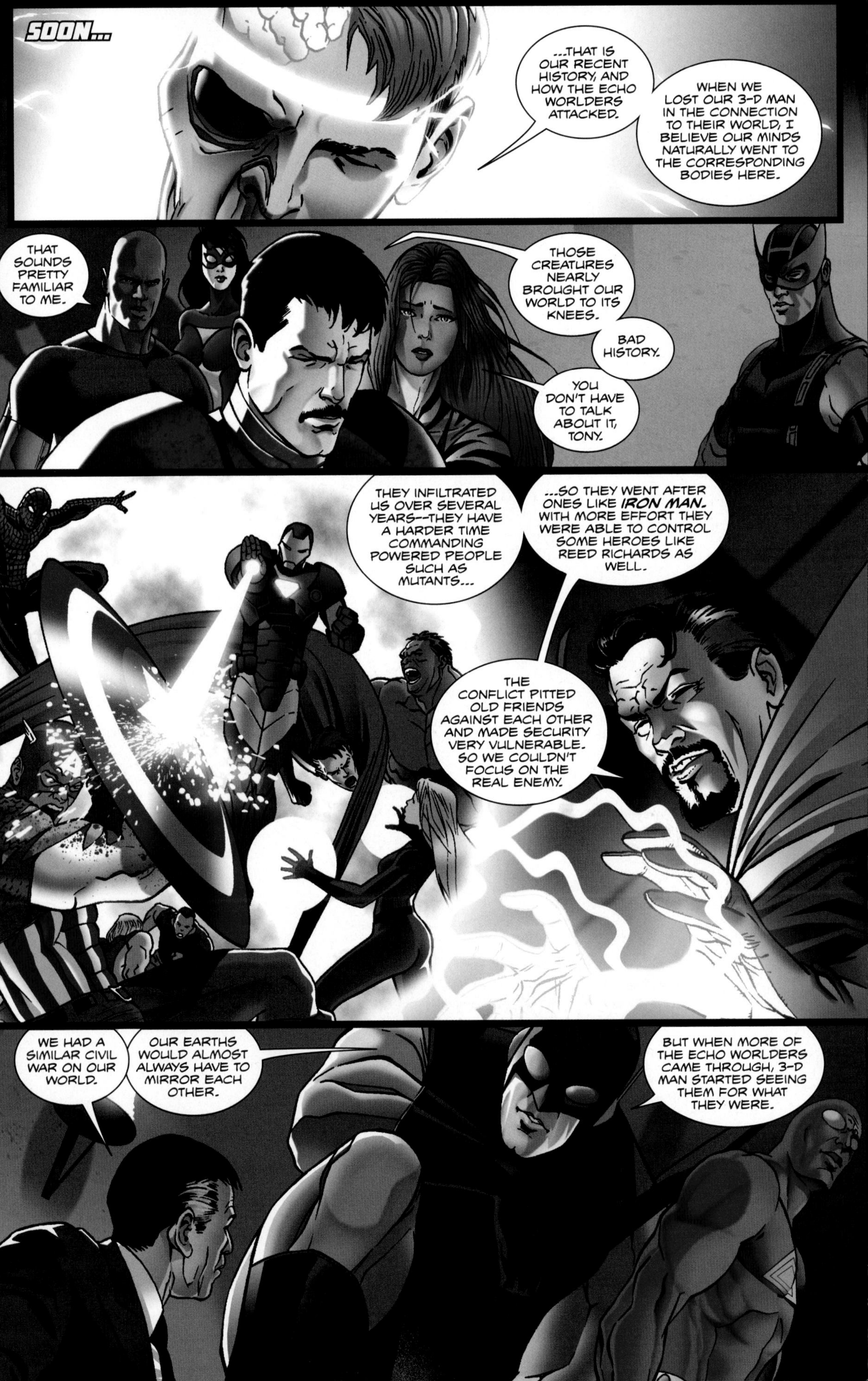
SOON...
...THAT IS OUR RECENT HISTORY, AND HOW THE ECHO WORLDERS ATTACKED.
WHEN WE LOST OUR 3-D MAN IN THE CONNECTION TO THEIR WORLD, I BELIEVE OUR MINDS NATURALLY WENT TO THE CORRESPONDING BODIES HERE.
THAT SOUNDS PRETTY FAMILIAR TO ME.
THOSE CREATURES NEARLY BROUGHT OUR WORLD TO ITS KNEES.
BAD HISTORY.
YOU DON'T HAVE TO TALK ABOUT IT, TONY.
THEY INFILTRATED US OVER SEVERAL YEARS--THEY HAVE A HARDER TIME COMMANDING POWERED PEOPLE SUCH AS MUTANTS...
...SO THEY WENT AFTER ONES LIKE *IRON MAN*. WITH MORE EFFORT THEY WERE ABLE TO CONTROL SOME HEROES LIKE REED RICHARDS AS WELL.
THE CONFLICT PITTED OLD FRIENDS AGAINST EACH OTHER AND MADE SECURITY VERY VULNERABLE. SO WE COULDN'T FOCUS ON THE REAL ENEMY.
WE HAD A SIMILAR CIVIL WAR ON OUR WORLD.
OUR EARTHS WOULD ALMOST ALWAYS HAVE TO MIRROR EACH OTHER.
BUT WHEN MORE OF THE ECHO WORLDERS CAME THROUGH, 3-D MAN STARTED SEEING THEM FOR WHAT THEY WERE.

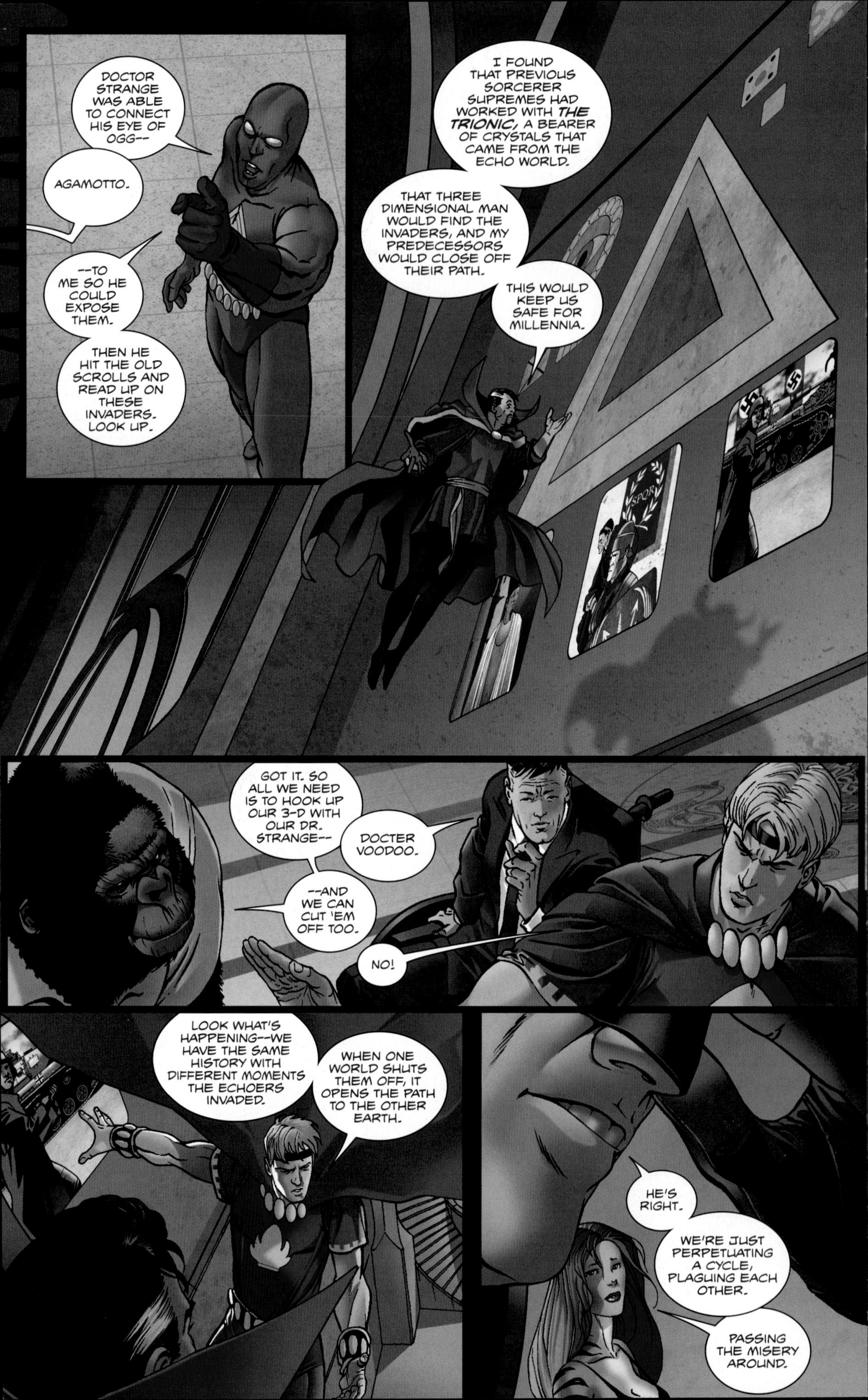
DOCTOR STRANGE WAS ABLE TO CONNECT HIS EYE OF OGG--
AGAMOTTO.
--TO ME SO HE COULD EXPOSE THEM.
THEN HE HIT THE OLD SCROLLS AND READ UP ON THESE INVADERS. LOOK UP.
I FOUND THAT PREVIOUS SORCERER SUPREMES HAD WORKED WITH THE TRIONIC, A BEARER OF CRYSTALS THAT CAME FROM THE ECHO WORLD.
THAT THREE DIMENSIONAL MAN WOULD FIND THE INVADERS, AND MY PREDECESSORS WOULD CLOSE OFF THEIR PATH.
THIS WOULD KEEP US SAFE FOR MILLENNIA.
SPQR
GOT IT. SO ALL WE NEED IS TO HOOK UP OUR 3-D WITH OUR DR. STRANGE--
DOCTER VOODOO.
--AND WE CAN CUT 'EM OFF TOO.
NO!
LOOK WHAT'S HAPPENING--WE HAVE THE SAME HISTORY WITH DIFFERENT MOMENTS THE ECHOERS INVADED.
WHEN ONE WORLD SHUTS THEM OFF, IT OPENS THE PATH TO THE OTHER EARTH.
HE'S RIGHT.
WE'RE JUST PERPETUATING A CYCLE, PLAGUING EACH OTHER.
PASSING THE MISERY AROUND.

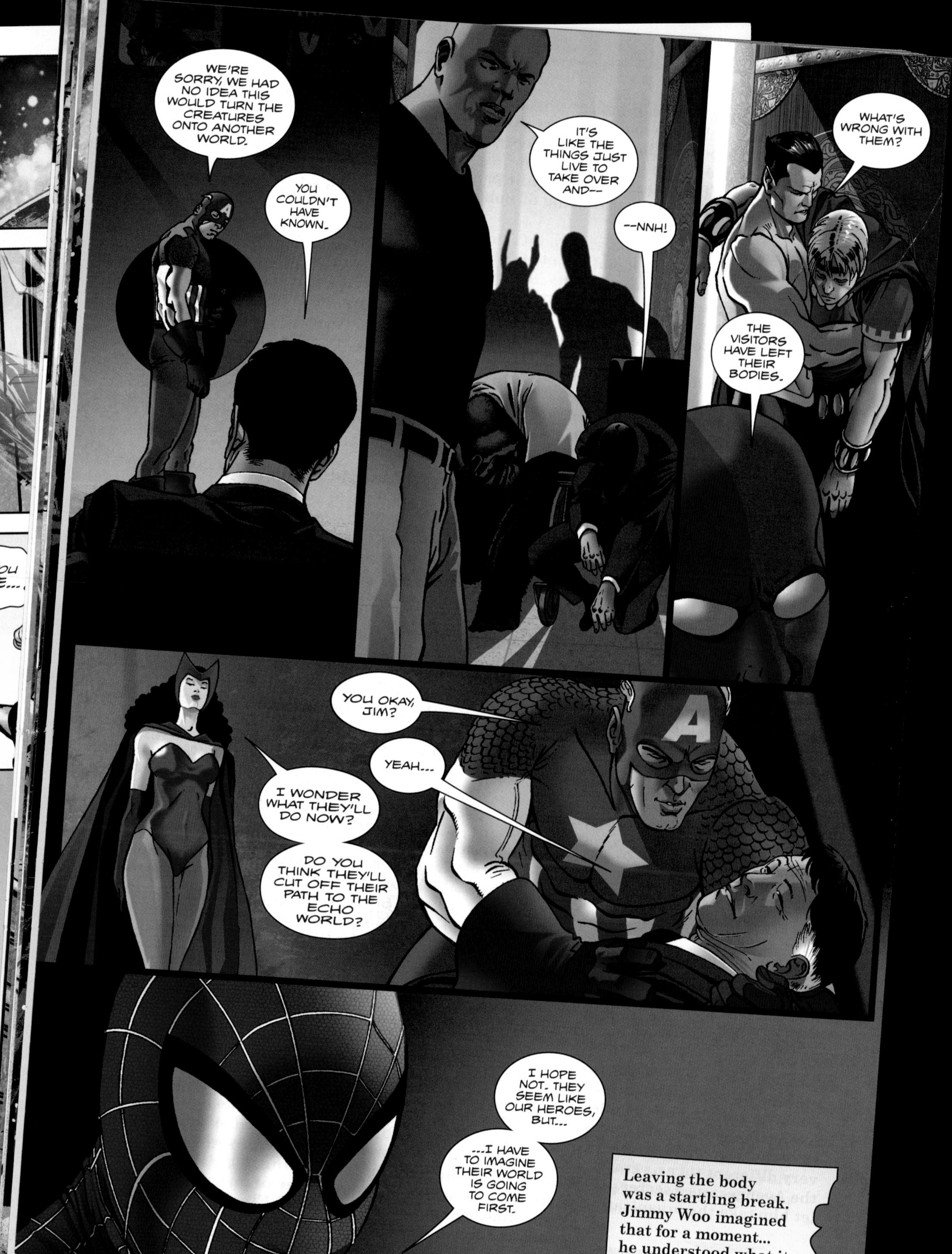
WE'RE SORRY, WE HAD NO IDEA THIS WOULD TURN THE CREATURES ONTO ANOTHER WORLD.
YOU COULDN'T HAVE KNOWN.
IT'S LIKE THE THINGS JUST LIVE TO TAKE OVER AND--
--NNH!
WHAT'S WRONG WITH THEM?
THE VISITORS HAVE LEFT THEIR BODIES.
YOU OKAY, JIM?
YEAH...
I WONDER WHAT THEY'LL DO NOW?
DO YOU THINK THEY'LL CUT OFF THEIR PATH TO THE ECHO WORLD?
I HOPE NOT. THEY SEEM LIKE OUR HEROES, BUT...
...I HAVE TO IMAGINE THEIR WORLD IS GOING TO COME FIRST.
Leaving the body was a startling break. Jimmy Woo imagined that for a moment... he understood what it would be like to die.

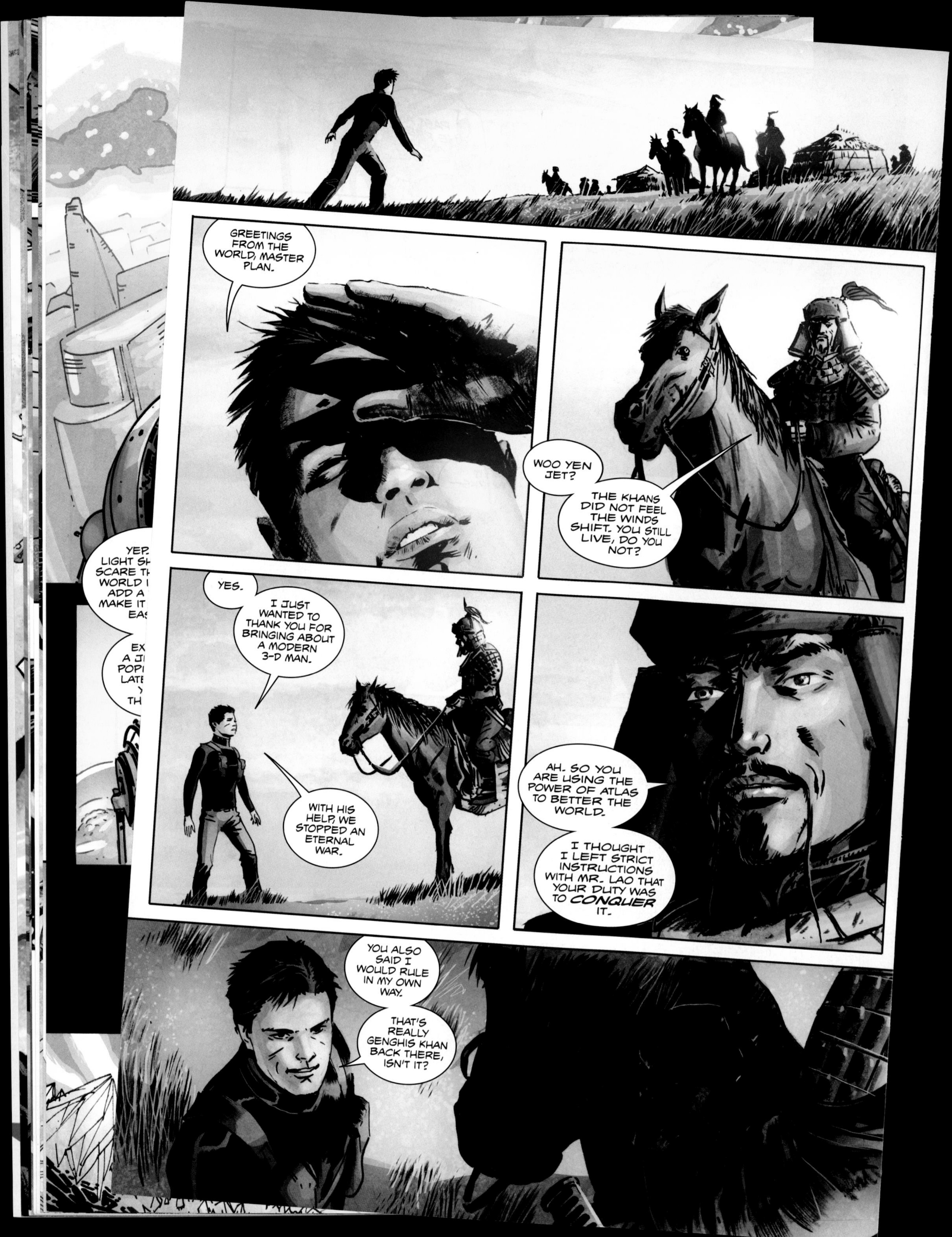

GREETINGS FROM THE WORLD, MASTER PLAN.
WOO YEN JET?
THE KHANS DID NOT FEEL THE WINDS SHIFT. YOU STILL LIVE, DO YOU NOT?
YES.
I JUST WANTED TO THANK YOU FOR BRINGING ABOUT A MODERN 3-D MAN.
WITH HIS HELP, WE STOPPED AN ETERNAL WAR.
AH. SO YOU ARE USING THE POWER OF ATLAS TO BETTER THE WORLD.
I THOUGHT I LEFT STRICT INSTRUCTIONS WITH MR. LAO THAT YOUR DUTY WAS TO CONQUER IT.
YOU ALSO SAID I WOULD RULE IN MY OWN WAY.
THAT'S REALLY GENGHIS KHAN BACK THERE, ISN'T IT?

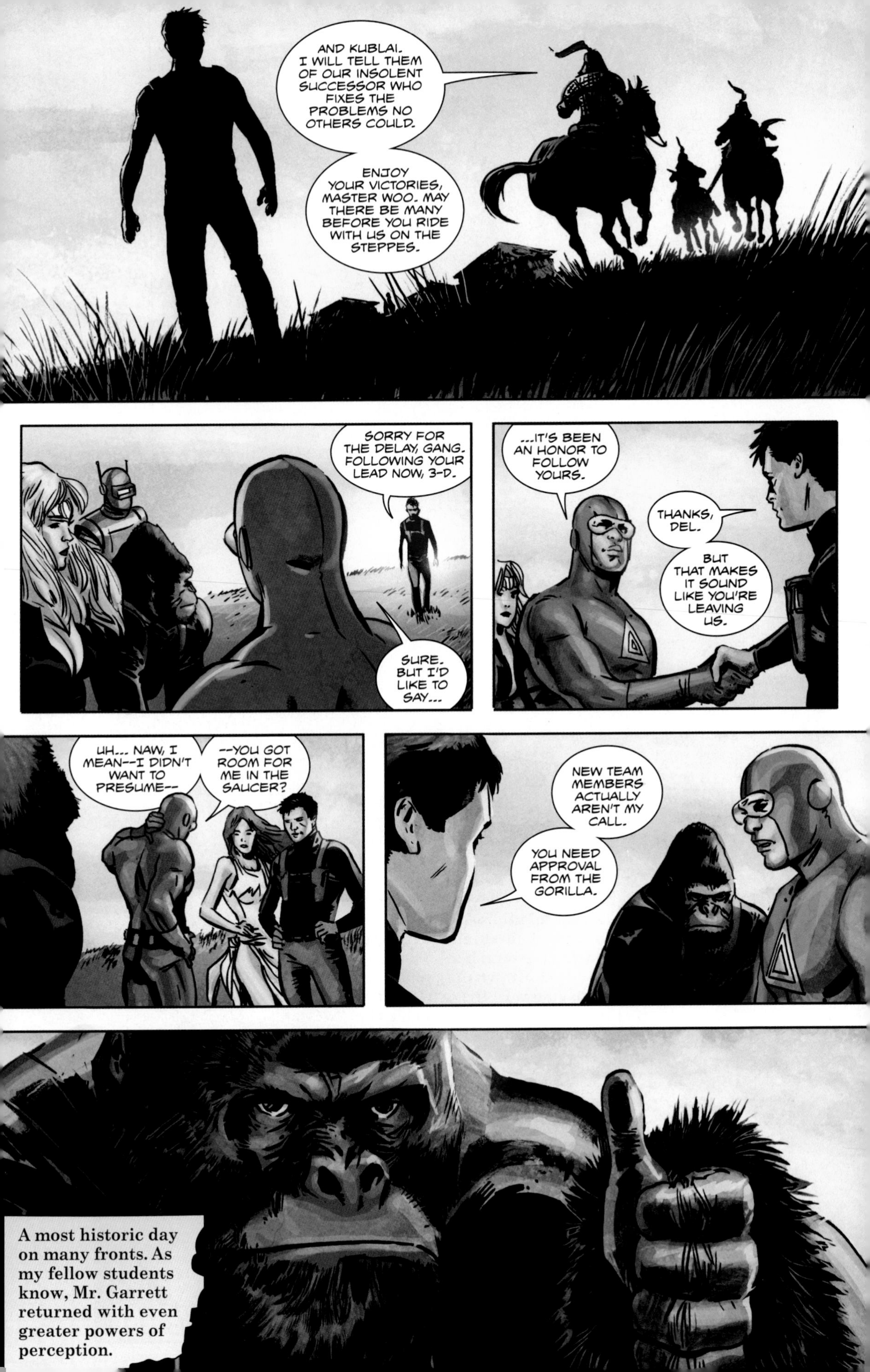
AND KUBLAI. I WILL TELL THEM OF OUR INSOLENT SUCCESSOR WHO FIXES THE PROBLEMS NO OTHERS COULD.
ENJOY YOUR VICTORIES, MASTER WOO. MAY THERE BE MANY BEFORE YOU RIDE WITH US ON THE STEPPES.
SORRY FOR THE DELAY, GANG. FOLLOWING YOUR LEAD NOW, 3-D.
SURE. BUT I'D LIKE TO SAY...
...IT'S BEEN AN HONOR TO FOLLOW YOURS.
THANKS, DEL.
BUT THAT MAKES IT SOUND LIKE YOU'RE LEAVING US.
UH... NAW, I MEAN--I DIDN'T WANT TO PRESUME--
--YOU GOT ROOM FOR ME IN THE SAUCER?
NEW TEAM MEMBERS ACTUALLY AREN'T MY CALL.
YOU NEED APPROVAL FROM THE GORILLA.
A most historic day on many fronts. As my fellow students know, Mr. Garrett returned with even greater powers of perception.

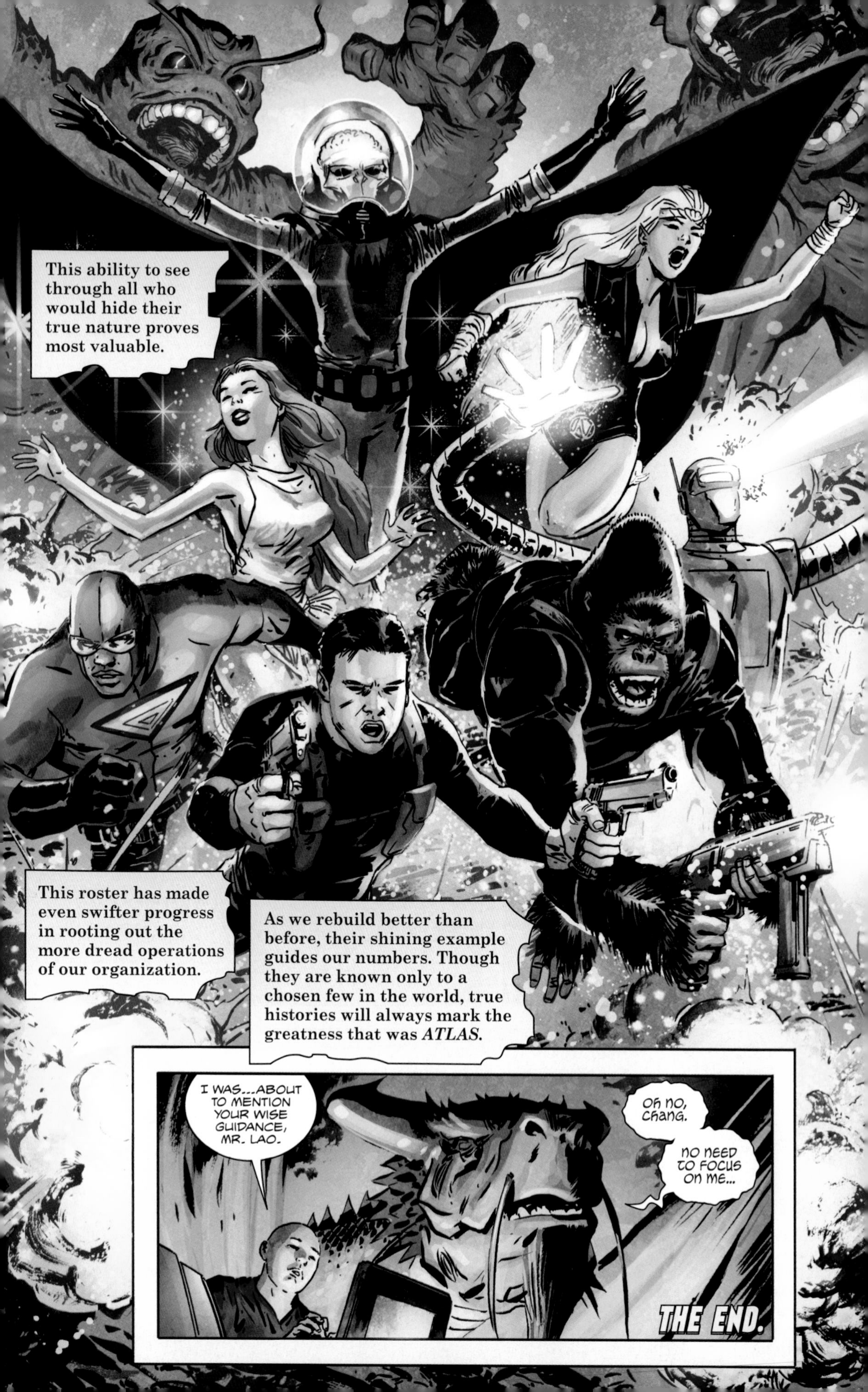
This ability to see through all who would hide their true nature proves most valuable.
This roster has made even swifter progress in rooting out the more dread operations of our organization.
As we rebuild better than before, their shining example guides our numbers. Though they are known only to a chosen few in the world, true histories will always mark the greatness that was *ATLAS*.
I WAS...ABOUT TO MENTION YOUR WISE GUIDANCE, MR. LAO.
OH NO, CHANG.
NO NEED TO FOCUS ON ME...
THE END.

3-D MAN (GARRETT)

HISTORY: A gifted young sprinter, Delroy Garrett, Jr. won three Olympic gold medals before he was exposed as a steroid user. Stripped of his awards and livelihood, Garrett sought new direction in the Triune Understanding, a philosophical movement that preached the fulfilment of one's innate potential through balancing various aspects of environment and self. Unbeknownst to Garrett, however, the seemingly benevolent Triune leader Jonathan Tremont was a power-hungry narcissist with a secret agenda built around an alien menace known as the Triple-Evil. When the Triple-Evil first manifested, the universe had formed three cosmic energy shards as "cosmic antibodies" designed to neutralize it; one of these shards empowered an alien hero slain and absorbed by the Triple-Evil. The other two shards landed on Earth, where one empowered the 3-D Man (a triple-powered super hero formed by the merger of brothers Hal and Chuck Chandler) in the 1950s. When a long-retired Hal Chandler sought the third shard in recent years, he came to the Himalayas, where a then-obscure Tremont arranged to serve as Chandler's guide. Having had prophetic dreams of the shard but needing Chandler to locate it, Tremont assaulted and imprisoned Chandler shortly after they found the third shard. Tremont soon mastered the third shard's energies, but having foreseen the coming of the Triple-Evil, he felt he must amass more power to face it. Tremont founded the Triune Understanding movement, secretly using his shard-derived abilities to drain spiritual energy from his unwitting followers as well as from the captive Chandler. When Garrett joined the Triunes, Tremont sensed the ex-athlete was spiritually similar to the Chandler brothers and saw an opportunity to create a powerful servant. After months of Triune studies and rituals designed to soothe Garrett's troubled spirit and make it more receptive, Tremont succeeded in transferring the Chandler brothers' energies into Garrett, who unwittingly absorbed the Chandlers' dormant spirits as well. Unaware of the Chandlers' involvement in this process, Garrett believed his Triune beliefs and training had unlocked his own latent superhuman potential, and he became the costumed hero Triathlon while serving as a celebrity spokesman for the Triune Understanding. Like the 3-D Man, Garrett had superhuman physical abilities three times as formidable as those of an athlete in peak human condition.

While aiding the Avengers against rogue arms dealer Moses Magnum, Triathlon worked well with the group; however, Tremont's plans soon came into conflict with the team, albeit covertly at first. Tremont's own quasi-resurrected dead brothers served him as Lord Templar and Pagan, two seemingly unconnected superhuman menaces whose apparently random crimes were designed to undermine public faith in traditional institutions and boost Triune recruiting. After clashes with both Templar and Pagan, the Avengers traced Templar to a Triune Understanding facility, where Triathlon and most of the other Triune followers present resented the Avengers' intrusion and refused to allow any search of the premises, fearing the heroes might be trying to implicate them in a crime. Before the dispute could be settled, Tremont had Pagan attack the site as a distraction, holding off all the heroes single-handedly until Lord Templar appeared and "defeated" Pagan with apparent ease, making the Avengers look weak by comparison. Tremont's subsequent speech subtly implied that the Avengers were persecuting the Understanding to mask their own inadequacies. This marked the beginning of a months-long smear campaign against the Avengers secretly orchestrated by Tremont and his corrupt inner circle, an ongoing effort to paint the Avengers as religiously intolerant and racially biased in an attempt to win sympathy for the Triunes, whose members included many visible minorities.

Unaware of Tremont's true nature and plans, Triathlon feared that the increasingly hostile Avengers might be intolerant, even racist; but the feud ended abruptly when the Avengers' government liaison Duane Freeman — another Triune follower — convinced the Avengers to recruit Triathlon, since he was a capable hero whose visible minority status and Triune background would help defuse much of the negative publicity. Determined to prove the Avengers wrong about the Triunes, Triathlon joined the team. Tremont, feeling the Triunes had milked their anti-Avengers campaign for all it was worth, publicly praised this development and ceased to stir up public opinion against the team; however, though neither Triathlon nor Freeman knew it, Tremont's ability to read their minds during certain Triune rituals gave him two unwitting spies within the Avengers. Wary of his fellow Avengers and resenting the circumstances of his recruitment, Garrett was a bitter and disruptive presence within the group at first; but he gradually became a valued and enthusiastic Avenger, thanks in part to advice and support from Avengers butler Edwin Jarvis and teammates

REAL NAME: Delroy Garrett, Jr.
ALIASES: Triathlon
IDENTITY: Publicly known
OCCUPATION: Licensed super hero; former adventurer, spokesman, Olympic athlete
CITIZENSHIP: USA
PLACE OF BIRTH: Philadelphia, Pennsylvania
KNOWN RELATIVES: None
GROUP AFFILIATION: Initiative, Avengers (inactive); formerly Skrull Kill Krew, Point Men, Triune Understanding
EDUCATION: Camp Hammond basic training graduate; also some college studies (full extent unknown) and extensive Triune teachings
FIRST APPEARANCE: (Triathlon) Avengers #8 (1998); (3-D Man) Avengers: the Initiative #12 (2008)

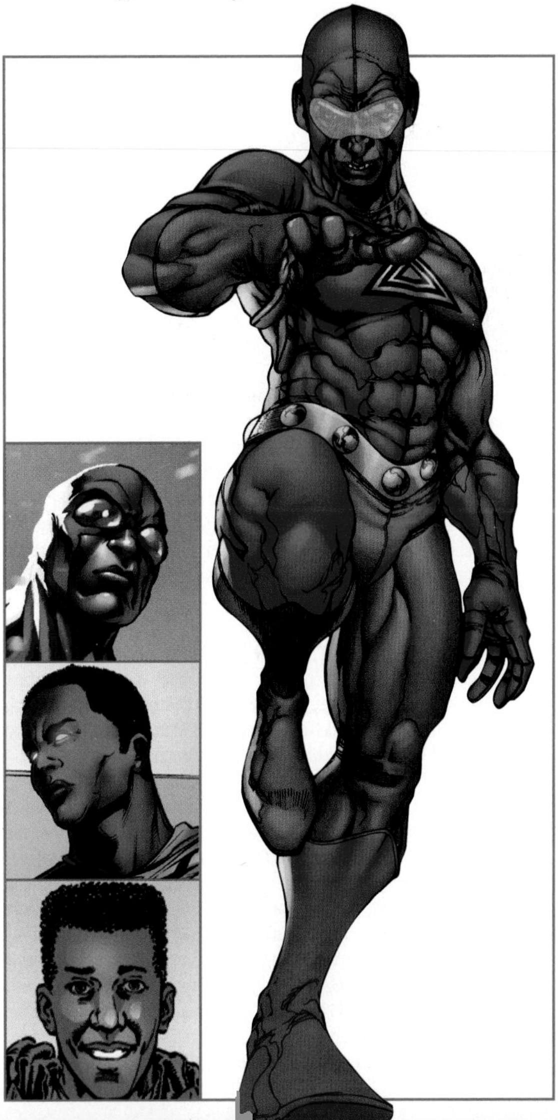

1ST TRIATHLON COSTUME

such as Warbird (Carol Danvers) and Photon (Monica Rambeau). He eventually began to prioritize his Avengers duties over his Triune commitments, and made friends within the group such as Wonder Man and fellow new recruit Jack of Hearts (Jack Hart).

When the Triple-Evil finally threatened Earth, Tremont faced it alongside the Avengers, exposing all his secrets to a greatly disillusioned Triathlon in the process. Finding the first cosmic shard within the Triple-Evil, Tremont tried to usurp the Garrett/Chandler shard as well and take all three shards for himself, but Triathlon — still merged with the Chandlers, whose spirits had newly awakened — sensed that the shards needed a selfless wielder to be effective, not the power-hungry Tremont. Absorbing all three shards and assuming a new triple form consisting of huge energy effigies of himself and the Chandler brothers, the newly cosmic-powered Triathlon banished the Triple-Evil and helped liberate Earth from Kang; he then gave up his cosmic powers — largely because they had been fuelled by the souls of the Triple-Evil's countless victims — and used the last of his cosmic energy to restore the Chandlers to their separate human forms, regaining his own normal form in the process. Declining to help the Triunes reorganize after Tremont's death in battle with the forces of Kang, Triathlon soon left the Avengers as well, though he later returned to aid them against threats such as Scorpio and an insane Scarlet Witch.

Garrett found a new purpose in the Fifty-State Initiative, a federal program training and regulating super heroes to be stationed throughout America. During his studies as an Initiative cadet at Camp Hammond, Triathlon was promoted to a leadership trainee position, leading other cadets in various exercises and field missions such as running crowd control when Hulk's Warbound attacked Manhattan, or capturing rogue android Dragon Man. When Garrett graduated to fully licensed super hero status, he adopted the 3-D Man costumed identity with the blessing of the warmly supportive Chandler brothers. For a graduation gift, they gave Garrett the original flight suit Chuck Chandler had worn during the mission that first transformed him and Hal into the 3-D Man. Realizing the mostly black suit was a poor match for his 3-D Man alias but wanting to show his appreciation for the gift, Garrett added the old flight suit's golden goggles to his 3-D Man costume when he reported for his prestigious new assignment as leader of the Point Men, Hawaii's state Initiative team.

Within minutes of starting his new job, Garrett made two surprising discoveries: that his new goggles could detect alien shape-shifting Skrulls no matter what form they assumed (Skrull technology having been involved in the Chandlers' original 3-D Man transformation), and that one of his new Point Men teammates, Magnitude, was secretly a Skrull spy. Though unable to prevent "Magnitude" from seriously injuring their partners Paydirt and Star Sign, Triathlon and the Point Men's supernatural specialist Devil-Slayer (Eric Payne) exposed and slew the Skrull after a brief struggle. Correctly deducing that Magnitude was part of a larger Skrull plot to subvert the Initiative, Garrett rushed to Camp Hammond to warn of this; however, new Hammond cadet Crusader (Z'reg) was secretly a Skrull, albeit an Earth-loving one who was genuinely loyal to the Initiative. Fearing discovery, Crusader temporarily reversed the polarity of Garrett's goggles so that anyone human looked like a Skrull to Garrett and any Skrull looked human. Mistakenly believing nearly all of Hammond's personnel had been replaced by Skrulls, Garrett set out for other Initiative bases in search of allies.

Nearly slain by a Skrull posing as She-Thing of the Initiative's Maverick team in New Mexico, 3-D Man was rescued by the Skrull Kill Krew, a Skrull-killing militia whose members derived their super-powers from the unwitting consumption of Skrulls that had entered the human food chain while disguised as animals. Krew leader Ryder drafted 3-D Man into the Skrull extermination campaign, and Garrett took to the work surprisingly eagerly — partly because the USA and the Initiative were now at war with the Skrulls since the aliens' new "Secret Invasion," but also because of the original 3-D Man's history as one of Earth's foremost Skrull fighters. Aided in non-combat capacities by the Chandlers, 3-D Man and the Krew went from state to state, exposing and killing Skrull infiltrators within the various Initiative teams, and recruiting other Initiative heroes to aid them as they went along. When Garrett's goggles were smashed during one skirmish, the Chandlers coached him in how to channel his "Tri-Force" energy into his eyes so that he could now detect Skrulls without artificial aids.

In the final battle between the Skrulls and Initiative forces at Camp Hammond, a still-disguised Crusader proved his true allegiance by neutralizing the Skrulls' doomsday weapon, playing a key role in the Initiative's victory; but 3-D Man, seeing through Crusader's disguise and assuming an enemy soldier, fatally shot the heroic Skrull. A subsequent investigation cleared Garrett of any wrongdoing, but it left 3-D Man feeling bitter and unwelcome since many within the Initiative now considered Crusader a hero and Garrett a murderer. Stepping down from active Initiative service, he joined seemingly sole remaining Skrull Kill Krew survivor Ryder in continuing to hunt down Skrulls for a time; however

TRIATHLON

Ryder eventually became uncomfortable around Garrett, perhaps because Ryder subconsciously realized his own evolving physical condition was slowly converting him into a more Skrull-like form which Garrett might detect. Frozen out of the Krew by Ryder, Garrett has since returned to more conventional heroics as the 3-D Man.

HEIGHT: 6'2"
WEIGHT: 200 lbs.
EYES: Brown
HAIR: Black

ABILITIES/ACCESSORIES: Triathlon's physical abilities are all enhanced to roughly three times peak human potential, notably his strength (lifting about one ton), speed (running up to 90 mph), stamina, agility and sensory acuity. When he channels his body's "Tri-Force" energy into his eyes, they glow red (left eye) and green (right eye) and enable him to identify Skrulls visually no matter how they disguise themselves. The Initiative trained him in leadership skills, first aid, lifesaving techniques, unarmed combat, battle strategy, aquatics, marksmanship and other skills. A good motorcyclist, a capable pilot of the Avengers' supersonic Quinjets, a skilled wielder of conventional firearms and a veteran track & field athlete, Garrett has taken acting lessons from Wonder Man for use in undercover work.

POWER GRID	1	2	3	4	5	6	7
INTELLIGENCE							
STRENGTH							
SPEED							
DURABILITY							
ENERGY PROJECTION							
FIGHTING SKILLS							